# MEN, BOOKS, AND MOUNTAINS

# MEN, BOOKS,
# AND MOUNTAINS

ESSAYS BY

Leslie Stephen

*Collected, and
with an Introduction, by*
S. O. A. Ullmann

GREENWOOD PRESS, PUBLISHERS
WESTPORT, CONNECTICUT

Library of Congress Cataloging in Publication Data

Stephen, Leslie, Sir, 1832-1904.
  Men, books, and mountains.

    Reprint of the ed. published by Hogarth Press,
London.
    "A check-list of works by Leslie Stephen":  p.
    I.  Title.
[PR5473.S6A67 1978]              824'.8      78-1861
ISBN 0-313-20262-1

Reprinted with the permission of The Hogarth Press Ltd.

Reprinted in 1978 by Greenwood Press, Inc.
51 Riverside Avenue, Westport, CT. 06880

Printed in the United States of America

10 9 8 7 6 5 4 3 2 1

# Contents

# Acknowledgments

It is a pleasure to record my debt to Professor Howard Mumford Jones, who first interested me in Stephen and who read an early draft of my introduction. For generous advice and assistance of various kinds, I am also greatly indebted to Professors Murray Krieger and Harold C. Martin, and to my cousin, Dr. Ruth Kahn. My thanks go also to Dr. Clyde Enroth for generously helping to read proofs, and to Sir John Murray and the British Museum for assistance in connection with the check-list.

Minneapolis, Minnesota                               S.O.A.U.
        May, 1956

# Introduction

SELDOM has a gifted writer tried as hard as Leslie Stephen to court neglect or been as successful in achieving that aim. Although specialists know his *History of English Thought in the Eighteenth Century* and lovers of mountaineering literature still enjoy his *Playground of Europe*, many well-educated readers remember him, if at all, only as the first editor of the *Dictionary of National Biography* or as the father of Vanessa Bell and Virginia Woolf.

When Victoria came to the throne in 1837, Stephen was only a somewhat sickly boy of four, the youngest son of mighty James, the able Under-Secretary of the Colonial Office. Twenty years later Cambridge knew him as the Reverend Leslie Stephen, an unorthodox Trinity Hall don, an outstanding rowing coach, and a prodigious hiker and climber. By the late sixties another transformation had occurred. The agnostic had replaced the cleric. The Cambridge celibate had gone to London and become the husband of Thackeray's daughter Minnie. Overnight Stephen had become a successful journalist, writing for some of the most influential periodicals of the day, among them *The Saturday Review*, *The Pall Mall Gazette*, and the New York *Nation*. John Morley and George Meredith became his lifelong friends. Browning and Tennyson, Darwin, Huxley, George Eliot, Henry James, and Hardy all knew and liked him. Young men like Henley and Stevenson were glad to acknowledge the help he had given them. Americans like Charles Eliot Norton; his "beloved Yankee," Holmes the younger; and James Russell Lowell, the godfather of his daughter Virginia, corresponded with him for years. In the closing decades of the century he was known to everyone as a brilliant and versatile man of letters. Yet at his death in 1904 his reputation began to decline rapidly.

Surprisingly, Stephen himself was largely responsible for the neglect accorded his work. He made it difficult for critics to look upon him as really first-rate because he habitually scoffed at his own works. His innate hypersensitivity and his almost morbid awareness of his slightest shortcomings led him to deny all claims to originality and consider himself a failure and even at times an impostor. Although he loved poetry and as a boy had literally become so intoxicated by it that doctors had prescribed a diet of prose, in his criticism he pretended to be a prosaic person, humbly feeling his way amid the mysteries of high poetic art. He insisted that he was only a sensible man of the world writing for other sensible men, subscribers to *The Cornhill Magazine* and *The National Review*. This approach to literature was well suited to win the confidence of his readers. By posing as an "outsider" instead of a man of letters, he not only could attack the excesses of æstheticism, but also could snipe at the Philistines themselves, who were quite willing to listen to friendly criticism from one of their own number. By the turn of the century, however, with a change in public taste, his critical forthrightness and his apparent insensibility had become more of a liability than an asset. To-day much of his work is almost entirely unknown, and some of his best goes unread because readers now accept uncritically his statements about himself and look upon him as a kind of blunt John Bull in a china shop: a man ill at ease in the literary world, a critic who was impartial because he had no strong sympathies and who avoided extremes because he was thoroughly commonplace. But just recently the twentieth century has begun to understand and appreciate the Victorians, and Stephen's slumbers are being disturbed. A number of his books have come back into print, and a full-length study of his works has at last appeared, Mr. Noël Annan's *Leslie Stephen*.

Because Stephen thought so little of his own work, he was naturally hesitant about collecting his articles. His four volumes of *Studies of a Biographer* with their fine critiques

of men like Arnold and Bagehot, Wordsworth and Tennyson, Emerson and Holmes, Trollope and Stevenson would
still lie buried in periodicals had he not, as he said, "swept
up some magazine twaddlings" at the request of his stepson,
who was starting a publishing house. It is hardly surprising,
then, that Stephen never reprinted some of his best essays.

Still uncollected, in fact, are hundreds of articles that
appeared in over two dozen periodicals in the course of
more than forty years, from 1861 to 1902. They represent
the full range of his interests: literature, biography, mountaineering, politics, history, education, philosophy, religion,
and contemporary manners and morals. Since no selection is likely to be wholly satisfactory to anyone but its
compiler, I have appended a list of Stephen's major articles
(many identified in print for the first time). Industrious
readers may use it to assemble their own collections. This
volume is not an attempt to represent all aspects of his work.
Some of Stephen's fine prefatory essays, especially those on
Fielding and Thackeray, are too long to reprint in a collection; many of his most characteristic essays deal with topics
which are now of interest to only a few; and others, although
excellent, repeat much that is available in one or another of
his many books. Instead, I have chosen essays that show
him at his best on topics which are still of general interest.
In addition, the selections emphasise aspects of his work
that are not sufficiently appreciated: his ability as a literary
critic and his dry wit and shrewdness in the informal
essay.

Stephen's most consistently entertaining essays are probably those on mountaineering. Climbing was a passion
with him for more than thirty years. By the time that his
health had forced him to lead a more sedentary life, he had
many difficult ascents to his credit and had long ago been
honoured by election to the presidency of the Alpine Club.
In his mountaineering essays he gave literary distinction to a
new genre. By turns exciting and ironic, exalted and whim-
sical, these essays have never been surpassed. "A Substitute

for the Alps," his last and one of his best, is more timely to-day than when it first appeared some sixty years ago. Now that teams of experts, employing hundreds of porters carrying tons of equipment, have at last painfully hoisted themselves to the top of Mount Everest and Mount Godwin Austen (K-2), it is amusing to read Stephen's mock onslaught upon these "new-fangled monstrosities." He writes as a vacationing amateur for whom mountain-climbing means a pleasant day's perpendicular jaunt up an alp in the company of a friend and two or three congenial guides. His essay good-naturedly pokes fun at Asian mountaineering, which seems to him much more like a military expedition or a Gargantuan scientific experiment than like a sport.

In addition to the Alpine essays, this collection contains two pieces of social criticism. Stephen rarely reprinted articles like these. Perhaps he mistakenly considered them too trivial or ephemeral. As he once half-humorously remarked about preserving work by writers like himself: "We should be content, and even eager, to pass into oblivion as soon as the temporary purpose of amusing an idle hour has been fulfilled. . . . Immortality in print is not only a superfluity; the bare suggestion of its possibility is a positive injury to one's feelings."* But Stephen's essays on social questions have kept their freshness and show us a side of him seldom as clearly revealed elsewhere. In 1869–1870, during his early days with *The Cornhill Magazine* before he became its editor, he wrote a series of twelve essays signed "A Cynic." He never reprinted any of them, although the first, "A Cynic's Apology," has appeared in several anthologies. "Vacations" belongs to this series, and "International Prejudices" is in a similar vein. They are not earnest attempts to reform society, but merely playful though dexterous thrusts at contemporary cant. Many of the follies that Stephen pokes fun at are, alas, still with us: our self-deception, our blind worship of science, and our tendency

* "Perishable Books," in *Among My Books*, ed. H. D. Traill (London [1898]), p. 43. Reprinted from *Literature*, I (1897), 178.

to make superficial and hasty generalisations about other nations and other races.

What passes for cynicism in these early essays is only an attempt to expose conceit, hypocrisy, and sentimentalism. Even though he calls himself a cynic, his prevailing tone is ironic rather than cynical. This irony is a counterpart of his agnosticism and implies that to go too far in any direction is to get into an area where one can talk only nonsense. Stephen turns his brand of irony to particularly good use in his only literary satire, "Did Shakespeare Write Bacon?" In it he examines an ingenious hypothesis which, as he remarks with deceptive gravity, "should only require a brief exposition to secure its acceptance by some people."

Most of his literary essays, however, are somewhat more serious. They dominate this collection because it is as a critic that I believe Stephen will be remembered longest. Except for Matthew Arnold, no other Victorian produced so large a body of distinguished criticism. Although critics as different as Carlyle and Swinburne have written an occasional essay that is finer than any of Stephen's, none of his contemporaries maintains so uniform a standard of excellence. Nor does any inspire as great confidence in his judgments, for none is so careful to explain the basis for his opinions. Stephen is sensitive yet incisive, sympathetic yet ultimately disinterested. He knows what he wants to say and says it without obscurity, without arrogance, and without trying to substitute bombast for critical insight. When literary historians sum up Stephen's criticism as rationalistic, utilitarian, agnostic, positivistic, their sweeping generalisations overlook the sources of his vital strength: his keen sensibility, his critical impartiality, his breadth of view, and his lively and vigorous style. One of the primary aims of this collection is to call attention to these virtues.

Stephen was wrong when he said that the best critic is the one who "makes the fewest mistakes." By modern standards he made fewer "mistakes" than Arnold and far fewer than Dr. Johnson; yet his criticism is not therefore superior to theirs. Like all good prose, the best criticism possesses the kind of literary excellence that transcends mere utility. Such excellence depends far more upon the qualities of mind and sensibility which the critic displays than upon the ultimate validity of his judgments. I am not trying to excuse Stephen for exercising bad judgment. He needs no such excuse, since he probably wrote a larger number of judicious critiques than any other Victorian. But far more important, all of them bear the personal stamp of an alert and sensitive mind, without which criticism has little permanent value.

Although usually not an innovator, Stephen was the first to give serious consideration to most of the major English novelists. He was also among the first to emphasise the influence of social structure upon literature. He pointed out the many ways in which a writer's sense of his audience affects his work, and by so doing Stephen helped prepare the way for the modern school of sociological criticism. Still more important, he played a leading part in the rehabilitation of the eighteenth century. He admired it because by temperament and intellectual heritage he was almost as much a man of the Enlightenment as of his own age. He shared the eighteenth-century's hatred of pedantry, its distrust of "enthusiasm" and fanaticism, its respect for common sense, its tolerance. His knowledge of intellectual history made him realise how much he owed to the ideas of men like Burke and Hume. His own *History of English Thought in the Eighteenth Century* was primarily an attempt to make his contemporaries as aware as he was of their intellectual debt to their predecessors. It is easy enough now to point out the limitations of Stephen's appreciation of men like Pope and Swift, but measured by the standards of his day, as set by Carlyle and Arnold, Stephen's praise of the Augustans seems generous indeed. Moreover, his criticism helped to convince many of his contemporaries that there was no justification for superciliously dismissing the eighteenth century as an age without imagination or literary distinction.

Stephen's own interest in the historical method as applied to philosophy, religion, and government antedated his career as a writer. It was thus natural for him to make use of this method once he began to write about literature. Not only in his historical essays but also in his criticism he conveys the impression that he sees literature in relation to society as a whole and fully understands the relation of any particular work to the history of literature. His unusually harsh review of Taine's *History of English Literature*, however, shows how strongly he disapproved of criticism which seemed to him to abuse even a sound method. He had no respect for Taine's *a priori* theories, his hasty generalisations, and his pseudo-scientific pretences. Stephen was quite aware, moreover, as some modern scholars are not, of "the vast difference between what is called knowing a thing's history and knowing the thing itself." Although generally more interested in understanding works than in passing judgment on them, he was careful to treat the historical method simply as a useful auxiliary, not as a substitute for critical judgment and individual taste.

He had his weaknesses, of course, particularly his inability to discuss poetic technique, a subject on which usually he remained wisely silent; his frequent failure to distinguish between an author and his work; and, by modern standards, his excessive attention to "the moral element in literature," though in this respect he was far more temperate than most of his contemporaries.

Stephen was, nevertheless, a remarkably fine critic. Neither dilettante nor pedant, he approached literature as a cultured man of the world. Although making use of many of the insights provided by advances in history, science, and sociology, he avoided becoming overcommitted to any one of them. His criticism holds a middle course between critical extremes. It tries to be both sympathetic and impartial, and refrains from using either a blackjack or a censer. Stephen never attempts to bludgeon readers into agreement or to awe them by dogmatic assertions. When he finally pronounces judgment he speaks with assurance, because he knows his own mind and never pretends to be speaking for anyone but himself. Stephen claimed that criticism was not his "proper line," but a friend came nearer to the truth when he called him "a critic blind to no literary merit save his own."*

\* The novelist James Payn, Stephen's successor as editor of *The Cornhill Magazine*, used this phrase in the dedication of *Some Literary Recollections* (London, 1884).

# A NOTE ON THE TEXT

"I have such a gift for misprints as few people can boast," Stephen admitted in a letter to James Russell Lowell. "I never look at an article of mine after it has been published without finding a bushel."* Stephen, alas, was not given to exaggeration. Few printers or editors seem to have been wholly successful in deciphering his handwriting. Since the text of this collection is based, not upon manuscripts but upon highly inaccurate texts that appeared in periodicals, it would have been doing Stephen a disservice to have reprinted the essays without emendation. I have tried, therefore, to provide the kind of text that he himself would have produced had he possessed the patience to proof read with care. I have silently corrected obvious misprints, normalised titles and proper names, and tried to make spellings consistent throughout the volume. Since punctuation with Stephen was often a matter of personal taste, I have made few changes, even at the risk of perpetuating printers' errors. I have also reprinted his quotations without alteration, since their inaccuracies reveal Stephen's habit of quoting from memory or altering quotations to fit

\* Frederick William Maitland, *The Life and Letters of Leslie Stephen* (London, 1906), p. 291.

his context. These passages also provide a yardstick for measuring the accuracy of the periodical texts. In the long quotation on page 73, for example, which Stephen doubtless copied verbatim from Hazlitt, "plashy sedges" becomes "flashing ridges" and "exhalation" appears as "inhalation." Other less glaring inaccuracies in the passage are too numerous to list here.

# The Study of English Literature[*]

I AM to speak of a well-worn topic, and I begin by saying that I do not purpose to dwell upon one of its aspects. I shall not consider the proper place of English literature in our school and university studies. My reason is simply that I have not the practical experience which would enable me to pass beyond the ordinary commonplaces. I have more prejudices than reasoned convictions upon that subject. I take for granted, indeed, as an undeniable proposition, that familiarity with our literature is desirable. It is desirable for us all to have the personal acquaintance of men better, wiser, more highly endowed than ourselves. Acquaintance with such men is not less desirable after their death. In some respects it is even more desirable. The dead man cannot, it is true, answer our questions or thrill us by his bodily presence; but neither can he alarm our modesty or repel us by accidental infirmities. If we could consciously meet a Shakespeare we should be struck dumb; but we are quite at ease with that essence of Shakespeare which is compressed into a book. We can put him in our pockets, admit him to an audience when we are in the humour, and treat him as familiarly as a college chum. We can meet Dr. Johnson without the least fear that he will be personally rude, and stop Macaulay's excessive flow of information by simply shutting up his pages. The man may be only unfortunate who, in his youth, has not been stimulated by the personal acquaintance of some revered contemporary. He is more than unfortunate, he is blameworthy, if he do not make the acquaintance of some of the great men from Chaucer to Lord Tennyson, from Bacon to Carlyle, who speak to us across the gulf of time or from regions inaccessible to us in person.

[*] A lecture delivered to the Students' Association of St. Andrews, March 26, 1887.

The true object of the study of a man's writings is, according to my definition, to make a personal friend of the author. You have not studied him thoroughly till you know the very trick of his speech, the turn of his thoughts, the characteristic peculiarities of his sentiments, of his imagery, of his mode of contemplating the world or human life. You should breathe a familiar atmosphere when you open his pages. If you meet a stray phrase of his, it should ring in your ears with the accent of an old acquaintance; you should be able to swear to it as part of his coinage. You should "have learnt his great language, caught his clear accents, made him your pattern to live and to die," and, I will venture to add, you should have then passed beyond this stage of idolatry—which is good as a phase, but bad as a permanent state of mind—into that of sane and reasonable appreciation. Addison, in an often quoted passage, ridicules the reader who wants to know whether his author is short or tall, black or fair. Perhaps such a demand is excessive; but I do not feel that I really know an author till I almost fancy that I should recognise him if I met him at a railway station. That indeed proves that I know very few; but it marks what is my own ideal. How, then, to attain such knowledge? I begin by replying, that before reaching the root of the matter there are certain auxiliary studies which are obviously necessary and yet obviously external. They give the key, they do not lead us into the sanctuary. For example, one necessary preliminary is to learn our letters. But a bare power of reading does not take us very far. That part of our education was probably completed in our nurseries. In our nurseries also we generally suppose ourselves to have learnt the English language. Now it is thought superfluous to insist upon a study of the alphabet, but a good deal is said of the importance of that scientific study of language which acquires the more sounding title, philology. For the study of a foreign literature it is, of course, indispensably necessary to learn the language, and generally at a comparatively late period. But for the study of English

literature the question occurs whether we may not be pre-
sumed to have learnt more from our nurses than we shall
ever acquire from our teachers. Philology is, of course, a
most important and interesting study. An investigation of
the great instrument of thought and of its processes of development has a genuine interest for philosophers, logicians,
and even for historians and antiquaries, as well as for literary
students. Philologists have to study the same documents as
men of letters. They have to read Chaucer and Shakespeare,
though with a very different purpose. So a chemist may
study a picture as well as an art critic. The main interest of
the one is in the pigments to which it owes its colour, as the
main interest of the other is in the effect upon the imagination of a particular combination of colours. The philologist,
as such, can tell you the history of a word used by Shakespeare, but as a philologist he has nothing to do with the
imaginative force of the sentence in which the word occurs.
So far as the language is obsolete, so far as it has become a
dead language, he can do something for you. He can supplement the instruction which, as to the great bulk of the language, was already given in your nursery. Here and there he
clears away an obscurity or points some allusion no longer
manifest; and we will, if you please, be duly thankful to
him, and tell him that he has rendered us a real service. But,
however valuable for other purposes, we must admit that he
is not a guide to the kind of knowledge which we desire,
but an humble attendant who has cleared a few stumbling-
blocks from our path.

There are other studies which make greater claims, and
of which I must speak more fully. Literature is made up of
words. It is a combination of raw materials which are all to
be found in the dictionary. But it is, as we know, a combination governed by peculiar laws of its own. To study those
laws scientifically must, therefore, it is urged, be an essential
aim of the literary student. The historical method is now in
the ascendant. It affects not only history in the old sense, but
philosophy, political and social theory, and every other

branch of inquiry which has to do with the development of living beings. No one would assert this more emphatically than I should do. One corollary is that we should study the history of our own literature, that we should not only trace it back to its origin in our own islands, but also to the great foreign literatures which have had so profound an influence upon our own. Especially, it is urged, no one can appreciate English literature without a knowledge of classical literature. You cannot, says one authority, fully estimate Chaucer unless you are familiar with Virgil, Statius, and Ovid. No one, says Mark Pattison, can follow Milton fully unless he has had at least a taste of Milton's training; that is, some knowledge of the authors whom Milton, we may not say plundered, but turned to account in every page of his poetry. The statement is not only plausible, but owes its plausibility to the fact that it contains a most important truth. Undoubtedly the sympathetic study of ancient masterpieces is a most admirable training for the literary student. Really to appropriate the great writers of Greece or Rome is to acquire a valuable possession. It is a great thing to know how the real masters take hold of a subject, in order to feel the vast difference between the great creative genius and the mere man of talent. The great classical works have an advantage not only as being recognised masterpieces, but as being foreign. To know them is to recognise genius amongst unfamiliar shapes and surroundings. As an hour at Calais will put more fresh knowledge into your minds than a month in London, simply by making you realise that there are countries where babies talk French, so excursions into the wide expanse,

*Which deep-browed Homer ruled for his demesne,*

enables you to get rid of insular prejudices. It is a training in the art of recognising the essential quality of genius apart from the local and temporary accidents which go so far to determine our taste in ordinary cases. I would emphatically assert the advantages of classical study—if anyone disputed it—all the more ungrudgingly, I hope, because my own acquaintance with the classics is limited. But I shall not be therefore deterred from observing that even this study may be so conducted as to degenerate into mere cram. The average schoolboy gains little when he holds Latin to be an instrument of torture invented by some prehistoric Keate or Busby, and is painfully drilled into construing *arma*, the arms; *virumque*, and the man; *cano*, I sing. Nay, such men have been observed as the more scholarlike pedant who can unravel every crabbed passage in the most corrupt fragment of a Greek play, but has only learnt, like Thackeray's Bardolph, to despise everybody who can't put a slang song into Greek iambics or turn a police report into the language of Thucydides. I have known many classical scholars, of whom I can safely say that they excite my envy, because I can perceive how much their taste in modern has been refined and elevated by their study of ancient literature. But I have also, to be quite frank, known one or two who have only become better-trained schoolboys, and have become more finical and pedantic without any perceptible improvement of their powers of appreciating literature. From which I only infer that it is possible even to learn Latin and Greek in a sense—in such a sense as to be a formidable competitor in an examination, and yet to gain a very poor training indeed. Such a man acquires something. He has the power of explaining allusions or producing parallel passages. He can track Milton in his appropriations, or say how many Greek poets have anticipated Gray's remark about the rose which wastes its sweetness in the desert air. It is not only amusing but instructive to hunt out the curious coincidences of thought or phrase in great poets, or to see how a great writer makes his own of what he borrows. But the power of answering one of the stock examiners' questions, "explain the allusions in this passage," is consistent with complete insensibility to the merits of both passages. How far does such knowledge really aid your appreciation? Opening Milton at random, I find that the passage describing Satan,

*His spear, to equal which the tallest pine*
*Hewn on Norwegian hills to be the mast*
*Of some great ammiral, were but a wand,*

may imply recollections of the *Odyssey*, of the *Æneid*, and of
Tasso. The commentator is also good enough to tell us that
there are many pines in Norway. Does the passage sound
any the better or the worse? Pattison told us that only those
classically trained could follow Milton. It is only such persons, I fully agree, who catch the full Miltonic aroma. But if
I were asked to name someone whose soul would really ring
like an echo to the majestic language of the great Puritan, I
think that my mind, and the minds of a good many of us,
would spontaneously recur to the name of one who has told
us that he knows little Latin and no Greek—I mean Mr.
John Bright. He cannot, he says very frankly, and it is a
misfortune for him, appreciate Plato. But that defect is
clearly compatible with unequalled mastery of some of the
noblest strains of English eloquence, and it would be in-
credible that a man who can use the instrument so skilfully
should not appreciate its use by others. When, indeed, I am
told that a knowledge of classical literature is not only most
desirable, but even essential to a full appreciation of the
modern literatures, I cannot but think that there is a gap in
the logic. How do you learn to appreciate either? I know a
lady of remarkable beauty; I am told and I believe that she
inherits the beauty from her grandmother. Do you imagine
that I enjoy the sight of her beauty the less because I had
not the happiness to know her grandmother? The knowledge
of the fact is interesting to me as an humble disciple of Mr.
Darwin; it is a case of "heredity," and therefore relevant to
a scientific inquiry. Similarly, if I wish to explain how English literature comes to have certain peculiarities, I must
know the sources from which it is derived. But after all there
is a vast difference between what is called knowing a thing's
history and really knowing the thing itself, between really
having an ear for music and knowing how, for example,

modern harmony has grown out of strumming on some prehistoric barbarous tom-tom. No amount of such knowledge
will give you the ear; nor will any knowledge of the relations
between English and classical literature of itself endow you
with the true faculty for perceiving the beauties of either.
We cannot honestly deny the fact that many of our greatest
writers owed little or nothing to any classical training, even
when they possessed it. It is enough to run over the bare
names of Shakespeare and Bunyan and Defoe and Burns
and Dickens, to say nothing of many less distinguished.
Cobbett wrote incomparably better English than Dr. Parr,
and Mr. Bright has a style very superior to—I will not give a
name. Criticism requires a wider knowledge though less
genius than original authorship; but I cannot discover that
our finest critic of some of the most important English
literature—I mean Charles Lamb—owed anything to his
scanty scholarship.

Admitting, then, most heartily the great value of a genuine
study of classical literature, I yet am forced to regard it
rather as one of the studies by which our tastes may be improved and our perceptions refined than as an indispensable
mode of training. There is one other kind of study upon
which I may spend a word or two. Recent critics, I observe,
are fond of dwelling upon what they call the "form" as distinguished from the "content" of poetry, and are given to
insist that the important question is not what a man says
but how he says it. I will not diverge into a discussion of this
statement, which like many others may, as I hold, be true
and important or very much the reverse according to our
interpretation of its precise meaning. I will only note that,
on one acceptation, it amounts to recommending the most
barren and mechanical study as the only genuine study.
You are, it is sometimes suggested, to study a poet's metres
and neglect his meaning. The difference between successive
schools of poetry is not in the sentiments which they express,
but in the mechanism by which they contrive to express
them. And thus a literary revolution is explained like a

revolution in the practical sciences. Somebody invented a new scheme of versification as somebody invented a new application of steam or electricity. To which I shall only say that the metrical systems and so forth which appear in different periods are undoubtedly worth study, and here, as everywhere, so far as the knowledge is useful, we should be careful to have accurate knowledge. But it is a palpable mistake, as I think, to speak of such changes as a cause instead of a symptom. If Pope preferred a smooth and monotonous system of verse to the rougher but more varied versification of his predecessors, the fact is to be noted, but not to be assigned as an explanation. The system of Pope was not due to an invention of ten-syllabled couplets, as the change in weaving was due to Arkwright's invention of the spinning-machine. It came when it was wanted. It was wanted when a new order of thoughts and feelings had to be expressed. The new order of thought and feeling was not created by the new mechanism, but determined its adoption. The literary revolution, to which we give the name of Wordsworth or Coleridge, was no more caused by the invention of a new literary fashion than the great political revolution by the abandonment of wigs and laced coats. Wigs and laced coats went with other things of more importance as men's social and political and religious instincts underwent a change; and the minor change, too, is worth noting as a symptom. But to treat the symptom as the cause, or to suppose that the external changes can be studied to any purpose without reference to the underlying causes to which they were due, is to miss the whole significance of literary or any other kind of history.

And this leads to a further inquiry. Where are we to look for the real significance of such changes? Literature may be considered in two ways. A book is the utterance of an individual mind. It is the *sic cogitavit* of a Francis Bacon, a William Shakespeare, or an Alexander Pope. But it does not depend simply upon the individual mind. Every individual is a constituent part of a society. He transmutes as well as creates. He utters his own thoughts, but he is also the organ through which the spirit of the age utters its thoughts. He looks upon the world, but he is also, in part at least, a product of its development. His philosophy, the enthusiasms which stir him, the doubts which torment him, the answers which he supplies to them, the form in which he states the eternal problems and tries to utter a solution, are all in great measure determined for him by the social element in which he lives. This has become a commonplace. No one would now think that Shakespeare could be criticised fully without some knowledge of Elizabeth's time, or Pope without a knowledge of Anne's time, or Byron without a knowledge of the Revolutionary time. Literature in this aspect is simply one function of the social organism—if you will allow me to use the philosophical slang of the day—and any serious treatment of it must recognise the fact. The greatest men, it is true, say what is of interest for all times; but even the very greatest, the Homers and Dantes and Shakespeares, say it in the dialect and under all the conditions of their own time.

So far, then, as the study of literature can be—I will not say made truly scientific, for it is idle to speak of science in relation to the vague and tentative judgments which alone are possible now, but—treated in a scientific spirit, that is, examined impartially and placed in due correlation with all the truths known to us, it is essential to understand in some degree the time as well as the man, because only through the time can we fully understand the man. In this sense the special studies which I have mentioned are all in various degrees relevant; they are useful auxiliary studies: the study of the language, of the forms of expression, of the previous literatures which have influenced our own, all call attention either to the symptoms or to the causes of important facts which we have to take into account. But I think that we can see the importance of another kind of study still more intimately connected with our aims. Let me try to show how, as I conceive, it may be of real assistance, even at the price of repeating some very familiar truths. You should, I say, understand the spirit of the age, and by that I do not mean that you should study what is called the philosophy of history. There is, indeed, no more fascinating study; but, in the first place, the doctrines which it announces are still the guesses of clever men rather than the established conclusions of scientific observers; and, in the next place, true or false, they are abstract theories, not concrete pictures. What you require is not a clever analysis, but a vivid representation of the period. You should see it, not be full of formula about it. An architect upon glancing at an old building can tell you to what century or to what generation it belongs. When you turn over a book you should possess the instinct which enables you to give a shrewd guess as to whether, for example, it was written before or after 1760, in the days of George II or of George III. If, now, you were studying the period of which Dryden was the literary autocrat, I believe that few bits of reading would give you more real help than that admirable third chapter of Macaulay's history which, with all its faults, gives the most graphic and picturesque account of English society at the time. Or, if you go to contemporary documents, nothing would enable you to construct such a picture for yourselves as the diaries of Pepys or the memoirs of Gramont; or, if I may mention a favourite book of my own, the volumes of the State trials which deal with that period. Nothing enables you to see so clearly the various heterogeneous elements of which society was then composed, and to understand what was the audience whose tastes Dryden considered in every line that he wrote, the great seminal thoughts which were then fermenting and struggling for utterance, and the imagery which typified them most completely, as the documents which bring before you the men themselves, with all their hopes and fears and beliefs and doubts and passions. If English literature is more intelligible when read in conjunction with the classics, I certainly hold that our understanding is still more improved by reading it in conjunction with English history.

To explain myself more clearly, let me take a particular instance. Suppose, for example, that you wish to study Pope, who, of course, represents a most important moment in the development of English literature. Some peculiarities of Pope's poetry are set out in every manual upon English literature. There is his famous theory of "correctness"; there are the limitations which he accepted or introduced into English verse, and the so-called conventionality which produced the so-called reaction of Wordsworth and his school; and it is, of course, necessary to know what were the peculiarities thus indicated and what was the history of their growth and decay. But if it be necessary to know this, it is necessary also to pass beyond this knowledge. Why did he adopt these canons of taste, and why did they so impress his contemporaries? No answer can be suggested from the bare facts themselves; you must feel the relation between the facts and the whole spirit of the time. Pope, again, was, after a fashion, classical. Some of his best forms are his imitations of Horace; and his most popular was the translation of the *Iliad*. Some critics, indeed, tell us that you will like Pope's *Iliad* better in proportion to your ignorance of Homer's *Iliad*. We may grant, in spite of this, that the enjoyment of Pope is facilitated by a knowledge of Homer, and especially of Horace, to whom he had so close an affinity. Yet the question remains, why did Pope and his contemporaries venerate the classics? why, for example, did they use "Gothic" as simply a term of reproach? what was the spirit of the age which led them to set so high a value upon the qualities which they recognised in classical literature? Unless we can give some sort of answer to such questions we must fail to perceive the significance of the facts we observe, or to enter really into the spirit of our author. To give an answer we must be able not merely to use the proper formula about certain analogies, but to transport ourselves at will to the first half of the eighteenth century.

Now, I shall not attempt any answer, but I shall try to indicate briefly how an answer should, in my opinion, be sought. There are, as I conceive, two main directions of study relevant to such an inquiry. We want to know something of the philosophy and, still more, something of the social conditions of the time. Pope's most ambitious, though not most successful, work, is the *Essay on Man*. The *Essay on Man* is a kind of cento from the popular writers upon philosophy of the day. It is full of passages taken almost bodily from such men as Samuel Clarke and Lord Shaftesbury and Leibnitz, and a great part of it seems to have been a versification of the prose in which Bolingbroke very rashly expressed his views of contemporary philosophy. Reading it without some knowledge of these doctrines is like reading modern literature without having heard of Darwinism. But the importance of such knowledge is not confined to this particular work, still less to the explanation of particular phrases or allusions. It is important because the whole tone of Pope's poetry is determined by his immersion in the speculations of the day. Why is it, for example, that whereas Milton sought to "justify the ways of God to man" by giving a concrete history of the great events which revealed the Divine purpose, Pope, adopting the same phrase, and wishing to "vindicate the ways of God to man," proceeds to versify a number of abstract arguments? The difference was imposed by the conditions of the time, by all the differences to which we refer when we say that Milton was a Puritan and that Pope was what has been called a Christian Deist. To understand that difference we must understand something of the philosophical history of the day, and unless we understand it we shall never appreciate the curiously didactic tendency which is one of the marked characteristics not only of the *Essay on Man*, but of all Pope's best work, and of most of the best work of the time, and which leads to its greatest fault, the confusion between the proper spheres of poetry and of logic. To perceive Pope's drift, to understand why he adopts modes of utterance which to us seem to be essentially prosaic, and to recognise the poet under the dealer in epigrams and commonplaces, we must know something of the intellectual revolution; of the immense breach which had taken place between the new philosophy and the old teaching of the schools; of the vast impression upon the imagination as well as upon the reason of Newton's gigantic discoveries; of the change in the whole modes of reasoning involved in Locke's new departure; of the kind of deification of "common sense" characteristic of the philosophy, of the theology, of the politics, and therefore also of the literature of the time. We must appreciate the aspiration expressed in Berkeley's famous verses for a time when men shall cease to impose for truth and sense "the pedantry of courts and schools"; the aspiration which involved an appeal from learned recluses and monastics wrapped in mystery to the clear common sense of a circle of educated men. That spirit shows itself in all the men of the day—in Berkeley, in Addison, in Swift, in Shaftesbury, in Bishop Butler, in Bolingbroke, not less than in Pope; and without some sense of that fact you will be at a loss to understand either the aims or the methods of Pope and his contemporaries.

Briefly, to understand the literature you must know something of the philosophy; and this, though pre-eminently true of a period like Pope's, where the absence of a clear distinction is a special characteristic, is more or less true of all periods. Between Shakespeare and Bacon, between Dryden and Hobbes, between Shelley and Godwin, between Scott and Burke, between Wordsworth's poetry and Coleridge's philosophy, there is more than a relation of contemporaneity. I do not mean, however, that any profound philosophical study is needed. Far from it. I only mean that you must have some such acquaintance with the general drift of thought as Pope himself possessed—which, to say the truth, was superficial enough—before you can fairly appreciate him, or cease to be repelled by some otherwise unintelligible peculiarities. But still more necessary is a study which, in truth, is closely connected with this. The study of the philosophy is most intimately connected with the study of society. The philosophical movement was congenial to, if it was not due to, the peculiar conditions of society. No human being was ever more acutely sensitive to the opinions of the day than Pope. Nobody ever reflected more accurately the special phases of the social life. The *Rape of the Lock*, the *Dunciad*, or the prologue and epilogue to the Satires, all his most undeniable successes, first take their true colouring when you know the people for whom they were written; when you have a clear vision of Queen Anne "taking sometimes counsel and sometimes tea" at Hampton Court, quarrelling with the Duchess of Marlborough, and going to meet Harley at Mrs. Masham's; when you can elect yourself a member of Addison's "little senate," where Steele, listening reverentially over his cups, and Budgell and Tickell and namby-pamby Philips are sitting around in rapt admiration, or follow the great man to Holland House and watch him writing a *Spectator* and revolving round two foci, each marked by a bottle of port; or sit up with Swift when he gets under his blankets on a cold night to scribble off the last events of the day to Stella, or meet the "Brothers' Club" at dinner to discuss the proper policy of the Tory ministry; or drive over with Pope himself in a chariot to sit with Bolingbroke under a haystack and talk bad metaphysics in a pasture painted with spades and rakes; or let his waterman row you up from Westminster stairs to see his garden and present a crystal for his grotto, and talk to Gay and Swift till your host says, "Gentlemen, I leave you to your wine," and leaves three of you to finish the pint from which he has deducted two glasses. You must follow him invisibly to his bed, where he will have paper and pens by his side, lest he should wake in the night, parturient of a couplet, and have no proper cradle ready for its reception. He will awake raging over some smart saying attributed to Lady Mary or Lord Hervey, and excogitate a stinging retort to be remembered at this day by all educated men, though nine out of ten may have forgotten its origin. Or perhaps he will add a tinge of bitterness to one of the passages in the *Dunciad*, where he lashes his multitudinous foes. We should

see them, too, poor wretches, far away in the recesses of
Grub Street, in the garret where the printer's devil finds
them, robed in an old sack with holes for the passage of
their arms, and desperately tearing their way through the
translation of a French translation of a classic, with the help
of a dictionary. Nor must we forget to see Pope on his best
side; to see how his eye shines and his lip trembles when he
turns a delicate compliment to an old friend; with what
touching gentleness he fondles his old mother, as Walpole
sneeringly puts it, and wakes, perhaps, to write those exquisite verses which still show us what true feeling lurked
in the deformed and spiteful little bundle of nerves:

> *Me let the tender office long engage*
> *To rock the cradle of reposing age;*
> *With lenient arts, extend a mother's breath,*
> *Make languor smile, and soothe the bed of death;*
> *Explore the thought, explain the asking eye,*
> *And keep awhile one parent from the sky.*

Carlyle could never write about a man till he had framed a
credible portrait of his appearance. Macaulay used to ramble
in the streets of London, trying to reconstruct a vision of the
houses as occupied by the old generation so long vanished
from sensible perception. To make some such picture as a
background for our poet is, I hold, most essential for a
clear appreciation. We shall understand the conditions under
which Pope worked when we know the enemies, big and
small, whom he dreaded, and upon whom he took vengeance;
the greater men whose approval he courted with genuine
affection; the critical circles, who revered him as an authority
because he adopted and reflected their sentiments with unequalled skill. His best poetry is the incarnation of his and
their conversation: the refined and elaborated essence by a
man of genius, full of such epigrams as would tell with men
of the world, drinking at the coffee-houses or meeting for
friendly suppers to polish their wits by collision; deficient in
romance, for the romantic to such men suggested the ridicu-

lous and the old-fashioned; teaching by direct precept rather then by imagery, for they cared nothing for the old mythology; embodying commonplaces, for the talk of such men avoided the depths and the raptures of poetry, and yet superabundantly keen, sometimes even profound in substance, though never seeking the profound at the risk of obscurity; and far more often really tender, though shy in openly repressing tenderness, and dreading sentimentality as the deadly sin. Feel this; see these men as they were, and so you will understand why Pope uttered himself in his characteristic fashion, and see the real power which was hidden under an unfamiliar mask.

And how to feel this? By reading some of the most delightful books in the language. By reading Addison and Swift, and Pope's own correspondence, and Lady Mary's letters, and *Robinson Crusoe*, and *Gulliver's Travels*, and Gay and Parnell, and a crowd of smaller writers, just as they come in your way. Of all books—but I speak professionally, for I refer to my own trade—none are more delightful than good biographies. I will not suggest that you should read a certain dictionary of biography, because it is not yet finished, though when it is finished you will have, in fifty moderately thick volumes, a pretty full introduction to English literary history. But I do think that in the study of biography you are led by the pleasantest of paths into the fullest possession of that concrete picture of a man's surroundings which I should desire you to possess. I will take one example. Let me speak from my own experience. I had the good fortune, when a boy, to read what is to me, I will confess, the most purely delightful of all books—I mean Boswell's *Life of Johnson*. I read it from cover to cover, backwards and forwards, over an over, through and through, till I nearly knew it by heart; and I should like nothing better than to read it again to-morrow. Just consider to what a circle you are introduced. There are the two main figures, forming a contrast in real life scarcely surpassable by Don Quixote and Sancho Panza—Johnson, physically, a giant deformed by disease and infirmity; intellectually, one vast mass of common sense and humorous shrewdness, masked by outrageous prejudices, and morally, hiding a woman's tenderness and a hero's independence of spirit under the roughness of a street porter; a man who begins by disgusting you, who soon extorts your respect, and who ends by making you love him like a dear friend. And Boswell, the inimitable, who has something amiable in all his follies, even, if I may say so, in his vices; whose vanity is redeemed by an unstinted and hearty appreciation of excellence which amounts to genius; with whom we sympathise because he lays bare so unsparingly weaknesses of his own, which, as our own conscience tells us, are not quite without certain corresponding germs in our own bosoms, who thus makes a kind of vicarious confession for us, which we enjoy though we would not imitate; whose indomitable gaiety, whose boundless powers of enjoying every excitement, even the excitement of confessing his sins and making good resolutions for the future, disarms all our antipathies—this unparalleled fool of genius attracts us as much as the master whose steps he dogged, and whose very foibles he copied. And this delightful pair are only the centre of a circle. Boswell opens the door to the whole literary history of the century. Johnson comes into contact in his youth with Pope and Swift, who had known the wits of Charles's day, and in his age with Hannah More, who made a pet of Macaulay, and with Miss Burney, who lived long enough to have made, if she had chosen, a pet of me. By friendship or hostility he touches all the great Englishmen of his time. Think only of three friends, of all of whom Boswell gives us the most intimate glimpses: Burke, incomparably the greatest writer upon political philosophy whom these islands have ever produced; Goldsmith, who "touched nothing that he did not adorn," author of some of the most exquisite poetry and of the most exquisite idyll of country life in our language; and Reynolds, the first of English painters, who still preserves for us the most admirable representations of his great contemporaries, and whose art seems to admit us to the most charming domesticities of the day, and might teach even women to find a new charm in infancy. These are only the most conspicuous figures in a gallery including so many eminent figures, and full of characteristic touches even when we have to do with their hostile encounters. We smile now at Johnson's judgments of Rousseau, whom he would have sentenced to transportation, and of Homer, whose philosophy he regarded as an illustration of the folly of trying to milk the bull when you are not satisfied with the cow. To know an epoch we want to know its prejudices as well as its new ideas, and of the most dogged prejudices we certainly find an ample crop in Boswell. And where should we find a better illustration of the stalwart loyalty of the day than in Johnson's two famous interviews with George III and with the arch-demagogue Wilkes—the last the very gem of Boswell's unsurpassable book. "Johnson," says Carlyle, "was the last of the Tories." In studying Boswell you will learn to know what that means. When you have read it you have had a glimpse both of the tendencies, social and intellectual, which were thus bringing on the revolution, and of that huge mass of manly, pigheaded, prejudiced, stupid, judicious, selfish, patriotic, invincible common sense which crushed for a time the revolutionists of England, though it was far indeed from exterminating the seeds of a profound revolution. You might go far to complete your study by reading two delightful, though curiously contrasted, collections of letters—the letters of the lovable recluse Cowper, who incidentally reveals what was fermenting in quiet country circles, and the most admirable letters of the not-too-lovable Walpole, which will show you what was going on in circles which scarcely deigned to cast an eye upon Johnson. It will be set before you by an observer whom Macaulay chooses to ridicule as a fribble unworthy of serious attention, but who, if I be not greatly mistaken, had, beneath all his affectations, one of the keenest eyes of all his contemporaries, and who certainly wrote letters unsurpassable in the English language. If he had some of the failings generally attributed to the French, he had, what is far rarer, some of the high qualities which make the French unrivalled as memoir writers and correspondents.

Through such readings, I have said, you gain a vivid concrete picture of the men of the day. You will learn the folly of the fashion, now dying out, of simply abusing the eighteenth century. You will learn how many men then lived admirable domestic lives, how much there was of kindliness and good feeling, and sincere wish to grapple with the evils of the day. Such a study will help, as I have hinted, to a genuine appreciation of the political, the social, and the ecclesiastical movements of the time. And therefore by the same process it will enable you to enter into the literature—to understand Johnson's *Vanity of Human Wishes* and *Rasselas* and *Lives of the Poets*, even, it may be, his *Rambler*, which I admit is greatly in need of some shoeing-horn—to delight in Goldsmith's *Traveller*, and *Vicar of Wakefield*, to enjoy Gray's exquisite art, much as it was reviled by Johnson, at the same time that you will penetrate into the priceless treasure-trove of Burke's political wisdom, and even judge more wisely of Gibbon's monumental history, or of Adam Smith's *Wealth of Nations*.

You may be inclined to say that I am making large demands. For a Macaulay or a Carlyle, who wish to present a complete picture of the whole complex life of a period, such reading may be desirable or necessary. But most of us have neither the portentous memory of Macaulay nor the imaginative intensity of Carlyle, nor the opportunity of poring over the old records till we can reclothe the dead bones of history. To this I reply, first, that the time required is not so very great. To read Boswell and Walpole and Cowper, to glance over a few old periodicals like the *Gentleman's Magazine* and the *Annual Register*, to read the regular histories of the day, so as to have a skeleton map of dates and facts, requires no exclusive absorption in the study. A little leisure and a little enthusiasm will go a very long way. But I must next reply that study of this kind, like the others I have mentioned, is still in one respect not sufficient, and in another not necessary. It is not sufficient, because, after all, what a man wants for the appreciation of books is not so much to have this or that kind of knowledge as to be a clever fellow and to have a sensitive nature. A great though misunderstood philosopher, called Dogberry, observed that "to read and write comes by nature." With proper limits, that aphorism, as applied to the reading or writing of books, is very sound. You want faculties which cannot be put into you, if they are absent, by any education, and which have a provoking way of asserting their existence—to the great confusion of education theorists—when they have received none of the orthodox pabulum. I don't want to say a word against education. If I did, indeed, I should probably be here in some personal danger. In reality, I only wish to argue on behalf of a wide and thorough education. But we ought, in honesty, to recognise one fact sometimes neglected. A good education for literary purposes is by no means exclusively an education in literature. To appreciate Shakespeare you want something much more important than cramming with facts. To enjoy *Romeo and Juliet* the best qualification is to be one-and-twenty (which is compatible with being also thirty or forty). To enjoy *Hamlet* it is, perhaps, better to be, let us say, fifty-four. The education which comes through life, through the possession of certain passions and feelings, is the most important of all education. But, I hasten to observe, this does not tell against education in general, but only against a narrow education which fails to stimulate all our powers. The best way to learn military arts is not to be drilled in them from childhood, but to spend many childish hours in field sports and games which brace the nerves and sharpen the eyes. I will venture to say what may sound paradoxical. Of all studies that which has the least in common with literary study is, I suppose, the study of mathematics. I will add that mathematicians are apt to acquire certain rather mistaken prejudices in literary matters. But if

I were asked whether a young man would best fit himself for a literary career or for the study of literature by reading books about authors or by reading mathematics (supposing him to have only time for one pursuit), I should unhesitatingly advise mathematics. Not, of course, that he will learn anything directly useful. He will never require to apply the binomial theorem to the criticism of *Paradise Lost*. But an exclusive reading of mere criticism on literary history has a strong tendency to make a man a prig, to suppress all spontaneous and independent judgment, and to leave his general faculties undeveloped. A study of mathematics, on the other hand, has been, since Plato's days, the most admirable system of intellectual gymnastics ever devised; it braces and invigorates the mental fibre, it makes a man appreciate clear, vigorous, uncompromising reason, and familiarises him with the most perfectly adequate expression of certain forms of thought. Therefore, though he has not the information required, though he has not learnt a single applicable truth, he has so far the advantage of coming to any study with vigorous faculty, with a trained perception for certain essential qualities of all good work, scientific and literary, and without being sworn to the special tenets of any little critical school. He will at least appreciate the cardinal virtue of clearness. I confess that I attach more importance to the judgment of a man of vigorous intellect tackling a new book without any knowledge of previous critical dogmas than to the judgment of the professed critic of less vigour who utters his opinions in mortal fear of contradicting something that has been said by Ste.-Beuve or Mr. Matthew Arnold. And this brings me to the second point, that such training as I have suggested is not essential. I have tried to show, and it is my firm belief, that it is extremely useful, especially when combined with all other means of training. But I cannot conclude without also insisting upon the fact that even if it be not attainable there is still no reason why a man should not learn, within certain limits, to enjoy and appreciate the masterpieces of literature. This is rather a delicate subject, but I must seek very briefly to explain what I think. There is an old controversy as to the relative value of the critical and the vulgar judgment of books. At times, as in the familiar cases of Bunyan and Defoe, the vulgar have forced the critics to accept their verdict. At times the critical few have recognised merit which has only by degrees won acceptance with the multitude. The critics, like the vulgar, have special weaknesses and prejudices which often obscure their judgment. Without arguing the point, I am content to observe that, in my opinion, lasting success with either class is enough to prove merit, and that, in any case, the fact that the ignorant have sometimes had the best of it is enough to prove that an ignorant person may have a sound judgment. He has the great advantage of spontaneity—of admiring a thing because if affects him, not because he has been told that he ought to admire it.

To preserve this spontaneity in all our judgments should be one of our very first objects, however much training we may undergo. Sincerity in such matters is of the very essence of all sound opinion. There are, I think, two rules in this matter. Never persuade yourselves that you like what you don't like; not if it be *Faust* or *Hamlet*, or the *Divina Commedia*, or the *Iliad*. Sham liking is far worse than honest stupidity. But, again, do not presume to think that your dislike to an accepted masterpiece proves it not to be a masterpiece. The chances are a thousand or a million to one that you are wrong, and not all the generations which have accepted them. If Shakespeare was not a poet, Shakespeare's influence is as great a mystery as would be the elevation of Vesuvius without volcanic energy. Confess, therefore, your incapacity, and by all means confess it frankly, but do not parade it as a discovery. Try again, and see if Shakespeare will not improve. If he doesn't, try to explain why he has impressed other people, and calculate the chances of its being due to their folly or to your obtuseness.

But can we in any case expect a genuine appreciation without preparatory training—without knowing the history of a book, the age in which it was produced, the parallel phenomena in other literatures, and so forth? To that question I think that an answer may be suggested by one fact which is tolerably familiar to you here, and which I mention with all due reserve. You have all read *Old Mortality*. You are acquainted with Mause Headrigg and Ephraim Macbriar and Balfour of Burley. Each of those admirable types of the old Covenanters is familiar, beyond the familiarity of mere literary students, with the one book which to many Scots in their rank of life has been the whole of literature, and the study of which was the only preparatory study for one of the masterpieces of our language, the *Pilgrim's Progress*. The Bible is read by millions who know hardly any other book, and who know and care nothing for any auxiliary study. To them, of course, it is something far more than a mere literary study. But do they or do they not appreciate, for example, the Psalms of David—not simply as inspired documents, but as exalted poetry? If I may take Scott's judgment, as represented in such characters as Mause Headrigg or Davie Deans, the answer is not perfectly simple. Such people, he would obviously say, managed to find what they sought; the phrase about smiting the Amalekite hip and thigh suited them better than the precept of turning the second cheek; they found a pattern in Jael's treatment of Sisera, and somehow failed to pay equal attention to the parable of the Good Samaritan. And, moreover, Scott would have said, or we may certainly say for him, that their views of history would not have been those of the most judicious inquirers, and that they had very erroneous opinions as to the circumstances and times under which the Old and New Testaments were composed. Yet as evidently they were profoundly influenced by their studies; the Biblical language and history had entered into their very souls; and the narrative which they revered, the Psalms which became their battle-cry, had no small share in generating that heroic courage under torture and defeat which Scott, with all his Cavalier prejudices and all his abhorrence of Jacobinism, cannot help recognising, as a chivalrous antagonist, amongst the persecuted Covenanters.

Now, making all due corrections, we may, I think, deduce from this instance some of the limitations and merits of untrained reading. The man who reads "without note or comment," trusts to his own unaided sagacity, and makes no auxiliary studies, has undoubtedly some enormous disadvantages. He will be liable to error if he reasons upon the books he loves as historical documents; for, of course, it is essential in that view to know all that can be known of the time and conditions of authorship. He will be liable to blunder if he speaks as a critic; he may cite as proofs of original genius what is manifestly borrowed, and entirely misconceive the true relations of his favourite books to other literature. Lamb, who read the English drama as a lover, who entered into its spirit as no one has done, and interprets it with unrivalled felicity, only illustrated his own want of knowledge when he ventured upon asserting the superiority of Marlowe's *Dr. Faustus* to Goethe's *Faust*. The simple reader, again, who reads like Lamb, is specially likely to read into books where he should read out of them; to attribute to the authors his own thoughts, and to find edification like the proverbial old lady in the blessed word "Mesopotamia"—to confound between an author's meaning and the thoughts which he accidentally suggests. To be fair, we should perhaps add that the most ignorant of critics can hardly excel some philosophical commentators in this respect—German critics of Shakespeare, for example. But for mere literary purposes this failing is of less importance than the opposite error— the error of leaving out instead of adding; the ignorant reader not only misses special allusions to facts or to previous writers, but frequently a writer's whole drift: the covert satire which is really the vitalising salt of an epigram; the political or philosophical inference which is suggested instead of bluntly stated; he fails to perceive the intensity of passion which burns under a studiously compressed manner, or the sagacity which pierces some current sophism by the assertion of some obvious truth now looking like a common-place; and he is kept at a distance by some mannerism or conventional mode of speech which really only lies on the surface. Shakespeare's Ulysses speaks of that "touch of nature which makes the whole world kin," that

> *All with one consent praise newborn gauds,*
> *Though they are made and moulded of things past,*
> *And give to dust that is a little gilt*
> *More laud than gilt o'erdusted.*

We all more or less suffer from the illusion which leads us to value the coinage, not in proportion to its intrinsic value, but to the gloss of novelty and to the modernness of the image and superscription. It is the common error, in short, which makes us prefer the last volumes from the circulating library to Scott or Fielding, or to regard the last leading article as eclipsing Junius or even the *Letters on a Regicide Peace*. It is right, indeed, as well as almost inevitable, that we should be more interested by our contemporaries than by writers of the past; but it is undesirable, it is indeed fatal to true literary appreciation, that we should be deluded by this error of intellectual perspective into misconceiving the true magnitude of the fixed stars of literature when we are blinded by the meteors of to-day. And this is precisely the main use of those auxiliary studies of which I have spoken. Since the great men lose some influence by not being our contempora-ries, we must be able to make ourselves their contemporaries; to get rid of this common illusion; to overcome an obstacle which, though often trifling in itself, may frequently generate a complete incapacity for perceiving the true rela-tions of things, and permanently withhold from us posses-sions which, when we have once made a little effort, become invaluable. It is briefly the function of such study to rub off the dust which makes the gold less attractive than the base metal gilt.

In this sense, the use of such studies, however great, is yet negative. They remove a film from our eyes, but cannot of themselves give us eyesight. The reading of the ignorant man has often the superlative advantage, that it is a reading of love. The greatest writers show their power in nothing more than this, that they put so much inextinguishable fire into their work that even at the distance of centuries, with all the disadvantages of unfamiliar language and unintelligible allusions, and half-unintelligible purpose, the glow can be felt beneath the drift and accumulation of centuries by men who are congenial in soul though unprepared by culture. Keats could feel the charm of Homer through the translation of Chapman, though Chapman had been dead for two centuries and Homer belonged to an almost prehistoric world. The Psalms of David, I have said, stir millions who have no preparatory knowledge except of their own language. And frequently a man can wrestle and struggle into a perception of the essential meaning and beauty of a great author with surprisingly little training. But, as a rule, such a feat can only be achieved by men of abnormal intelligence. Judicious training can greatly diminish the impediments which keep at bay all but the keenest intelligence, and help to complete the knowledge and strengthen the perceptions even of the keenest. Most of us are absolutely in need of it, and everyone may be helped by it. Yet that is not enough unless the patient can also minister to himself; unless he has that intense appetite for the study which will sometimes overcome all apparent obstacles, though it will be the keener when the obstacles are removed. To teach so as to stimulate that appetite and not to quench it by irrelevant cram is the great problem for the teacher. And therefore I will add one corollary: as a rule, the best way of beginning the study of literature is to read that book which you can read with pleasure, or, if possible, with enthusiasm. I will not say—I wish I could—that there are no mischievous books. But (making obvious deductions) I am quite ready to accept with Gibbon the "tolerating maxim of the elder Pliny" that there is hardly any book from which you cannot derive some good. I am convinced that no reading is good which is not in some degree reading with an appetite. I am almost ready to invert the maxim, and to say that all reading with an appetite is necessarily good.

Some distinguished men have recently been amusing themselves with the insoluble problem, Which are the best hundred books? I say insoluble, because to my mind the best book for any man is that in which he takes most interest; and as men's powers and tastes vary indefinitely, and there is no power and no taste which may not be stimulated by reading, so the suitability of books depends upon the idiosyncrasy of the reader. One man prefers metaphysics and another poetry; one is a devourer of novels and another of biography, and a third of travels, and a fourth of history, and a fifth of antiquarian research, and a sixth of theological controversy, and a seventh of politics; one likes the classics and another Oriental or modern English literature; one is an enthusiast for Scott, and one for Coleridge, and a third for Alexandre Dumas, and so forth. Which is the best? That depends on the man; but all are good, and whichever rouses his mind most, and commands his sympathies most powerfully, is in all probability the best for him. Literature represents all the reasonings and feelings and passions of civilised men in all ages. As Coleridge says—

> *All thoughts, all passions, all desires,*
> *Whatever stirs this mortal frame,*
> *All are but ministers of Love,*
> *And feed his sacred flame.*

We may apply the words to genius. To select any particular variety as best for all is as absurd as to say that every man ought to be a priest or that every man ought to be a soldier. But this I may say, Take hold anywhere, read what you really like and not what someone tells you that you ought to like; let your reading be part of your lives. It may have a bearing upon your true interests and the function which you are to discharge in the world; or it may be a relief to the occupations in which you are immersed. Even if it be a mere recreation, let it be such a recreation as may be subservient to your highest development—a rule which is of course applicable to every employment, from preaching to playing football. But, in any case, remember that reading worthy of the name is not the acquisition of a set of dates and facts, or a knowledge of the correct critical labels, but an occupation which to be pursued to any purpose must be pursued with zeal—must become, if it should not begin by being, a real and keen enjoyment, and which should end by becoming not a mere luxury but a necessity of life. If there should be some people who find, after all, that reading anything is a bore, I shall simply point out to them that there are many occupations besides reading, and some of them quite as useful. You may study science and art, or be active philanthropists, though you never read anything more nearly approaching literature than Euclid or the reports of the association for the benefit of distressed washerwomen. Literature should be content with its genuine worshippers, and not stoop to enlist the services of mere hypocrites. But I am equally certain that most of us can find something to read, something the reading of which can become a ruling passion, something, too, which will please our intellects, give keenness to our perceptions and strength to our sympathies, something which will make us better specimens of the human race, and more fitted to discharge any of the duties which lie before us. And if fully to qualify ourselves requires a struggle, it is a struggle which will bring an ample reward.

(The Cornhill Magazine, 1887)

# The Essayists

ONE of our national characteristics, we are told, is a love of sermons of all varieties, from sermons in stone to sermons in rhyme. We have no reason, that I can see, to be ashamed of our taste. We make an awkward figure when we disavow or disguise it. The spectacle of a solid John Bull trying to give himself the airs of a graceful, sensitive, pleasure-loving creature, indifferent to the duties of life and content with the spontaneous utterance of emotion, is always ridiculous. We cannot do it—whether it be worth doing or not. We try desperately to be æsthetic, but we can't help laughing at ourselves in the very act: and the only result is that we sometimes substitute painfully immoral for painfully moral sermons. We are just as clumsy as before, and a good deal less natural. I accept the fact without seeking to justify it, and I hold that every Englishman loves a sermon in his heart. We grumble dreadfully, it is true, over the quality of the sermons provided by the official representatives of the art. In this, as in many previous long vacations, there will probably be a lively discussion in the papers as to the causes of the dullness of modern pulpits. I always wonder, for my part, that our hard-worked clergy can turn out so many entertaining and impressive discourses as they actually do.

At present I have nothing to say to the sermon properly so called. There is another kind of sermon, the demand for which is conclusively established by the exuberance of the supply. Few books, I fancy, have been more popular in modern times than certain lay-sermons, composed, as it seems to scoffers, of the very quintessence of commonplace. If such popularity were an adequate test of merit, we should have to reckon amongst the highest intellectual qualities the power of pouring forth a gentle and continuous maundering

about things in general. We swallow with unfailing appetite a
feeble dilution of harmless philanthropy mixed with a little
stingless satirising of anything that interrupts the current of
complacent optimism. We like to hear a thoroughly comfortable person purring contentedly in his armchair, and declaring that everything must be for the best in a world which
has provided him so liberally with buttered rolls and a
blazing fire. He hums out a satisfactory little string of platitudes as soothing as the voice of his own kettle singing on
the hob. If a man of sterner nature or more daring intellect
breaks in with a harsh declaration that there are evils too
deep to be remedied by a letter to the *Times*, mocks at our
ideal of petty domestic comfort, and even swears that some
of our heroes are charlatans and our pet nostrums mere
quackery, we are inexpressibly shocked, and unite to hoot
him down as a malevolent cynic. He professes, in sober
earnest, to disbelieve in us. Obviously he must be a disbe-
liever in all human virtue; and so, having settled his business,
we return to our comfortable philosopher, and lap ourselves
in his gentle eulogies of our established conventions. I do
not know, indeed, that we change very decidedly for the
better when we turn up our noses at a diet of mere milk and
water, and stimulate our jaded palate with an infusion of
literary bitters. The cynic and the sentimentalist who
preach to us by turns in the social essay, often differ very
slightly in the intrinsic merit or even in the substance of
their discourses. Respondent and opponent are really on the
same side in these little disputations, though they make a
great show of deadly antagonism. I have often felt it to be a
melancholy reflection that some of the most famous witticisms ever struck out—the saying about the use of language
or the definition of gratitude—have been made by what
seems to be almost a mechanical device—the inversion of a
truism. Nothing gives a stronger impression of the limited
range of the human intellect. In fact, it seems that the essay
writer has to make his choice between the platitude and the
paradox. If he wishes for immediate success he will probably

do best by choosing the platitude. One of the great secrets of popularity—though it requires a discreet application—is not to be too much afraid of boring your audience. The most popular of modern writers have acted upon the principle. You may learn from Dickens that you cannot make your jokes too obvious or repeat them too often; and from Macaulay that you should grudge no labour spent in proving that two and two make four. The public should be treated as a judicious barrister treats a common jury. It applauds most lustily the archer who is quite certain of hitting a haystack at ten paces: not the one who can sometimes split a willow wand at a hundred. Even the hardened essayist feels a little compunction at times. He is conscious that he has been anticipated in the remark that life is uncertain, and doubts whether he can season it with wit enough to get rid of the insipidity. "Of all the vices which degrade the human character," said the youthful Osborne in the essay which Amelia produced to Dobbin, "selfishness is the most odious and contemptible. An undue love of self leads to the most monstrous crimes, and occasions the greatest misfortunes both to States and families." Young Osborne succeeded in staggering through two or three sentences more, though he ends, it is true, by dropping into something like tautology. But really, when I consider the difficulty of saying anything, I am half-inclined to agree with his tutor's opinion that there was no office in the Bar or the Senate to which the lad might not aspire. How many sermons would reduce themselves to repeating this statement over and over again for the prescribed twenty minutes! And yet some skilful essayists have succeeded in giving a great charm to such remarks; and I rather wonder that amongst the various selections now so fashionable, someone has not thought of a selection of our best periodical essays. Between the days of Bacon and our own, a sufficient number have been produced to furnish some very interesting volumes.

The essay writer is the lay preacher upon that vague mass of doctrine which we dignify by the name of knowledge of

life or of human nature. He has to do with the science in
which we all graduate as we grow old, when we try to pack
our personal observations into a few sententious aphorisms
not quite identical with the old formulæ. It is a strange experience which happens to some people to grow old in a day,
and to find that some good old saying—"vanity of vanities,"
for example—which you have been repeating ever since you
first left college and gave yourself the airs of a man of the
world, has suddenly become a vivid and striking impression of
a novel truth, and has all the force of a sudden discovery. In
one of Poe's stories, a clever man hides an important document by placing it exactly in the most obvious and conspicuous place in the room. That is the principle, it would
sometimes seem, which accounts for the preservation of
certain important secrets of life. They are hidden from the
uninitiated just because the phrases in which they are couched
are so familiar. We fancy, in our youth, that our elders must
either be humbugs—which is the pleasantest and most
obvious theory—or that they must have some little store of
esoteric wisdom which they keep carefully to themselves.
The initiated become aware that neither hypothesis is true.
Experience teaches some real lessons; but they are taught
in the old words. The change required is in the mind of the
thinker, not in the symbols of his thought. Wordly wisdom is
summed up in the familiar currency which has passed from
hand to hand through the centuries; and we find on some
catastrophe, or by the gradual process of advancing years, that
mystic properties lurk unsuspected in the domestic halfpenny.

The essayist should be able, more or less, to anticipate
this change, and make us see what is before our eyes. It is
easy enough for the mere hawker of sterile platitudes to
imitate his procedure, and to put on airs of superhuman
wisdom when retailing the barren *exuviæ* of other men's
thought. But there are some rare books, in reading which
we slowly become aware that we have to do with the man
who has done all that can be done in this direction—that is,
rediscovered the old discoveries for himself. Chief, beyond

rivalry, amongst all such performances, in our own language, at least, is Bacon's *Essays*. Like Montaigne, he represents, of course, the mood in which the great aim of the ablest thinkers was precisely to see facts for themselves instead of taking them on trust. And though Bacon has not the delightful egotism or the shrewd humour of his predecessors, and substitutes the tersest method of presenting his thought for the discursive rambling characteristic of the prince of all essayists, the charm of his writing is almost equally due to his unconscious revelation of character. One can imagine a careless reader, indeed, skimming the book in a hurry, and setting down the author as a kind of Polonius—a venerable old person with a plentiful lack of wit and nothing on his tongue but "words, words, words." In spite of the weighty style, surcharged, as it seems, with thought and experience, we might quote maxim after maxim from its pages with a most suspicious air of Polonius wisdom; and though Polonius, doubtless, had been a wise man in his day, Hamlet clearly took him for an old bore, and dealt with him as we could all wish at moments to deal with bores. "He that is plentiful in expense of all kinds will hardly be preserved from decay." Does it require a "large-browed Verulam," one of the first "of those that know," to give us that valuable bit of information? Or—to dip into his pages at random—could we not have guessed for ourselves that if a man "easily pardons and remits offences, it shows"—what?— "that his mind is planted above injuries"; or, again, that "good thoughts are little better than good dreams except they be put in act"; or even that a man "should be sure to leave other men their turns to speak." "Here be truths," and set forth as solemnly as if they were calculated to throw a new light upon things in general. But it would be hard to demand even of a Bacon that he should refrain from all that has been said before. And the impression—if it ever crosses the mind of a perverse critic—that Bacon was a bit of a windbag, very rapidly disappears. It would be far less difficult to find pages free from platitude than to find one in which there is not some condensed saying which makes us acknowledge that the mark has been hit, and the definitive form imposed upon some hazy notion which has been vaguely hovering about the mind, and eluding all our attempts to grasp it. We have not thought just that, but something which clearly ought to have been that. Occasionally, of course, this is due to the singular power in which Bacon, whatever his other merits or defects, excels all other philosophic writers; the power which springs from a unique combination of the imaginative and speculative faculties, of finding some vivid concrete image to symbolise abstract truths. It is exhibited again in the perverted, but often delightful, ingenuity with which he reads philosophical meanings into old mythological legends, entirely innocent, as a matter of fact, of any such matter; which often makes us fancy that he was a new incarnation of Æsop, able to construct the most felicitous parables at a moment's notice, to illustrate any conceivable combination of ideas; a power, too, which is connected with his weakness, and helps to explain how he could be at once an almost inspired prophet of a coming scientific era, and yet curiously wanting in genuine aptitude for scientific inquiry. It is, perhaps, the more one-sided and colourless intellect which is best fitted for achievement, though incapable of clothing its ambition in the resplendent hues of Bacon's imagination.

In the *Essays* the compression of the style keeps this power in subordination. Analogies are suggested in a pregnant sentence, not elaborated and brought forward in the pomp of stately rhetoric. Only, as we become familiar with the book, we become more aware of the richness and versatility of intellect which it implies, and conscious of the extreme difficulty of characterising it or its author in any compendious phrase. That has hardly been done; or, what is worse, it has been misdone. Readers who do not shrink from Mr. Spedding's* seven solid volumes may learn to know Bacon;

* They may learn as much from the admirable *Evenings with a Reviewer*, which unfortunately remains a privately-printed book, not easy to get sight of.

and will admit at least that the picture drawn by that loving hand differs as much from Macaulay's slapdash blacks and whites as a portrait by a master from the audacious caricature of a contemporary satirist. But Mr. Spedding was characteristically anxious that his readers should draw their own conclusions. He left it to a successor, who has not hitherto appeared, to sum up the total impressions of the amazingly versatile and complex character, and to show how inadequately it is represented by simply heaping together a mass of contradictions, and calling them a judgment. Perhaps a thorough study of the *Essays* would be enough by itself to make us really intimate with their author. For we see as we read that Bacon is a typical example of one of the two great races between whom our allegiance is generally divided. He would be despised by the Puritan as worldly, and would retort by equal contempt for the narrow bigotry of Puritanism. You cannot admire him heartily if the objects of your hero-worship are men of the Cromwell or Luther type. The stern imperious man of action, who aims straight at the heart, who is efficient in proportion as he is one-sided, to whom the world presents itself as an internecine struggle between the powers of light and darkness, who can see nothing but eternal truths on one side and damnable lies on the other, who would reform by crushing his opponents to the dust, and regards all scruples that might trammel his energies as so much hollow cant, is undoubtedly an impressive phenomenon. But it is also plain that he must have suppressed half his nature; he has lost in breadth what he has gained in immensity; and the merits of a Bacon depend precisely upon the richness of his mind and the width of his culture. He cannot help sympathising with all the contemporary currents of thought. He is tempted to injustice only in regard to the systems which seem to imply the stagnation of thought. He hates bigotry, and bigotry alone, but bigotry in every possible phase, even when it is accidentally upon his own side. His sympathies are so wide that he cannot help taking all knowledge for his province. The one lesson which he cannot learn is Goethe's lesson of "renouncing." The whole universe is so interesting that every avenue for thought must be kept open. He is at once a philosopher, a statesman, a lawyer, a man of science, and an omnivorous student of literature. The widest theorising and the minutest experiment are equally welcome; he is as much interested in arranging a masque or laying out a garden, as in a political intrigue or a legal reform or a logical speculation. The weakness of such a man in political life is grossly misinterpreted when it is confounded with the baseness of a servile courtier. It is not that he is without aims, and lofty aims; but that they are complex, far-reaching, and too wide for vulgar comprehension. He cannot join the party of revolution or the party of obstruction, for he desires the equable development of the whole organisation. The danger is not that he will defy reason, but that he will succeed in finding reasons for any conceivable course. The world's business, as he well knows, has to be carried on with the help of the stupid and the vile; and he naturally errs on the side of indulgence and compliance, hoping to work men to the furtherance of views of which they are unable to grasp the importance. His tolerance is apt to slide into wordliness, and his sensibility to all manner of impulses makes him vulnerable upon many points, and often takes the form of timidity. The time-serving of the profligate means a desire for personal gratification; the time-serving of a Bacon means too great a readiness to take the world as it is, and to use questionable tools in the pursuit of vast and elevated designs.

The *Essays* reflect these characteristics. They are the thoughts of a philosopher who is not content to accept any commonplace without independent examination; but who is as little disposed to reject an opinion summarily because it has a slightly immoral aspect as to reject a scientific experiment because it contradicts an established theory. We must hear what the vicious man has to say for himself, as well as listen to the virtuous. He shows his tendency in the opening essay. The dearest of all virtues to the philosophic mind is truth, and there is no sincerer lover of such truth than Bacon. But he will not overlook the claims of falsehood. "Truth may, perhaps, come to the price of a pearl, that showeth best by day; but it will not rise to the price of a diamond or carbuncle, that showeth best in varied lights. A mixture of a lie doth ever add pleasure." That famous sentence is just one of the sayings which the decorous moralist is apt to denounce or to hide away in dexterous verbiage. Bacon's calm recognition of the fact is more impressive, and, perhaps, not really less moral. The essay upon *Simulation and Dissimulation* may suggest more qualms to the rigorous. Dissimulation, it is true, is condemned as a "faint kind of policy and wisdom"; it is the "weaker sort of politicians that are the great dissemblers." But this denunciation has to be refined and shaded away. For, in the first place, a habit of secrecy is both "moral and politic." But secrecy implies more; for "no man can be secret except he give himself a little scope of dissimulation; which is, as it were, but the skirts or train of secrecy." But if secrecy leads to dissimulation, will not dissimulation imply downright simulation—in plain English, lying? "That," replies Bacon, "I hold more culpable and less politic, except it be in rare and great matters." He enumerates their advantages, and their counter-balancing disadvantages; and the summing-up is one of his characteristic sentences. "The best composition and temperature is to love openness in fame and opinion; secrecy in habit; dissimulation in seasonable use; and a power to feign if there be no remedy."

How skilfully the claims of morality and policy are blended! How delicately we slide from the virtue of holding our tongues to the advisability of occasional lying! "You old rogue!" exclaims the severe moralist, "your advice is simply —don't lie, unless you can lie to your advantage, and without loss of credit." And yet it really seems, if we follow Mr. Spedding's elaborate investigations, that Bacon lied remarkably little for a statesman—especially for a timid statesman —in an age of elaborate intrigues. I fancy that the student of

recent history would admit that the art of dexterous equivo-
cation had not fallen entirely out of use, and is not judged
with great severity when an opponent asks an awkward
question in Parliament. A cynic might even declare the
chief difference to be that we now disavow the principles
upon which we really act, and so lie to ourselves as well as to
others; whereas Bacon was at least true to himself, and, if
forced to adopt a theory of expediency, would not blink the
fact. It is this kind of sincerity to which the *Essays* owe part
of their charm to every thoughtful reader. We must not go
to them for lofty or romantic morality—for sayings satisfactory to the purist or the enthusiast. We have a morality,
rather, which has been refracted through a mind thoroughly
imbued with worldly wisdom, and ready to accept the com-
promises which a man who mixes with his fellows on equal
terms must often make with his conscience. He is no hermit
to renounce the world, for the world is, after all, a great
fact; nor to retire to a desert because the air of cities is taint-
ed by the lungs of his fellows. He accepts the code which is
workable, not that which is ideally pure. He loves in all
things the true *via media*. He objects to atheism, for religion
is politically useful; but he is quite as severe upon superstition, which is apt to generate a more dangerous fanaticism.
He considers love to be a kind of excusable weakness, so
long as men "sever it wholly from their serious affairs and
actions of life"; but he is eloquent and forcible in exalting
friendship, without which a man may as well "quit the stage."
In this, indeed, Bacon (we will take Mr. Spedding's view of
that little affair about Essex) seems to have spoken from his
own experience; and in spite of the taint of wordliness, the
feeling that there is something tepid in their author's nature,
a certain want of cordiality in the grasp of his hand—we feel
that the *Essays* have a merit beyond that which belongs to
them as genuine records of the observation of life at first
hand by a man of vast ability and varied and prolonged experience. They show, too, a marvellously rich and sensitive
nature, capable of wide sympathies, with all manner of in-

terests, devoted to a grand and far-reaching ambition, though not sufficiently contemptuous of immediate expediency, and fully appreciative of the really valuable elements in human life. If he has the weaknesses—he has also, in a surpassing degree, the merits—of a true cosmopolitan, or citizen of this world, whose wisdom, if not as childlike as the Christian preacher requires, is most certainly not childish. When we add the literary genius which has coined so many pregnant aphorisms, and stamped even truisms with his own image and superscription, we can understand why the *Essays* have come home to men's business and bosoms.

It is amusing to compare Bacon with the always delightful Fuller, in regard to whom Coleridge declares that his amazing wit has deprived him of the credit due to his soundness of judgment. The statement does not quite cover the ground. Fuller in the *Holy and Profane State* and Bacon in the *Essays* have each given us a short sermon upon the text *Be angry and sin not.* Fuller undoubtedly makes the greatest display of intellectual fireworks. In half-a-dozen short paragraphs, he gets off as many witticisms, good, bad, and inimitable. A man who can't be angry, he says, is like the Caspian Sea which never ebbs or flows: to be angry on slight cause, is to fire the beacons at the landing of every cockboat: you should beware of doing irrevocable mischief when you are angry, for Samson's hair grew again, but not his eyes: he tells us that manna did not corrupt when left over the Sabbath, whereas anger then corrupts most of all: and then we have that irresistible piece of absurdity which so delighted Charles Lamb; we are warned not to take too literally the apostle's direction not to let the sun go down upon our wrath, for "then might our wrath lengthen with the days, and men in Greenland, where day lasts above a quarter of the year, might have plentiful scope of revenge." Undoubtedly Fuller's astonishing ingenuity in striking out illustrations of this kind, excites, as Coleridge says, our sense of the wonderful. If we read in search of amusement, we are rewarded at every page; we shall never fail to make a bag in beating his coverts: and beyond a doubt we shall bring back as well a healthy liking for the shrewd lively simplicity which has provided them. But it is equally undeniable that Fuller never takes the trouble to distinguish between an illustration which really gives light to our feet and a sudden flash of brilliancy which disappears to leave the obscurity unchanged. He cannot refrain from a ludicrous analogy, which is often all the more amusing just because it is preposterously inapplicable. Here and there we have a really brilliant stroke and then an audacious pun, not, perhaps, a play upon words, but a play upon ideas which is quite as superficial. At bottom we feel that the excellent man has expended his energy, not in "chewing and digesting" the formula which serves him for a text, but in overlaying it with quaint conceits. Bacon gives us no such flashes of wit, though certainly not from inability to supply them; but he says a thing which we remember: "Men must beware that they carry their anger rather with scorn than with fear, so that they may seem to be rather above the injury than below it; which is a thing easily done, if a man will give a law to himself in it." The remark is doubtless old enough in substance; but it reveals at once the man who does not allow a truism to run through his mind without weighing or testing it; who has impartially considered the uses of anger and the proper mode of disciplining it; and who can aid us with a judicious hint or two as to the best plan of making others angry, an art of great utility, whatever its morality, in many affairs of life.

The essay, as Bacon understood it, is indeed a trying form of utterance. A man must be very confident of the value of his own meditations upon things in general, and of his capacity for "looking wiser than any man ever really was," before he should venture to adopt his form. I cannot remember any English book deserving to be put in the same class, unless it be Sir Henry Taylor's essays, the *Statesman* and *Notes upon Life*, which have the resemblance at least of reflecting, in admirably graceful English, the

mellowed wisdom of a cultivated and meditative mind, which
has tested commonplaces by the realities of the world and its
business. But a few men have thoughts which will bear
being presented simply and straightforwardly, and which
have specific gravity enough to dispense with adventitious
aids. A Frenchman can always season his wisdom with
epigram, and coins his reflections into the form of detached
*pensées*. But our language or our intellect is too blunt for
such jewellery in words. We cannot match Pascal, or Roche-
foucauld, or Vauvenargues, or Chamfort. Our modes of
expression are lumbering, and seem to have been developed
rather in the pulpit than in the rapid interchange of animated
conversation. The essay after Bacon did not crystallise into
separate drops of sparkling wit, but became more continuous, less epigrammatic, and easier in its flow. Cowley
just tried his hand at the art enough to make us regret that
he did not give us more prose and fewer Pindarics. Sir
William Temple's essays give an interesting picture of the
statesman who has for once realised the dream so often
cherished in vain, of a retirement to books and gardens;
but the thought is too superficial and the style too slipshod
for enduring popularity; and that sturdy, hot-headed,
pugnacious, and rather priggish moralist, Jeremy Collier,
poured out some hearty, rugged essays, which make us like
the man, but feel that he is too much of the pedagogue,
brandishing a birch-rod wherewith to whip our sins out of
us. The genuine essayist appeared with Steele and Addison
and their countless imitators. Some salvage from the vast
mass of periodicals which have sunk into the abysses appears
upon our shelves in the shape of forty-odd volumes, duly
annotated and expounded by laborious commentators. It is
amusing to glance over the row, from the *Tatler* to the
*Looker-on*, from the days of Steele to those of Cumberland
and Mackenzie, the "Man of Feeling," and reflect upon the
simple-mindedness of our great-grandfathers. Nothing
brings back to us more vividly the time of the good old
British "gentlewoman"; the contemporary of the admirable

Mrs. Chapone and Mrs. Carter, who even contributed short papers to the *Rambler*, and regarded the honour as a patent of immortality; who formed Richardson's court, and made tea for Johnson; who wrote letters about the "improvement of the mind," and at times ventured upon a translation of a classical moralist, but inquired with some anxiety whether a knowledge of Latin was consistent with the delicacy of the female sex; and thought it a piece of delicate flattery when a male author condescended to write down to the level of their comprehension. Lady Mary seems to have been the only woman of the century who really felt herself entitled to a claim of intellectual equality; and the feminine author was regarded much in the same way as a modern lady in the hunting-field. It was a question whether she should be treated with exceptional forbearance, or warned off a pursuit rather too rough for a true womanly occupation. Johnson's famous comparison of the preaching women to the dancing dogs gives the general sentiment. They were not admired for writing well, but for writing at all.

We have changed all this, and there is something pathetic in the tentative and modest approaches of our grandmothers to the pursuits in which their granddaughters have achieved the rights and responsibilities of equal treatment.

But it is necessary to remember, in reading the whole *Spectator* and its successors, that this audience is always in the background. It is literature written by gentlemen for ladies—that is, for persons disposed to sit at gentlemen's feet. Bacon is delivering his thoughts for the guidance of thoughtful aspirants to fame; and Temple is acting the polished statesman in the imagined presence of wits and courtiers. But Steele and Addison make it their express boast that they write for the good of women, who have hitherto been limited to an intellectual diet of decent devotional works or of plays and romances. The *Spectator* is to lie on the table by the side of the morning dish of chocolate; and every writer in a periodical knows how carefully he must bear in mind the audience for which he is catering.

The form once fixed was preserved throughout the century with a persistency characteristic of the sheep-like race of authors. Every successor tried to walk in Addison's footsteps. The *World*, as somebody tells us, was the Ulysses bow in which all the wits of the day tried their strength. The fine gentlemen, like Chesterfield and Walpole, too nice to rub shoulders with the ordinary denizens of Grub Street, ventured into this select arena with the encouragement of some easily dropped mask of anonymity. It is amusing to observe on what easy terms glory was to be won by such achievements. There was the exemplary Mr. Grove, of Taunton, who wrote a paper in the *Spectator*, which, according to Johnson, was "one of the finest pieces in the English language," though I suppose but few of my readers can recollect a word of it, and Mr. Ince, of Gray's Inn, who frequented Tom's Coffee House, and was apparently revered by other frequenters on the strength of a compliment from Steele to some contributions never identified. Nay, a certain Mr. Elphinstone, seen in the flesh by Hazlitt, was surrounded for fifty years by a kind of faint halo of literary fame, because he had discharged the humble duty of translating the mottoes to the *Rambler*. The fame, indeed, has not been very enduring. We have lost our appetite for this simple food. Very few people, we may suspect, give their days and nights to the study of Addison, any more than a youthful versifier tries to catch the echo of Pope. We are rather disposed to laugh at the classical motto which serves in place of a text, and must have given infinite trouble to some unfortunate scribblers. The gentle raillery of feminine foibles in dress or manners requires to be renewed in every generation with the fashions to which it refers. The novelettes are of that kind of literature which are too much like tracts, insipid to tastes accustomed to the full-blown novel developed in later times. A classical allegory or a so-called Eastern tale has become a puerility like the old-fashioned pastoral. We half regret the days when a man with a taste for fossils or butterflies was called a *virtuoso*, and considered an unfailing butt for easy ridicule; but we are too much under the thumb of the scientific world to reveal our sentiments. And as for the criticism, with its elaborate inanities about the unities and the rules of epic poetry, and the authority of Aristotle and M. Bossu, we look down upon it from the heights of philosophical æsthetics, and rejoice complacently in the infallibility of modern tastes. Were it not for *Sir Roger de Coverley*, the old-fashioned essay would be wellnigh forgotten, except by some examiner who wants a bit of pure English to be turned into Latin prose.

Oblivion of this kind is the natural penalty of labouring upon another man's foundations. There is clearly a presumption that the form struck out by Addison would not precisely suit Fielding or Johnson or Goldsmith; and accordingly we read *Tom Jones* and the *Vicar of Wakefield* and the *Lives of the Poets* without troubling ourselves to glance at the *Champion* or the *Covent Garden Journal*. We make a perfunctory study even of the *Bee* and the *Citizen of the World*, and are irreverent about the *Rambler*. We may find in them, indeed, abundant traces of Fielding's rough irony and hearty common sense, and of Goldsmith's delicate humour and felicity of touch; but Goldsmith, when forced to continuous dissertation, has to spin his thread too fine, and Fielding seems to be uncomfortably cramped within the narrow limits of the essay. The *Rambler* should not have a superfluous word said against it; for the very name has become a kind of scarecrow; and yet anyone who will skip most of the criticisms and all the amusing passages may suck much profitable and not unpleasing melancholy out of its ponderous pages. It is all the pleasanter for its contrast to the kind of jaunty optimism which most essayists adopt as most congenial to easy-going readers. I like to come upon one of Johnson's solemn utterances of a conviction of the radical wretchedness of life. "The cure for the greatest part of human miseries is not radical but palliative. Infelicity is involved in corporeal nature, and interwoven with our being; all attempts, therefore, to decline it wholly are useless and vain; the armies of pain send their arrows against us on every side; the choice is only between those which are more or less sharp, or tinged with poison of greater or less malignity; and the strongest armour which reason can supply will only blunt their points, but cannot repel them." This melancholy monotone of sadness, coming from a brave and much-enduring nature, is impressive, but it must be admitted that it would make rather severe reading at a tea-table—even when presided over by that ornament to her sex, the translator of Epictetus. And poor Johnson, being painfully sensible that he must not deviate too far from his Addison, makes an elephantine gambol or two with a very wry face; and is only comical by his failure.

I take it, in fact, to be established that within his special and narrow province Addison was unique. Hazlitt and Leigh Hunt tried to exalt Steele above his colleague. We can perfectly understand their affection for the chivalrous, warm-hearted Irishman. When a virtuous person rebukes the extravagance of a thoughtless friend by the broad hint of putting an execution into his house, we naturally take part with the offender. We have a sense that Addison got a little more than his deserts in this world, whilst Steele got a little less, and we wish to make the balance even. And to some extent this applies in a literary sense. Steele has more warmth and pathos than Addison; he can speak of women without the patronising tone of his leader, and would hardly, like him, have quoted for their benefit the famous theory of Pericles as to their true glory. And, yet, it does not want any refined criticism to recognise Addison's superiority. Steele's admirers have tried to vindicate for him a share in Sir Roger; but anyone who reads the papers in which that memorable character is described, will see that all the really fine touches are contributed by Addison. Steele took one of the most promising incidents, the courtship of the widow, and the paper in which this appears is the furthest below the general level. To have created Sir Roger—the forefather of so many exquisite characters, for surely he is closely related to

Parson Adams, and Uncle Toby, and Doctor Primrose, and
Colonel Newcome—is Addison's greatest achievement, and
the most characteristic of the man. For it is impossible not to
feel that some injustice is done to Addison when grave
writers like M. Taine, for example, treat him seriously as a
novelist or a political theorist, or even as a critic. Judged by
any severe standard, his morality and his political disserta-
tions and his critical disquisitions—the immortal papers, for
example, upon the Imagination and upon *Paradise Lost*—
are puerile enough. With all our love of sermons, we can be
almost as much bored as M. Taine himself by some of
Addison's prosings. The charm of the man is just in the
admirable simplicity of which Sir Roger is only an imaginative projection. Addison, it is true, smiles at the knight's
little absurdities from the platform of superior scholarship.
He feels himself to be on the highest level of the culture of
his time—a scholar, a gentleman—fit to sit in council with
Somers, or to interpret the speculations of Locke. But at
bottom he is precisely of the same material as the fine old
squire with whom he sympathises. His simplicity is not
destroyed by learning to write Latin verses or even by becoming a Secretary of State. Sir Roger does not accept the
teaching of his chaplain with more reverence than Addison
feels for Tillotson and the admirable Dr. Scott, whose
authority has become very faded for us. The squire accepts
Baker's chronicle as his sole and infallible authority in all
matters of history; but Addison's history would pass muster
just as little with Mr. Freeman or Dr. Stubbs. We smile at
Sir Roger's satisfaction with the progress of the Church of
England when a rigid dissenter eats plentifully of his
Christmas plum-porridge; but there is something almost
equally simple-minded in Addison's conviction that the
prosecutors of Sacheverell had spoken the very last words of
political wisdom, and even the good Sir Roger's criticisms of
the *Distressed Mother* are not much simpler in substance,
though less ambitious in form, than Addison's lectures upon
similar topics. Time has put us as much beyond the artist

as the artist was beyond his model, and, though he is in part
the accomplice, he must also be taken as partly the object of
some good-humoured ridicule. We cannot sit at his feet as a
political teacher; but we see that his politics really mean
the spontaneous sympathy of a kindly and generous nature,
which receives a painful jar from the sight of bigotry and
oppression. His theology, as M. Taine rather superfluously
insists, represents the frigid and prosaic type of contemporary divines; but it is only the external covering of that
tender sentiment of natural piety to which we owe some of
the most exquisite hymns in the language. In short, the
occasional pretentiousness of the man, when he wants to
deliver *ex cathedra* judgments upon points of criticism and
morality, becomes a very venial and rather amusing bit of
affectation. It shows only the docility—perhaps rather
excessive—with which a gentle and rather timid intellect
accepts, at their own valuation, the accepted teachers of his
day; and, having put away all thoughts of judging him by an
inapplicable standard, we can enjoy him for what he really is
without further qualification; we can delight in the urbanity
which is the indication of a childlike nature unspoilt by
familiarity with the world; we can admire equally the tenderness, guided by playful fancy, of the Vision of Mirza, or the
legend of Marraton and Yaratilda, and the passages in which
he amuses himself with some such trifle as ladies' patches,
handling his plaything so dexterously as never to be too
ponderous, whilst somehow preserving, by mere unconscious
wit, an air as of amiable wisdom relaxing for a moment from
severer thought. Addison's imitators flounder awkwardly
enough, for the most part, in attempting to repeat a performance which looks so easy after its execution; but in
truth, the secret, though it may be an open one, is not easily
appropriated. You have only to acquire Addison's peculiar
nature, his delicacy of perception, his tenderness of nature
held in check by excessive sensibility, his generosity of
feeling which can never hurry him out of the safe entrenchment of thorough respectability, his intense appreciation of

all that is pure and beautiful so long as it is also of good report—you must have, in short, the fine qualities along with the limitations of his character, and then you will spontaneously express, in this kind of lambent humour, the quiet, sub-sarcastic playfulness which could gleam out so delightfully when he was alone with a friend, or with his pen, and a bottle of port to give him courage.

Essay-writing, thus understood, is as much one of the lost arts as good letter-writing or good talk. We are too distracted, too hurried. The town about which these essayists are always talking, meant a limited society; it has now become a vast chaos of distracted atoms, whirled into momentary contact, but not coalescing into permanent groups. A sensitive, reserved Addison would go to his club in the days when a club meant a social gathering instead of an oppressive house of call for 1,200 gentlemen, glaring mutual distrust across their newspaper. He has his recognised corner at the coffee-house, where he could listen undisturbed to the gossip of the regular frequenters. He would retire to his lodgings with a chosen friend, and gradually thaw under the influence of his bottle and his pipe of tobacco, till he poured out his little speculations to his companion, or wrote them down for an audience which he knew as a country parson knows his congregation. He could make little confidential jokes to the public, for the public was only an enlarged circle of friends. At the present day, such a man, for he was a man of taste and reflection, finds society an intolerable bore. He goes into it to be one of a crowd assembled for a moment to be dispersed in a dozen different crowds to-morrow; he is stuck down at a dinner-table between a couple of strangers, and has not time to break the ice or get beyond the conventional twaddle, unless, indeed, he meets some intrepid talker, who asks him between the soup and the fish whether he believes in the equality of the sexes or the existence of a Deity. He is lucky if he can count upon meeting his best friends once in a fortnight. He becomes famous, not to be the cherished companion of the day, but to be mobbed by a crowd. He may become a recluse, nowhere more easily than in London; but then he can hardly write effective essays upon life; or he may throw himself into some of the countless "movements" of the day, and will have to be in too deadly earnest for the pleasant interchange of social persiflage with a skilful blending of lively and severe. The little friendly circle of sympathetic hearers is broken up for good or bad, dissolved into fragments and whirled into mad confusion; and the talker on paper must change his tone as his audience is dispersed. Undoubtedly in some ways the present day is not merely favourable to essay-writing but a very paradise for essayists. Our magazines and journals are full of excellent performances. But their character is radically changed. They are serious discussions of important questions, where a man puts a whole system of philosophy into a dozen pages. Or else they differ from the old-fashioned essay as the address of a mob-orator differs from a speech to an organised assembly. The writer has not in his eye a little coterie of recognised authority, but is competing with countless rivals to catch the ear of that vague and capricious personage, the general reader. Sometimes the general reader likes slow twaddle, and sometimes a spice of scandal; but he is terribly apt to take irony for a personal insult, and to mistake delicacy for insipidity. It is true, indeed, that one kind of authority has become more imposing than ever. We are greatly exercised in our minds by the claims of the scientific critic; but that only explains why it is so much easier to write about essay-writing than to write an essay oneself.

Some men, indeed, have enough of the humourist or the philosopher to withdraw from the crush and indulge in very admirable speculations. Essays may be mentioned which, though less popular than some downright twaddle, have a better chance of endurance. But, apart from the most modern performances, some of the very best of English essays came from the school which in some sense continued the old traditions. The "cockneys" of the first quarter of the century, still talked about the "town," as a distinct entity. Charles Lamb's supper parties were probably the last representatives of the old-fashioned club. Lamb, indeed, was the pet of a little clique of familiars, standing apart from the great world—not like Addison, the favourite of a society, including the chief political and social leaders of the day. The cockneys formed only a small and a rather despised section of society; but they had not been swamped and overwhelmed in the crowd. London was not a shifting caravanserai, a vague aggregate of human beings, from which all traces of organic unity had disappeared. Names like Kensington or Hampstead still suggested real places, with oldest inhabitants and local associations, not confusing paraphrases for arbitrary fragments of S. or N.W. The Temple had its old benchers, men who had lived there under the eyes of neighbours, and whose personal characteristics were known as accurately as in any country village. The theatre of Lamb's day was not one amongst many places of amusement, with only such claims as may be derived from the star of the moment; but a body with imposing historical associations, which could trace back its continuity through a dynasty of managers, from Sheridan to Garrick, and so to Cibber and Betterton, and the companies which exulted in the name of the King's servants. When sitting in the pit, he seemed to be taking the very place of Steele, and might still listen to the old "artificial comedy," for which we have become too moral or too squeamish. To read Elia's essays is to breathe that atmosphere again; and to see that if Lamb did not write for so definite a circle as the old essayists, he is still representing a class with cherished associations, and a distinctive character. One should be a bit of a cockney fully to enjoy his writing; to be able to reconstruct the picturesque old London with its quaint and grotesque aspects. For Lamb is nowhere more himself than in the humorous pathos with which he dwells upon the rapidly vanishing peculiarities of the old-fashioned world.

Lamb, Leigh Hunt, and Hazlitt may be taken to represent

this last phase of the old town life before the town had become a wilderness. They have all written admirable essays, though Hunt's pure taste and graceful style scarcely atone for the want of force or idiosyncrasy. No such criticism could be made against his friends. Lamb was not only the pet of his own clique, but the pet of all subsequent critics. To say anything against him would be to provoke indignant remonstrance. An attack upon him would resemble an insult to a child. Yet I will venture to confess that Lamb has some of the faults from which no favourite of a little circle is ever quite free. He is always on the verge of affectation, and sometimes trespasses beyond the verge. There is a self-consciousness about him which in some moods is provoking. There is a certain bigotry about most humourists (as of a spoilt child) which has become a little tiresome. People have come to talk as if a sense of humour were one of the cardinal virtues. To have it is to be free of a privileged class, possessed of an esoteric system of critical wisdom. To be without it is to be a wretched matter-of-fact utilitarian pedant. The professed humorist considers the rest of mankind as though they were deprived of a faculty, incapable of a relish for the finest literary flavours. Lamb was one of the first representatives of this theory, and is always tacitly warning off the profane vulgar, typified by the prosaic Scotchman who pointed out that his wish to see Burns instead of Burns' son was impracticable, inasmuch as the poet himself was dead. The pretension is, of course, put forward by Lamb in the most amiable way, but it remains a pretension. Most people are docile enough to accept at his own valuation, or at that of his admirers, any man who claims a special privilege, and think it wise to hold their tongues if they do not perceive it to be fully justified by the facts. But I admit that, after a certain quantity of Lamb, I begin to feel a sympathy for the unimaginative Scotchman. I think that he has something to say for himself. Lamb, for example, was a most exquisite critic of the authors in whom he delighted. Nobody has said such admirable things about the old English dramatists, and

a little exaggeration may be forgiven to so genuine a wor-
shipper. But he helped to start the nuisance of "appreciative
criticism," which proceeds on the assumptive fancy that it
necessarily shows equal insight and geniality to pick up
pebbles or real jewels from the rubbish-heaps of time. Lamb
certainly is not to be blamed for the extravagance of his
followers. But this exaltation of the tastes or fancies of a little
coterie has always its dangers, and that is what limits one's
affection for Lamb. Nobody can delight too much in the
essay upon roast pig—the apologue in which contains as
much sound philosophy as fine humour—or in Mrs. Battle's
opinions upon whist, or the description of Christ's Hospital,
or the old benchers of the Temple, or Oxford in the Long
Vacation. Only I cannot get rid of the feeling which besets
me when I am ordered to worship the idol of any small sect.
Accept their shibboleths, and everything will go pleasantly.
The underlying conceit and dogmatism will only turn its
pleasanter side towards you, and show itself in tinging the
admirable sentiments with a slight affectation. Yet, one
wants a little more fresh air, and one does not like to admire
upon compulsion. Lamb's manner is inimitably graceful;
but it reminds one just a little too much of an ancient beau,
retailing his exquisite compliments, and putting his hearers
on their best behaviour. Perhaps it shows the corruption of
human nature, but I should be glad if now and then he could
drop his falsetto and come out of his little entrenchment of
elaborate reserve. I should feel certain that I see the natural
man. "I am all over sophisticated," says Lamb, accounting
for his imperfect sympathy with Quakers, "with humours,
fancies craving hourly sympathy. I must have books,
pictures, theatres, chitchat, scandal, jokes, antiquities, and a
thousand whimwhams which their simpler taste could do
without." There are times when the simpler taste is a
pleasant relief to the most skilful dandling of whimwhams;
and it is at those times that one revolts not exactly against
Lamb, but against the intolerance of true Lamb worshippers.

The reader who is tired of Lamb's delicate confections, and wants a bit of genuine nature, a straightforward uncompromising utterance of antipathy and indignation, need not go far. Hazlitt will serve his turn; and for that reason I can very often read Hazlitt with admiration when Lamb rather palls upon me. If Hazlitt has the weaknesses of a cockney, they take a very different form. He could hardly have been the ideal of any sect which did not enjoy frequent slaps in the face from the object of its worship. He has acquired, to an irritating degree, the temper characteristic of a narrow provincial sect. He has cherished and brooded over the antipathies with which he started, and, from time to time, has added new dislikes and taken up grudges against his old friends. He has not sufficient culture to understand fully the bearing of his own theories; and quarrels with those who should be his allies. He has another characteristic which, to my mind, is less pardonable. He is not only egotistical, which one may forgive, but there is something rather ungentlemanlike about his egotism. There is a rather offensive tone of self-assertion, thickly masked as self-depreciation. I should be slow to say that he was envious, for that is one of the accusations most easily made and least capable of being proved, against anyone who takes an independent view of contemporary celebrities; but he has the tone of a man with a grievance; and the grievances are the shocks which his vanity has received from a want of general appreciation. There is something petty in the spirit which takes the world into its confidence upon such matters; and his want of reticence takes at times a more offensive form. He is one of the earliest "interviewers," and revenges himself upon men who have been more popular than himself by cutting portraits of them as they appeared to him. Altogether he is a man whom it is impossible to regard without a certain distrust; and that, as I fancy, is the true reason for his want of popularity. No literary skill will make average readers take kindly to a man who does not attract by some amiable quality.

In fact, some explanation is needed, for otherwise we

could hardly account for the comparative neglect of some of the ablest essays in the language. We may be very fine fellows now, but we cannot write like Hazlitt, says a critic who is more likely than anyone to falsify his own assertions. And when I take up one of Hazlitt's volumes of essays, I am very much inclined at times to agree with the assertion. They are apt, it is true, to leave a rather unpleasant flavour upon the palate. There is a certain acidity; a rather petulant putting forwards of little crotchets or personal dislikes; the arrogance belonging to all cliquishness is not softened into tacit assumption, but rather dashed in your face. But, putting this aside, the nervous vigour of the writing, the tone of strong conviction and passion which vibrates through his phrases, the genuine enthusiasm with which he celebrates the books and pictures which he really loves; the intense enjoyment of the beauties which he really comprehends, has in it something inspiring and contagious. There is at any rate nothing finicking or affected; if he is crotchety, he really believes in his crotchets; if he deals in paradoxes, it is not that he wishes to exhibit his skill, or to insinuate a claim to originality, but that he is a vehement and passionate believer in certain prejudices which have sunk into his mind or become ingrained in his nature. If every essayist is bound to be a dealer in commonplace or in the inverse commonplace which we call a paradox, Hazlitt succeeds in giving them an interest, by a new method. It is not that he is a man of ripened meditative wisdom who has thought over them and tested them for himself; nor a man of delicate sensibility from whose lips they come with the freshness of perfect simplicity; nor a man of strong sense, who tears away the conventional illusions by which we work ourselves into complacency; not a gentle humourist, who is playing with absurdities and appeals to us to share his enjoyable consciousness of his own nonsense; it is simply that he is a man of marked idiosyncrasy whose feelings are so strong, though confined within narrow channels, that his utterances have always the emphatic ring of true passion. When he talks about one of his favourites, whether Rousseau or Mrs. Inchbald, he has not perhaps much to add to the established criticisms, but he speaks as one who knows the book by heart, who has pored over it like a lover, come to it again and again, relished the little touches which escape the hasty reader, and in writing about it is reviving the old passionate gush of admiration. He cannot make such fine remarks as Lamb; and his judgments are still more personal and dependent upon the accidents of his early studies. But they stimulate still more strongly the illusion that one has only to turn to the original in order to enjoy a similar rapture. Lamb speaks as the epicure; and lets one know that one must be a man of taste to share his fine discrimination. But Hazlitt speaks of his old enjoyments as a traveller might speak of the gush of fresh water which saved him from dying of thirst in the wilderness. The delight seems so spontaneous and natural that we fancy—very erroneously for the most part—that the spring must be as refreshing to our lips as it was to his. We are ashamed after it when we are bored by the *Nouvelle Héloïse*.

There is the same kind of charm in the non-critical essays. We share for the moment Hazlitt's enthusiasm for the Indian jugglers, or for Cavanagh, the fives-player, whom he celebrates with an enthusiasm astonishing in pre-athletic days, and which could hardly be rivalled by a boyish idolater of Dr. Grace. We forget all our acquired prejudices to throw ourselves into the sport of the famous prize-fight between the gasman and Bill Neate; and see no incongruity between the pleasure of seeing one side of Mr. Hickman's face dashed into "a red ruin" by a single blow, and of taking a volume of Rousseau's sentimentalism in your pocket to solace the necessary hours of waiting.

It is the same, again, when Hazlitt comes to deal with the well-worn topics of commonplace essayists. He preaches upon threadbare texts, but they always have for him a strong personal interest. A commonplace maxim occurs to him, not to be calmly considered or to be ornamented with fresh illustrations, but as if it were incarnated in a flesh and blood representative, to be grappled, wrestled with, overthrown, and trampled under foot. He talks about the conduct of life to his son, and begins with the proper aphorisms about industry, civility, and so forth, but as he warms to his work, he grows passionate and pours out his own prejudices with the energy of personal conviction. He talks about "effeminacy," about the "fear of death," about the "main chance," about "envy," about "egotism," about "success in life," about "depth and superficiality," and a dozen other equally unpromising subjects. We know too well what dreary and edifying meditations they would suggest to some popular essayists, and how prettily others might play with them. But nothing turns to platitude with Hazlitt; he is always idiosyncratic, racy, vigorous, and intensely eager, not so much to convince you, perhaps, as to get the better of you as presumably an antagonist. He does not address himself to the gentle reader of more popular writers, but to an imaginary opponent always ready to take up the gauntlet and to get the worst of it. Most people rather object to assuming that position, and to be pounded as if it were a matter of course that they were priggish adherents of some objectionable theory. But if you can take him for the nonce on his own terms and enjoy conversation which courts contradiction, you may be sure of a good bout in the intellectual ring. And even his paradoxes are more than mere wanton desire to dazzle. Read, for example, the characteristic essay upon *The Pleasure of Hating*, with its perverse vindication of infidelity to our old friends, and old books, and you feel that Hazlitt, though arguing himself for the moment into a conviction which he cannot seriously hold, has really given utterance to a genuine sentiment which is more impressive than many a volume of average reflection. A more frequent contrast of general sentiment might, indeed, be agreeable. And yet, in spite of the undertone of rather sullen melancholy, we must be hard to please if we are not charmed with the occasional occurrence of such passages as these:

I remember once strolling along the margin of a stream, skirted with willows and flashing ridges, in one of those sequestered valleys on Salisbury plain, where the monks of former ages had planted chapels and built hermit's cells. There was a little parish church near, but tall elms and quivering alders hid it from my sight; when, all of a sudden, I was startled by the sound of a full organ pealing on the ear, accompanied by the rustic voices and the rolling quire of village maids and children. It rose, indeed, like an inhalation of rich distilled perfumes. The dew from a thousand pastures was gathered in its softness, the silence of a thousand years spoke in it. It came upon the heart like the calm beauty of death; fancy caught the sound and faith mounted on it to the skies. It filled the valley like a mist, and still poured out its endless chant, and still it swells upon the ear and wraps me in a golden trance, drowning the noisy tumult of the world.

If the spirit of clique were invariably productive of good essay-writing, we should never be in danger of any deficiency in our supplies. But our modern cliques are so anxious to be cosmopolitan, and on a level with the last new utterance of the accepted prophet, that somehow their disquisitions seem to be wanting in individual flavour. Perhaps we have unknown prophets amongst us whose works will be valued by our grandchildren. But I will not now venture upon the dangerous ground of contemporary criticism.

(*The Cornhill Magazine*, 1881)

# Did Shakespeare Write Bacon?

W ERE Shakespeare and Bacon identical? A new answer was recently suggested to me by a friend, and a consideration of his hypothesis led to the discovery of such corroborative arguments that it should only require a brief exposition to secure its acceptance by some people. I may briefly recall certain well-known facts. Bacon had conceived in very early youth an ambitious plan for a great philosophical reform. He had been immediately plunged into business, and at the accession of James I, when a little over forty, had been for many years a barrister and a Member of Parliament, and had moreover taken a very active part in great affairs of State. He was already lamenting, as he continued to lament, the many distractions which had forced him to sacrifice literary and philosophical to political ambition. Now that a second Solomon was to mount the throne, he naturally wished to show that he was a profound thinker, deserving the patronage of a wise monarch. Besides merely selfish reasons he hoped that James would help him to carry out his great schemes for the promotion of scientific research. He resolved, therefore, to publish a book setting forth his new philosophic ideas. He had not as yet found time to prepare any statement of them, or even to reduce them to order. He was still immersed in business and harassed by many anxieties. Now Bacon, if there be any truth in Pope's epigram or Macaulay's essay, was not above questionable manœuvres. If he had not time to write, he could get a book written for him. We know in fact that he afterwards employed assistants, such as Hobbes and George Herbert, in preparing some of his literary work. It is plain, however, from the full account of his early life in Spedding's volumes that he had as yet no connection with the famous men of letters of his time. Not one of them is mentioned in his letters, though at a later time he became known to Ben Jonson, who has celebrated the charms of his conversation. Jonson's friendship with Shakespeare gives some significance, as we shall see, to this circumstance. Bacon took a significant step. He had recently incurred reproach by taking part in the prosecution of his former patron, Essex. He now (1603) made conciliatory overtures to Southampton, who had not only been a friend of Essex, but had been under sentence for complicity in the rising for which Essex was beheaded. Why did Bacon approach a man so certain to be prejudiced against him? One reason suggests itself. Southampton was a patron of men of letters, and especially the one man whom we know to have been helpful to Shakespeare. If Bacon was desirous of hiring an author, Southampton would be able to recommend a competent person, and there was no one whom he was more likely to recommend than Shakespeare. Shakespeare was by this time at the height of his powers, and had shown by *Hamlet* his philosophical as well as his poetical tendencies. He was recognised as an able writer, capable of turning his hand to many employments. He could vamp old plays and presumably new philosophies. If Bacon wanted a man who should have the necessary power of writing and yet not be hampered by any such scientific doctrine of his own as would make him anxious to claim independence, he could not make a better choice. Southampton is said, on pretty good authority, to have made a present of £1,000 to Shakespeare. The story is intelligible if we suppose that he paid the money on Bacon's account, and for some service of such a nature that any trace of Bacon's interest in it was to be concealed.

At any rate somebody wrote a book. The famous *Advancement of Learning* appeared in the autumn of 1605. It is dedicated to James, and gives a general survey of the state of knowledge at the time; or, as the last paragraph states, is "a small globe of the intellectual world." It shows literary genius and general knowledge, but not the minute information of a specialist. Who wrote the book? I need not rely upon the probabilities already mentioned, however strong they may be, which point to Shakespeare. If Shakespeare wrote it he might naturally try to insert some intimation of the authorship to which he could appeal in case of necessity. One of the common amusements of the time was the composition of anagrams; and I accordingly inquired whether such a thing might be discoverable in the *Advancement*. It would most probably be at the beginning, and I was rewarded by finding in the first two lines a distinct claim of Shakespeare's own authorship and a repudiation of Bacon's. Naturally, when a man is writing two sentences in one set of letters he has to be a little obscure, and will probably employ a redundant word or two to include all that are required. Shakespeare's style, therefore, if perceptible, is partly veiled. The opening words are "There were under the law, excellent King, both daily sacrifices and free-will offerings, the one pro(ceeding, &c.)." To the end of "pro" there are eighty-one letters. Re-arrange them and they make the following: "Crede Will Shakespere, green innocent reader; he was author of excellent writing; F. B. N. fifth idol, Lye."* I won't try to explain why the reader should be called green and innocent, but the meaning of the whole will be perfectly clear when the last words are explained. F. B. N., of course, means Francis Bacon. "Fifth idol" refers to one of the most famous passages in a book hitherto ascribed to Bacon. In the aphorisms prefaced to the *Novum Organum* the causes of human error are described as belonging to *four* classes of "idols." False systems of philosophy, for example, generate what are curiously (though the word would naturally occur to a dramatist) called "idols of the theatre." Of the others I need only say that they do not include one fertile source of

* If anyone cares to verify this, he may be helped by the statement that in both cases A occurs in four places, B in one, C in three, D in three, E in fifteen, F in four, G in two, H in four, I in six, K in one, L in six, N in six, O in four, P in one, R in seven, S in three, T in five, U in one, W in three, X in one, and Y in one.

deception, namely, direct lying. Shakespeare intimates that his employer was illustrating this additional or fifth kind of idol by his false claim to the authorship. The aphorisms, however, were for the present held back. The book was published, we may presume, before Bacon had discovered this transparent artifice. Shakespeare would chuckle when calling his attention to it afterwards. Bacon would be vexed, but naturally could not take public notice of the trap in which he had been caught. His feelings may be inferred from his later action. When Shakespeare's plays were collected after the author's death, Bacon we know got at the printers and persuaded them to insert a cryptogram claiming the authorship for himself. The claim was obviously preposterous, but the fact that he made it is interesting to the moralist. It is a melancholy illustration of a familiar truth. Bacon had probably come to believe his own lie, and to fancy that he had really written the *Advancement of Learning*, or that, having bought it, he had a right to it. Then, he thought, he would make sure of a posthumous revenge should the anagram be deciphered. "If Shakespeare succeeds in claiming my philosophy, I will take his plays in exchange." He had become demoralised to the point at which he could cheat his conscience by such lamentable casuistry.

Meanwhile Bacon's fame was growing; and so was his immersion in business. In 1607 he became Solicitor-General and a comparatively rich man. In the next year he makes references to a proposed continuation of his great philosophical work. In other words, he was thinking of procuring its continuation. Probably there was some little difficulty in getting over the misunderstandings which would inevitably arise from these dark and dangerous dealings. The bargain might be hard to strike. In 1611, however, we know that Shakespeare gave up the stage and retired to pass the last five years of his life at Stratford. All his biographers have thought this retirement strange, and have been puzzled to account for the supposed cessation of authorship. No successful writer ever gives up writing. The explanation is now clear. Shakespeare retired because Bacon, who had grown rich, could make it worth his while to retreat to a quiet place where he would not be tempted to write plays, or drink at the "Mermaid," or make indiscreet revelations. If it be asked what he was doing, the answer is obvious. He was writing the *Novum Organum*. It was all but impossible for Bacon in the midst of all his astonishing political and legal activity to find time to write a philosophical work. No doubt he did something: he made notes and procured collections of various observations upon natural phenomena with which he supplied his co-operator. We may even suppose that he persuaded himself that he was thus substantially the author of the book which he prompted. Shakespeare died in 1616, leaving the work as a fragment. Bacon, who not long afterwards became Lord Chancellor, put the papers together, had them translated into Latin (which would obliterate any lurking anagram), and was able to publish the book in 1620. I leave it to critics to show the true authorship from internal evidence. It is enough here to note certain obvious characteristics. The book in the first place, as is generally admitted, shows that the author was not only an amateur in science, but curiously ignorant of what was being done in his own day. That was quite natural at Stratford-on-Avon, while Bacon in London had ample means for hearing of the achievements of leading men of science, even if he could not appreciate their work. In the next place the *Novum Organum* is the work of a poet. The scientific formulæ are given in the shape of weighty concrete maxims—"Man is the servant and interpreter of Nature," and so forth. So in classifying the various kinds of experiments, the writer does not elaborate an abstract logical scheme, but represents each class (there are no less than twenty-seven) by some vivid concrete emblem. One class suggests the analogy of a signpost at crossroads and receives the famous name of *Instantiae crucis*, the origin of our common phrase, "crucial experiments." Bacon was not a poet—as anyone may see

78

who looks at his version of the Psalms—Shakespeare certainly was.

After publishing this "magnificent fragment," as an accomplished critic calls it, Bacon was convicted of corrupt practices, and passed his few remaining years in trying to proceed with his philosophical work. The result was significant. He had no official duties to distract him, but also he had no Shakespeare to help him. His later publications added a little or nothing in substance. The chief of them was *De Augmentis*. This is simply an enlarged edition in Latin (the anagram of course disappearing) of the *Advancement of Learning*. The early book, as the same critic says, has an advantage over the "more pretentious" version from the "noble and flowing" (shall we say the Shakespearean?) "English," while the additions are of questionable value. I will only notice one point. The *Advancement of Learning* speaks of the state of poetry at the time. "In poesy," says the author, "I can report no deficience. . . . For the expression of affections, passions, corruptions, and customs we are beholden to poets more than to the philosophers' works: and for wit and eloquence not much less than to orators' harangues." That was a very natural opinion to be expressed by Shakespeare. In the *De Augmentis* the last sentence disappears; but a fresh paragraph is inserted upon dramatic poetry. The theatre might be useful, it says, either for corruption or for discipline; but in modern times there is plenty of corruption on the stage and no discipline.

Bacon, it may be noticed, was aiming this backhanded blow at Shakespeare in the same year in which he was inserting the cryptogram in the first folio. It may appear, at first sight, that he was inconsistent in condemning the very works which he was claiming, and it may even be said by the captious that the fact throws some doubt upon the cryptogram. A deeper insight into human nature will suggest that such an inconsistency is characteristic. Bacon wishes at once to appropriate Shakespeare's work and to depreciate it so long as it is still ascribed to Shakespeare. I omit, however, the obvious psychological reflections and will only remark that other works ascribed to this period, the *Sylva Sylvarum* and so forth, no doubt represent the collections which, as I have said, Bacon formed to be used as materials by his collaborator.

I have told my story as briefly as may be, and leave details to be filled up by anyone who pleases. Plenty of writers have insisted upon Shakespeare's logical subtlety and powers of philosophical reflection. They will be ready to believe that the author of *Hamlet* was also the author of the *Novum Organum*, and will be relieved from the necessity of accepting the old paradox that the "wisest" was also the "meanest" man of his time. The meanness may all be ascribed to one man, and the wisdom to the man from whom he stole it.

*(The National Review,* 1901)

# Taine's History of English Literature

M. TAINE'S history of English literature has attained a degree of popularity which is in some sense a sufficient proof of its merits. M. Taine's critical judgments are at times irritating; his philosophy may be questionable; and his leading principles are sometimes overlaid with such a mass of epigrammatic illustration that we have some difficulty in distinctly grasping their meanings. To protest against some of these faults is indeed the purpose of this paper. And yet, whatever his faults, it is impossible not to be grateful to him. He has done for us what no native author had done, or, it may be, was able to do. Most of our home-bred critics, however keen their insight, failed to supplement their microscopic acuteness of vision by the application of a genuine comparative method. We still frequently discuss Shakespeare as we discuss the Bible; we regard him, that is, as an isolated phenomenon unrelated to the general movement of European, or even of English thought. M. Taine has done much to inculcate a sounder method, and to widen our intellectual horizon. He has the force which belongs to the apostle of a new theory, who preaches it in season and out of season, and inevitably rather exaggerates its value. Our thick English heads are all the better for incessant hammering upon a single point. With admirable persistence, one of our historians has managed to drill us into a faint belief in the truth that there were Englishmen before William the Conqueror; and M. Taine is rendering an analogous service in proving to us that as our history is continuous, so our great writers are the natural expressions of its dominant ideas. Let us add that he has that special felicity, characteristic of Frenchmen generally, that in spite of all his reiterations of a single doctrine, he is quite incapable of becoming a bore. Once taken up, it is always hard to lay him down.

That his fundamental doctrine is substantially true may be at once assumed. We ought to study the organism in connection with the medium. Botany becomes more fruitful as we investigate the relations between a given flora and the various conditions of its growth. In the same way a Dante, a Shakespeare, or a Goethe is a flower of literature in no merely fanciful metaphor. We first understand the full significance of their writings when we have made ourselves familiar with the intellectual soil from which they spring. There is, however, one obvious limitation upon the value of this truth. Briefly stated, it is that even Frenchmen are not omniscient and infallible. An angel might possibly predict the occurrence of a Shakespeare in the world as certainly as a chemist can foretell the appearance of a crystal in his crucible under given conditions. We, however, are a long way below the angels. We have not analysed human nature into its primary constituent elements; and still less can we say how they are affected by surrounding circumstances. Granting that a science of history is conceivable, its bases are scarcely laid. Trying to describe the peculiarities of a race or climate, we feel at once the absence of anything like a scientific nomenclature. Our words express mere rough popular generalisations, and at every step we say too little or too much. Far from having arrived at the stage of prediction, we have not yet arrived at the stage of trustworthy observation. We are limited to mere empirical statements, and are reduced to the unsatisfactory method of *ex post facto* explanations. We cannot predict a Shakespeare, though when he has actually come, we can give some ostensible proof that he must have appeared in this shape and no other. Indeed, the process is only too easy. An uncomfortable misgiving besets us when we read M. Taine's lucid explanations. Are they not too lucid? Is he not accounting for the planetary orbits before he has discovered the theory of gravitation? Suppose, to make a wild hypothesis, that he had somehow been under the delusion that Balzac, Pascal, and Montaigne were Englishmen, and that Byron, Pope, and Hobbes were Frenchmen, would not his ingenuity have been equal to the task of reconciling the phenomenon to his theories? His theories, in short, may be admirable, but they are of necessity liable to the objection that, having been made after the facts, they are not susceptible of independent verification.

The difficulty grows as we examine M. Taine's arguments in greater detail. The national character, he tells us, is determined by three causes—the race, the *milieu*, the epoch. Giving a sufficiently wide interpretation to these words, there can be no doubt of it. If you understand the nature of a plum-pudding (Englishmen, M. Taine tells us, like homely illustrations), the temperature of the water in which it is placed, and the stage of cooking at which it has arrived, you can tell pretty well how it will taste. But when for a plum-pudding you substitute the more complex phenomenon of a race, and the cooking process is represented by the infinitely complex forces which mould human character, the problem becomes something of the hardest. By the *milieu* M. Taine seems generally to understand the climate. The influence of climate upon constitution is itself a problem of vast perplexity; even such a simple generalisation as the connection between drunkenness and fogs, of which M. Taine elsewhere assumes the truth, would require to be tested by a whole series of observations, never yet made. Climate, again, is but one condition amongst many. How many peculiarities of the English political and social constitution, and therefore indirectly of our modes of thought and literature, result from our insularity and from the geological conditions of our soil? It is easy to trace the reflection of English scenery in the descriptive passages of Spenser, Thomson, and Wordsworth; but this is at most a superficial influence, and is far removed indeed from supplying a base for scientific theories. M. Taine carries his remarks rather further than Voltaire's crude statement that there are certain days of east wind in London when it is customary for people to hang themselves; but his criticism does not always go much deeper. M. Taine, indeed, does not really trouble himself to trace back English peculiarities to the source which he indicates. He is content in practice to start from a lower point; and to regard the race as already acclimatised. He assumes our idiosyncrasy to be sufficiently well known, and only suggests vaguely the general conditions by which it may have been developed.

Is this idiosyncrasy sufficiently known? Can we really say with any precision in what respects an Englishman differs from a Frenchman? Is our knowledge of the subject really entitled to be called in any sense scientific, or does it merely consist of those rough, empirical approximations, which may give some practical guidance, but fail to supply sufficient rules for satisfactory theorising? M. Taine's main distinction is certainly vague enough. He habitually contrasts the northern with what he sometimes calls the classical races, and seems to assume that each race conforms to a well-ascertained type. Can there, we are prompted to ask, be much value in so rough a division? On the one side we have the English races considered as a single unit. Yet it is plain that in spite of all the levelling influences of civilisation, the inhabitants of the British Islands are as far as possible from being homogeneous. The Englishman differs from the Irishman as widely as he differs from the Frenchman. Climate has not extinguished all contrasts between the Celtic and the Teutonic imaginations. M. Taine does not condescend to take account of these minutiæ. He illustrates some of his theories, for example, by the English parliamentary speakers of the last century. These orators, he tells us, "love the coarse vulgarity of gaudy colours. They hunt out accumulations of big words, contrasts symmetrically protracted, vast and resounding periods"; and his proof of these rather questionable statements is drawn from the younger Pitt, from the "acrimonious rhetoric and forced declamation of Sheridan," and above all from Burke. Any Englishman would reply that Burke was an Irishman, that Sheridan was a typical Irishman, and that the love of florid rhetoric and the "coarse vulgarity of gaudy colours" is precisely one of the points on which the average Englishman most emphatically differs from the Irishman. What can be the value of a description of national character which would make such men as Burke, Sheridan, Grattan, and O'Connell typical representatives of English peculiarities? The qualities which distinguish them are just the qualities in which Englishmen are most strikingly deficient. Granting, however, that in these cases the feebler race has been overpowered by the stronger, and that Burke and Sheridan were addressing an English audience, let us look at the other branch of the contrast. M. Taine constantly uses the French and the classical texts as interchangeable phases. Corneille and Racine are the legitimate representatives of the Greek dramatists. The French taste in art and literature is identified with the Athenian. The doctrine would certainly be disputed in this form by most English and German critics. We may assume, however, that M. Taine is pointing to a real distinction. There is probably some quality present in all "classical" dramatists from Æschylus to M. Sardou, and absent from all "Germanic" dramatists, from Marlowe to Mr. Tom Taylor. But surely it requires to be carefully defined before we can use it for "scientific psychology." M. Taine speaks as though the distinction were as palpable as the difference between a black skin and a white. His language, again, would put the French and Italian poetry into one class to be contrasted with the English in another. The difference between the English poetry of the Renaissance and the classical period may be expressed by saying that in one case we were under Italian, and in the other under French influences. How can the difference be satisfactorily explained by a writer who constantly speaks as if the two influences were identical? M. Taine is, of course, fully conscious of these distinctions, and could doubtless give a brilliant, and perhaps an accurate account of their nature. I merely urge that, if his science penetrated much below the surface, he should at least favour us with some definition of this "classical spirit" of which he speaks so constantly. His utterances are not very clear. When, for example, he tells us *à propos* of Mr. Carlyle, that the "classical ages and Latin races" generally adopt an analytical method, and the "romantic ages and the Germanic races" an intuitive method (I use the words roughly), one is beset by a whole host of doubts; and to say the truth, one is inclined to think that this brilliant generalisation may pair off with Mr. Buckle's theory that the Scotch intellect is essentially deductive and the English inductive. It is one of those clever guesses at truth which will not bear serious examination. Such modes of reasoning suggest that after all M. Taine is, like the rest of us, in the days of superficial classification. A physicist who has only got so far as to divide the material world into four elements, is not yet capable of making a really scientific statement. We are still in the analogous position in regard to races of men. That even with such rough generalities, a man may make very instructive remarks is possible enough. I only observe that it is altogether premature to give ourselves the airs of scientific accuracy. Our efforts to make faithful portraits are too much like trying to paint miniatures with a mop. Endless confusion is produced, and the apparently precise statements crumble in our hands. M. Taine is better than his philosophy; but it is because his showy generalities generally cover clever remarks about the difference between Englishmen and Frenchmen; and here, if not scientific, he can be picturesque and approximately accurate.

Before examining his account of the English character, however, it is necessary to say a word or two upon his third condition. The epoch, it is undeniable, must be taken into account in discussing the psychology of a people. What, then, is the epoch? M. Taine speaks of the mediæval period, the renaissance, the classical and the modern periods. To each of those periods belongs an appropriate philosophy, an appropriate social organisation, and, as the result of both,

an appropriate tone of sentiment which expresses itself in
the contemporary literature. For the most part, M. Taine
is content to give rather a picturesque description than a
philosophical analysis of the peculiarities of the time. He
accumulates a number of vivid details and acute critical
remarks which show how the English nobleman in a wig
is the old feudal baron in disguise; how Puritanism was
already latent in our mediæval religion; and how Byron was
but a new avatar of the old Berserker spirit. One mode of
characterisation is comparatively neglected. As he was not
writing a history of thought, but of literature, it is of course
natural that he should dwell rather upon the general temper
of the period than upon the particular dogmas which were
current. He has therefore occupied himself more with our
poets and novelists than with our theologians and philosophers. Hobbes and Locke interest him as illustrations of
character rather than as landmarks for the history of speculation. The plan of his book imposed this restriction upon him;
but at times it seems to lead him into a certain injustice, or,
at least, incompleteness of view. The epoch cannot be fairly
understood without taking into account the speculative
stage which has been reached. As M. Taine truly says,
"beneath every literature there is a philosophy"; and, if you
put the philosophy out of sight, you are apt to misunderstand
the literature. When, therefore, M. Taine takes the degraded theatre of the Restoration for his chief authority as
to English manners of the period, and spends many pages
in proving what is obvious enough, that Wycherley was a
very poor creature beside Molière, he seems to be sinking
to the level of the old-fashioned historians, who identified
the court with the nation, and argued that, because Charles
II was a scapegrace, the English people were corrupt at
heart. He touches upon Barrow and Tillotson principally
by way of showing what dull sermons Englishmen can
write; and he finds in Bunyan a good representative of the
later Puritans. Yet a fuller reference to such men as Locke
and Cudworth, and Leighton and Baxter, though it might

have involved some dull writing, would have been but a
fair balance to the full-length likeness of the ribald play-
wrights. Periods, moreover, are run together rather vaguely.
Hobbes is introduced as the natural product of this degraded
society, and is contrasted with Descartes. The French
philosopher, "in the midst of a purified society and religion,
noble and calm, enthroned intelligence and elevated man;
whereas Hobbes, in the midst of an overthrown society and
a religion run mad, degraded man and enthroned matter."
Yet Hobbes published his *Leviathan* in 1651, at the age of
sixty-three; and his treatise on human nature was composed
in 1640. Like Descartes, his junior by eight years, he really
belongs to the first half of the seventeenth century; and it is
not evident that the social state which led to the Fronde was
nobler and purer than that which produced the English
civil war. To represent him as the product of the Restoration
period is obviously erroneous, though he may be regarded as
the teacher of many of its politicians. The chief writers of the
time represent the reaction from his principles. M. Taine's
indifference to our speculative literature leads him to a
greater injustice to the eighteenth century. Incapacity for
the loftier philosophy is one of our unfortunate characteristics. Accordingly Locke, Berkeley, and Hume, are dis-
patched in a few sentences. Berkeley lights upon a single
idea, but does not know how to use it. Locke is "almost as
poor" and a hesitating and inconclusive thinker. Hume, a
bolder inquirer, ends in a complete pyrrhonism. "Rarely,
in this world," says M. Taine, "has speculation fallen lower."
This judgment will be admitted in some sense by people
who still believe in the possibility of framing a science of
ontology. The great English thinkers just noticed were of
the destructive order; and the result of their labours was so
far negative. And yet I do not think that M. Taine has a
right to treat them with this sublime contempt. Whatever
their faults, they represented for the time the main current
of the European movement of thought; Locke, with all his
shortcomings, was the great prophet of the century, and

Hume's scepticism was necessary, if for nothing else, to supply a basis for Kant's attempt at a reconstruction of the metaphysical edifice. But, moreover, M. Taine has himself expressed a very different view. In his essay on Mr. Mill, which, having received the warm praise of Mr. Mill himself, may dispense with mine, he comes, after an elaborate investigation, to the conclusion that the English and German methods of inquiry represent two tendencies which require to be combined in order to bring out the complete philosophy of the future. Mr. Mill, as representing the English method, is the greatest master since Hegel. Now Mr. Mill's legitimate intellectual ancestors are plainly Locke, Berkeley, and Hume, to whom we may add Hartley and his disciple, James Mill. If this be true, we may deny to the English sceptics the title of philosophers, but we cannot possibly deny that they represent a most important intellectual movement. To declare that speculation never fell lower is to use a rather ambiguous phrase; but it is clearly unjust if it means that the thinkers of the time were feeble as well as destructive. The theological speculation of the same period is dismissed with equal contempt, as so much prosaic moralising. The divines were "apologists, not inquirers," and "busied themselves with morality not with truth." Deism and atheism are a mere passing eruption; the freethinkers, under the guidance of Collins, Tindal, and Bolingbroke, "attack the clergy by the same instinct which leads them to beat the watch." M. Taine is right enough in insisting upon the strong tendency of the divines and their opponents to ethical discussions, and in declaring that their love of truth was clouded by theological prejudices; whilst he can scarcely exaggerate the narrowness of their critical methods. When, however, he compares them with Voltaire, Montesquieu, and Diderot, he reminds us that the weapons of the French assailants of orthodoxy were really forged in England. To say that Collins and Tindal were simple assailants of morality is to adopt the coarsest mis-representations of their adversaries. They were really discussing, though with infinitely inferior knowledge and ability, the same problems which have occupied Strauss and Renan in later years. Their criticism was feeble because it was premature; but with such methods as were open to them, they argued the truth of the Christian doctrine with extraordinary eagerness; and, if their reasoning was generally cramped and narrow, they anticipated the substance of many later inquiries. If deism expired, it was chiefly because theology had become so leavened with the deistic spirit that it was scarcely burdensome even to sceptics. The arguments of the deists and their opponents would be as useless at the present day as bows and arrows in modern warfare; but M. Taine too easily assumes that the worthlessness of the argument shows the incapacity of the disputants. Like Hampden with his forty shillings, they were raising very deep questions in very narrow issues; and at least one theologian of the time was as good a representative of English thought as contemporary essayists and novelists. Butler is not a philosopher of a high order; but he certainly represents a vein of genuine and very characteristic speculation. His extreme contempt for the whole of this vigorous, though narrow school of thinkers, whose faults are after all chiefly the faults of the times, makes M. Taine rather unjust even to Pope and Addison. Their moralising and their references to the popular theology are set down by him to the natural propensity of English writers to run into prosy and irrelevant sermons. Rather they are a natural corollary from the intense interest which all their contemporaries were naturally taking in the most absorbing controversies of the time. A fuller reference, in short, to the condition under which men were then labouring, by such means as were open to them, to frame a rational theory of the universe would have explained many things which are ascribed too summarily to the innate prosiness and utilitarianism of the English character.

What, however, is this character upon which M. Taine discourses so copiously? It is not altogether easy to pack into

a distinct logical formula the numerous brilliant remarks of
which we are the subjects. Much that he says is but the
reproduction, in a more pretentious form, of the good old
theory symbolised by the figure of John Bull. Hogarth, in
one of his pictures, represents the jovial Englishman con-
fronted by the wretched frog-eaters at Calais; and M. Taine
gives us the frog-eaters' view of the contrast. We are large,
overfed, beer, port wine, and gin swilling animals; coarse,
burly, and pachydermatous, with little external sensibility,
and no love for things of the intellect; but yet with strong
passions which sometimes express themselves in broad
humour, and sometimes give birth to a rich but overcharged
poetry. All this, however, which sometimes verges upon
caricature, is no more than we have heard before. It does
not require a philosopher, with theories about race, climate,
and epoch, to tell us as much. The first drawing in *Charivari*
of a British Goddam gives the same theory in a coarser
shape; and it has certainly been familiar since the days of
Froissart. That there is a great deal of truth in the doctrine
is indeed undeniable. Vague as are most international
judgments, there are yet some contrasts too striking not to
be perceived. A man must be extremely inferior to M. Taine
who could not roughly indicate the difference between
Shakespeare and Corneille, or between Voltaire and Dr.
Johnson. On the other hand, such general remarks do not
take us very far. When M. Taine has pointed out that an
English writer is more harsh and positive than the analogous
Frenchman, he has gone but a little way towards defining
his real character. Beneath the qualities which make a man
English there lie the qualities which make him a man; and
if you stop short at the specific differences you do not reach
the essence. M. Taine's criticism is thus apt to become
superficial. A French critic of the old school was satisfied to
point out that in the English drama murders were committed on the stage, and ribaldry mixed with the most solemn
sentiments; and then summarily condemned us as hopeless
barbarians. M. Taine is too scientific in spirit and too gener-

ous in feeling to agree in these rash judgments; and yet he is often content to stop at the same point. The want of classical taste is the one fact which occurs to him about many of our writers, and that failing, though it does not make him deliberately unjust, prevents him from really sympathising with their spirit. Too often we see the old Frenchman under the mask of the modern psychologist, and we feel that, with all his philosophy, he can only hold up his hands in amazement at our grotesque modes of thought. Addison remarks in one of the *Spectators*, that an Englishman often complains that French actors all "speak in a tone," not considering that Frenchmen make the same complaint about himself. His reason, of course is, that each language has a system of expression of its own, which is not appreciated by anyone not brought up to it from infancy. Now careful observation may enable us to recognise the existence of this natural "tone"; but it cannot give us the ear which is spontaneously susceptible to the impressions. M. Taine has laboured conscientiously and sometimes with remarkable success, to train himself in the English taste; but we are frequently conscious that an innate insensibility to our specific methods renders him an incompetent judge of the finer literary essences. His judgment of our poets often implies a misconception—such at least it appears to me—of the relative positions which they really occupy in the opinion of competent judges. Mr. Tennyson's *In Memoriam* appears to him to be the cold and monotonous lamentation of a "correct gentleman, with bran new gloves," who wipes away his tears at a funeral with a cambric handkerchief; whilst he speaks of the idylls with rather an exaggerated enthusiasm. This opinion, as I fancy, follows rather from a theory as to what Mr. Tennyson ought to be, than from a perception of what he really is. Time, however, must decide in this instance. His view of the earlier poets of this century touches upon less debatable ground. He treats at length of the unreadable epics of Southey—the "illustrious poet," as he elsewhere calls that most elegant writer of prose—and the tinsel finery of Moore, whilst he scarcely condescends to notice Keats, an infinitely superior poet, as need hardly be said, and one whose influence on succeeding writers has been far more deeply marked. Wordsworth is with him simply the tiresome, though occasionally eloquent moralist of the *Excursion*, and the rebel against the conventionalities of poetic diction. That Wordsworth ever deserted his theories in practice, and that his greatest claims are founded upon the sonnets and the odes, does not seem to occur to him. *Lycidas* is only mentioned as showing that Milton was beginning to injure his poetry by an admixture of theological passion. Denham's *Cooper's Hill*, originally published in 1643, is questionably introduced as showing that a true vein of poetry existed in the Restoration period, whilst no notice is taken of Marvell. But, not to dwell upon small oversights in so comprehensive a work, this want of that more intimate appreciation which we observe in a perfect critic, may be illustrated from another case. It is curious to compare M. Taine's remarks upon Hogarth with Charles Lamb's well-known essay. M. Taine tells us that Hogarth's pictures are a mass of hideous grotesques. "Detestable yahoos that you are," he exclaims to the actors in the Hogarthean world, "who presume to usurp the blessed light; in what brain can you have arisen, and why did a painter sully his eyes with the sight of you? It is," he replies, "because his eyes were English, and the senses are barbarous." M. Taine, therefore, holding his nose, as it were, succeeds in forcing himself to contemplate these brutalities, and kindly excuses Hogarth to the Frenchmen whose delicate feelings are shocked by such crudities, on the ground that moralists are useful, and that Hogarth has preached a lesson admirably adapted to barbarians. We turn to Lamb, and find that these pictures, whatever their faults, are regarded as displaying extraordinary intensity of imagination; that the Frenchmen who are shocked at a St. Giles's must yet admit that Hogarth's "Gin Lane" shows more genius than Poussin's literal representation of the "Plague at

93

Athens"; that some of his figures are as "terrible as anything that Michelangelo ever drew; that the madman in Hogarth's "Bedlam" shows as much tragic power as the demoniacs in Raphael; and, in short, that Hogarth is a pictorial Shakespeare. Then Hogarth's faces are never mean or insignificant; even in the midst of horrors, he always shows a sense of beauty, and is specially fond of introducing the innocence of childhood to relieve the mind oppressed by spectacles of crime and misery. The "Stages of Cruelty," on which M. Taine dwells as emphatically characteristic, are dismissed as mere worthless caricatures, "the offspring of his fancy in some wayward humour"; but in nearly all the other pictures Lamb finds infinite kindliness, humour, and, in short, that "sprinkling of the better nature, which, like holy water, chases away and disperses the contagion of the bad." M. Taine remarks of one of Hogarth's pictures, the "Modern Midnight Conversation," that, "wickedness, stupidity, all the vile poison of the vilest human passions, drops and distils from" the figures. Lamb falls into raptures over the joviality, and the wealth of humour and fancy displayed in the "Election Entertainment." Now if I wished to define Hogarth's place relatively to Raphael and Michelangelo, I should certainly prefer M. Taine's judgment to Lamb's. Lamb knew and cared as little as possible for any art except that which embodied his favourite modes of sentiment. Very possibly, too, he puts more into Hogarth than can be really found in him, and is wilfully blind to his defects. But if I wanted to know the genuine Hogarth, I should as decidedly prefer the testimony of the man who has loved him heartily, who sympathises with all his prejudices, and pored over him with tender affection. To make Lamb's criticism perfectly sound, it requires to be toned down and corrected; whilst M. Taine's requires to be supplemented by an entirely new set of observations. He has only touched the outside of the man. His psychology has merely informed him of the obvious fact that Hogarth is coarse, and would shock French nerves; to which we may perhaps add, that he now shocks English nerves. Lamb, without any psychology to speak of, has instinctively discovered the source of Hogarth's power, and explains why we love him with perhaps a rather indiscriminating affection. He sees the tenderness and the humour, and in consideration of them forgives the brutality, which to M. Taine is the single quality worth noticing. That English are in some sense coarser than French nerves is probable enough; but M. Taine's treatment of Hogarth, and it is too often paralleled in his other criticism, would lead to the exaggerated conclusion that we are nothing but ferocious brutes, whose solid imaginations can only be stimulated by vivid representations of hell or the gallows. If we could accept this as a faithful portrait of the nation at large, it would scarcely supply us with a sufficient method for judging individual character.

Beyond these commonplaces, however, M. Taine has certain theories which, though not systematically expounded, are frequently indicated with more or less clearness. The Englishman, so far as I can venture to state his doctrine, is a combination of two distinct characters. Sometimes, he tells us, we give up everything to liberty, sometimes we enslave everything to rule. Our frames are too vigorous and too unyielding. Some of us, "alarmed by the fire of an overfed temperament and by the energy of unsocial passions," regard nature as dangerous, and place her in a strait-waistcoat of propriety, morality, and religion. The restraint gradually becomes too severe; and then nature breaks her fetters and gives herself up to excesses. Shakespeare, we are told, led to the reaction of the Puritans, Milton produced Wycherley, Congreve Defoe, and Wilberforce Lord Byron. This struggle is represented in the period of which he is speaking by Fielding and Richardson. An Englishman is always oscillating vehemently between these two extremes. He is a Berserker (M. Taine is fond of the Berserkers) in a black coat and white tie. He behaves for a long time with an overstrained decorum, which makes him rather ridiculous and very tiresome to his neighbours; and then suddenly the old madness fires his blood, and, like a half-reclaimed savage, he throws off his decent apparel and furiously runs amuck, hewing down every impediment that comes in his way. The theory has certainly some conveniences. At first sight it seems to be so wide as to include almost every conceivable case. Every Englishman, and indeed every human being, must be somewhere between the extremes of obedience to law and revolt from law, and it is easy enough to recognise in every writer an admixture of these two different elements. M. Taine, however, means to express something more than this. He means to say that the characteristic of English writers is an incapacity for obeying the dictates of that moderate good sense which gives laws to French literature. If the Puritan element predominates in him he becomes a bore, and preaches eternal sermons of flat morality. If he has a dash of Berserker blood, he takes leave of all decency, and plunges into artistic as well as moral extravagances. He is like an overfed horse, who can be forced to walk by a strong hand, but, if allowed the least liberty, will break into a mad gallop. And therefore he is incapable of that regulated energy which is characteristic of the classical school. His merit is in his outbursts of demoniac power; and he is wanting in a sense of harmony and proportion. It would be curious to inquire how far this theory is confirmed by our political history, and whether, as it would seem to imply, Englishmen have been more remarkable than their neighbours for vehement alternations between tyranny and licence. Nothing, as we are frequently told, is more characteristic of Englishmen than their love of compromise. How is this tendency to be reconciled with a theory which should make them conspicuous for a love of extremes? The theory is picturesque rather than scientific, and though it enables M. Taine to describe certain aspects of English literature with great vividness, it breaks down when we try to interpret it too strictly. The thesis suggested seems to be in one respect fundamentally erroneous. If by the Berserker element in the English race he means their capacity for deep emotion and gloomy imagination, this capacity does not really involve an unwillingness to obey laws, but only to obey a particular kind of laws. M. Taine sometimes seems to mistake for mere licence conformity to a type differing from his own ideal. This confusion, if it be a confusion, runs through a good many of his criticisms, and may be best explained by his judgment in some individual cases.

M. Taine, for example, has devoted a very able and interesting essay to a criticism of Mr. Carlyle. It is one of the most curious, though not the most satisfactory, in his book. His sincere desire to be impartial and appreciative struggles with a radical incapacity for sympathising with a mind so different from his own. He describes very amusingly the perplexity of a Frenchman when brought into contact with this "extraordinary animal." By an energetic course of study M. Taine succeeds to some extent in solving the problem. He accounts for Mr. Carlyle as a Puritan who has somehow been profoundly influenced by German ideas. He is a hybrid between Hegel and John Knox. That is his vital formula; and M. Taine deduces all his peculiarities with great ingenuity and with many instructive comments. And yet he cannot really like the strange character whom he has analysed. He sometimes verges upon caricature, as when he says that "no ulcer, no filth is sufficient to disgust Carlyle"—a statement which, to say the least of it, is overstrained. He declares that Carlyle sees "nothing but evil in the French revolution," and condemns the French because they were not Puritans of the English variety. I do not maintain that Mr. Carlyle has done justice to the revolution; but, after all, he has said in his own dialect little more than has been said by Comte in France—namely, that the revolution, whilst necessary and useful on the destructive side, was deficient on the constructive side, and recent history perhaps shows that, if the judgment be inadequate, it is not one which implies a real want of insight. M. Taine retaliates the dislike, though he guards himself with praiseworthy care against yielding to his prejudice. Mr. Carlyle, on this theory, becomes a

Berserker-Puritan. His genuine forefathers, says M. Taine, were "the Norse pirates, the poets of the sixteenth century, the Puritans of the seventeenth." Many of them were madmen, and Mr. Carlyle has only been saved from madness by his love of facts—his "sentiment of actuality," as M. Taine calls it—and his religious spirit. If saved, however, he has been saved "so as by fire." He shows the frenzied eye, the overstrained imagination, the grotesque affectations which testify to a mind tottering on the verge of insanity. Mr. Carlyle, in fact, is an inspired madman. That is really M. Taine's verdict, though he covers it under a decorous phraseology.

We see here that, in this instance, the Puritan and the Berserker are not so irreconcilable as to be incapable of amalgamation. The fact may lead us to ask whether the Berserker element is not capable of recognising a law and an artistic theory of its own, though so strange to M. Taine that he confounds obedience to it with madness? His essay, painstaking and ingenious as it is, overlooks one side of Mr. Carlyle's writings. The Puritans, as has often been remarked, joined to their enthusiasm a strong vein of shrewd common sense; and that is a faculty which is conspicuous in Mr. Carlyle's writings to anyone who is not so astonished by the superficial strangeness of his style as to be unable to penetrate to their substance. Its expression in literature is that singular quality which we call humour, and which M. Taine pronounces, in accordance with a common, though, as I venture to think, a rather unsound opinion, to be unknown to and therefore unnamed by his countrymen. In a curious passage he endeavours to explain what humour means. It implies, he says, a taste for strong contrasts, which is undeniable; it implies further, that the writer gratifies his own whims in complete forgetfulness of his audience—a doctrine which is more disputable; and, finally, it implies a "violent joviality buried under a heap of sadness." Shakespeare's clowns making jests over a grave are typical instances of the faculty. To this I will add that it also implies, in a man of strong mind, a cool intellect presiding over the freaks of a warm imagination, and checking the tendency to extravagance by a keen perception of absurdity. This is the substratum which really underlies the strange excursions of the English intellect; and M. Taine's difficulty in recognising its manifestations explains the error of some of his critical judgments. A man is not the worse in many ways for being devoid of a sense of humour, but certainly he is disqualified to be a sound critic of much of our literature. Leave out Mr. Carlyle's humour, or regard it as simply distasteful, and his queer phrases and violent contrasts become a mere offence, if not actually indications of insanity. A critic who has to explain the phenomenon by a scientific analysis, instead of spontaneously delighting in its freshness, can see nothing but affectation and absurdity in much that is to others the real charm of Mr. Carlyle's writings; and therefore we are not surprised that after discussing, with great acuteness, Mr. Carlyle's relation to Hegel and to the Puritans, M. Taine is still unable to feel his merits, and speaks of him like a visitor to a lunatic asylum, who recognises flashes of genius in the ravings of one of its inmates. He ends very characteristically by expressing his preference for Macaulay's calm and solid reasoning over the "exaggerated and demoniac style, the marvellous and sickly philosophy, the sinister and furious politics" of his rival, though admitting that Macaulay has less genius.

Perhaps it would surprise M. Taine if we replied that we prefer Mr. Carlyle, not merely for his genius, but for the soundness of his judgment. A significant instance may be found in another case where we have to complain of M Taine's injustice. No English reader who has compared the essays of the two writers upon Johnson will deny that Mr. Carlyle has discovered a real man where Macaulay presents us with a heap of paradoxes. M. Taine would apparently take a different view, for he mentions Mr. Carlyle's admiration of Johnson as a proof of his extravagance, and his own portrait of the lexicographer is modelled upon that of

Macaulay. His account of Johnson is indeed a curiosity in its way. After describing the poor man's oddities in the fashion of Macaulay, he asks his readers what can possibly be the secret of the English admiration for this strange being. At length he finds an answer. We like Johnson, it seems, because we like sermons. "It is for this reason that the essays (that is, the *Rambler* and its like) are a national food. It is because they are insipid and dull for us that they suit the taste of an Englishman. We understand now why they take for a favourite the respectable, the unbearable Samuel Johnson." Surely a more hopeless answer was never given. Very few Englishmen ever read the essays, though we may possibly regret the fact; and the faults which have made Johnson unreadable to us are precisely the faults which, as M. Taine tells us, make them unbearable to a Frenchman. Why then do we love Johnson? As M. Taine has read Boswell, and is unable to answer the question, we may despair of giving any answer which will satisfy him. Englishmen, however, to whom that book has been a delight from the days of their childhood, and who can discuss few subjects without one of the old doctor's vigorous phrases rising to their lips, could give an account of their faith which would satisfy themselves. It is partly because, under a rough outside, Johnson had a noble nature, to which Mr. Carlyle has done justice in his admirable essay, and partly because he had that strong sense of humour which is the index of shrewd common sense. *Rasselas* is certainly not so lively as *Candide*, though it is a very powerful work in its way; but Johnson is no mere retailer of moral platitudes, but a man whose words, especially those reported by Boswell, always show the thinker who has really known men and manners, and been ennobled instead of embittered by his experience. What we love in him is not his prosing, but the sturdy hammer-strokes of his humour upon plausible nonsense. The man whose motto was "clear your mind of cant" was not a walking sermon, but a real human being of no ordinary force.

M. Taine's criticism on Johnson's style shows the same

want of appreciation. "Classical prose," he says, "attained the same perfection in him as classical poetry in Pope. Art cannot be more consummate or nature more forced." Johnson's prose, with its lumbering superfetation of verbal antithesis, is not the perfection of art, nor is it comparable to Pope's admirably compact English. It is really cognate to the grander style of Milton or Sir Thomas Browne; though the writer's ear was spoilt by the uncongenial atmosphere of his time. The remark may lead us to notice very briefly one or two of M. Taine's judgments upon our so-called classical school. Here, according to him, we have the Berserker in fetters. The rich English nature, cramped and confined by laws imposed from without, becomes intolerably prosy and affected, for genuine art, as he occasionally tells us, we have no capacity; as soon as we try to be artistic we lose our native wildness, and become hopelessly dull and pedantic.

There is some English poetry which might be quoted against M. Taine, and even with an appeal to his own authority. If neither Spenser, nor Milton, nor Pope, nor Gray, nor Keats, nor Mr. Tennyson had any artistic perception, then, not only the English critics but M. Taine himself must have made some gross mistakes. I will notice, however, one case which M. Taine considers to be typical. Richardson and Fielding are the representatives of the Puritan and the Berserker in their own time. M. Taine, after an amusing account of Richardson's prolixities and twaddle, ends by twitting him with his artistic weakness. "We love art," he says, "and you have a scant amount of it . . . . Art is different from nature; the latter draws out, the first condenses. . . . You are rendered heavy by your conscience, which drags you along step by step, and low on the ground," and, therefore, it would seem you are no more capable of loving nature than mere art. Nobody would deny at the present day that Richardson is intolerably long-winded and prosy. *Clarissa Harlowe* is almost as tiresome as her relation the *Nouvelle Héloïse*. Yet M. Taine would scarcely say that Rousseau's prolixity is incompatible with artistic sense; and I do not see how he can pass the same judgment upon Richardson. One thing at least is certain. He cannot condemn Richardson without condemning the taste of his own countrymen. Not only Diderot, but Balzac and Alfred de Musset, speak of *Clarissa Harlowe* (*le premier roman du monde,* as Musset calls it) with an admiration which sounds rather extravagent to an Englishman. I know not how M. Taine explains this strange attraction of the clumsy British moralist for brilliant Frenchmen; but I should venture to suggest that *Clarissa Harlowe*, with all its faults, is marked not only by a vigour of conception, but by a unity and harmony of design which entitles it to be called a genuine work of art of no mean order. Remembering that Richardson was an originator of a new style, I can only account for his success by believing that his artistic sense was as finely developed as that of any French novelist, though it had to work under unfavourable conditions and upon very prosaic materials. But if Richardson was really an artist, M. Taine's theory fails.

The doctrine that Englishmen who are not Berserkers must be dismal prosers has to encounter a still greater difficulty. Pope was clearly not a Berserker; nor, as it has been generally thought, was he by any means a bore. He was, we have been in the habit of saying, a man who beat his French contemporaries upon their own ground of brilliant epigram and delicate executive power. The English view of Pope, in short, contradicts M. Taine's theories as distinctly as the French view of Richardson; and, to say the truth, I can hardly resist the impression that if Boileau had been an Englishman and Pope a Frenchman, Pope's superiority would have been held up as a conclusive proof of the doctrine that English poets do "not easily get into the classical dress." "This gold-embroidered jacket, so well fitted for a Frenchman, hardly suits their figure: from time to time a hasty, awkward movement makes rents in the sleeves and elsewhere." Still, Pope's poetry stands in the way. Dislike it

as much as you please, but you can hardly doubt that it is a
very remarkable literary phenomenon; and I know not
which of the French writers who wear the jacket so naturally
have succeeded in surpassing him. The only way out of the
dilemma is to insist upon Pope's many grievous defects. M.
Taine dwells, with great cleverness, upon the artificiality
and the commonplace of Pope's writings, and I would not
deny that here, as in the case of Richardson, he hits a real
blot. I would simply suggest that, by reversing the old
precept,

> *Be to his faults a little blind,*
> *Be to his virtues very kind,*

you can make a caricature of anybody, and especially of one
so open to caricature as Pope. M. Taine is not often unfair
from downright mistake; but from dwelling too emphatically and exclusively upon the lights or the shades. Unluckily that is the most effective because the least easily answered mode of misrepresentation. To answer his criticism
upon Pope would require an essay at least as long as his own;
and, moreover, it is impossible to persuade a critic who can
only account for our admiration of the *Rape of the Lock* by
saying that "a Pekin mandarin vastly relishes a concert of
kettles"; who says of the *Dunciad*, that "rarely has so much
talent been spent to produce greater tedium"; and condemns
a mock-heroic poem because the writer brings in magnilo-
quent allusions disproportioned to his professed subject. M.
Taine, however, is bound to find something to praise in
Pope; for in truth his reputation must have had some cause,
if not some justification; and hitherto M. Taine has proved
that Pope's best jewellery is but stained glass. He therefore
observes, truly enough, that Pope was a great master of
language; upon which I shall only remark that real mastery
of language implies a command of the thoughts which are
symbolised by language. Pope, however, had a more truly
poetical merit than this power of manipulating words. He
was, we are glad to hear, capable of describing nature to

perfection. By this time, it seems, poets had produced a sufficient stock of descriptive phrases. "Every aspect of nature was observed; a sunrise, a landscape reflected in the water, a breeze amid the foliage, and so forth. Ask Pope to paint in verse an eel, a perch, or a trout, he has the exact phrase ready; you might glean from him the contents of a gradus. He gives the features so exactly, that at once you think you see the thing; he gives the expression so copiously, that your imagination, however obtuse, will end by seeing it." And in proof of this he quotes a description of a pheasant from *Windsor Forest*. The researches, in fact, of some generations of poets had proved that eels were silvery, and Pope's skill in versification enabled him to expand this observation in the phrase,—

*The silver eel, in shining volumes rolled.*

The most obtuse imagination will now be forced to see the shininess of eels.

That a brilliant critic who is bored by Pope's fancy, shocked by his humour, and indifferent to his wit, should have selected for special praise his faithful descriptions of natural objects, is one of those literary oddities which can only be explained in one way. M. Taine's theories must be true. Englishmen love nature; and are dull to art. Pope was an Englishman. Therefore his art was poor, and his descriptions of nature excellent. The only parallel to this is the argument by which Colonel Choke proved to Martin Chuzzlewit that the Queen must necessarily live in the Tower. An example of the same method may, however, be found in M. Taine's much more appreciative essay upon Addison. Poor Addison's unfortunate habit of writing lay-sermons in his Saturday *Spectators* is indeed turned to cruel account; and, were it not for our previous knowledge of the book, we should expect, from the prominence which M. Taine gives to Addison's sermonising, and to the rounded monotony of his phrases, that our gentle humourist was simply an earlier Johnson. He does justice, however, to

Addison's amiable character, and strives to do justice to his
humour. This "strange mode of painting human folly"—
which Englishmen call humour—"contains an incisive good
sense, the habit of restraint, business habits, but above all a
fundamental energy of invention." I do not consider this to
be a very felicitous analysis; but M. Taine's description of
the results is better than his account of the method. He even
remembers, towards the end of his essay, that Addison invented Sir Roger de Coverley, and some other admirable
characters. Addison, however, being an Englishman, must
have been brutal; and M. Taine, looking about for proofs of
this quality, manages to discover it in Addison's playful
description of the dissection of a beau's brain. "These an-
atomical details," says M. Taine, "which would disgust us,
amused a positive mind; crudity is for him only exactness; accustomed to precise images, he finds no objectionable colour
in the medical style." I will take M. Taine's word for it, that
things which seemed pleasant to London ladies would have
shocked people in Paris; though, to say the truth, I think that a
careful examination of French literature might reveal passages—say in Voltaire, or Diderot—which would be equally
disgusting to English ladies. Perhaps, however, their offen-
siveness belongs to a different category. I merely remark that
when a writer of so exquisitely delicate a nature as Addison
is condemned for coarseness, on the strength of a single
passage which ventures upon questionable ground, one begins to feel that by such criticism you may torture any facts
into apparent conformity with any theory. The fact is, that
M. Taine's incapacity for appreciating English humour
often hinders his perception of the guiding principle of our
best writers. Gothic architecture has its rules, as well as
Classical; though it may be that they are not so easily reduc-
ible to a simple code. A critic who fancies that it is purely
arbitrary because it allows certain liberties which he condemns, has merely abandoned the problem on account of its
complexity. Humour condemns certain faults as rigorously
as the "classical" taste condemns others. If our realism, our

tolerance of harsh contrasts, and our occasional buffoonery is disagreeable to M. Taine, so the frigid conventionalities, the empty generalities, and the irreverent intrusions of epigram of some French writers are disagreeable to us. Our sense of humour makes us laugh at the pompous declamation of a French tragedy, as his sense of proportion makes him laugh at our more highly coloured extravagances. With all his laudable anxiety to enter into the spirit of English writing, M. Taine can never really believe that our daring disregard of foreign conventionalities can be anything but wanton caprice. "Burke," he says, in his summary fashion, "has no taste, nor have his compeers." Burke certainly has not the French taste; but if M. Taine really believes that the grand rhetoric of Burke, of Jeremy Taylor, or Milton, or Sir Thomas Browne is produced by a kind of strange accident; that it is the result of a writer simply throwing the reins upon the neck of his imagination, and letting it carry him whither it will, he might believe that Westminster Abbey was built by mere wild fancy confined by an artistic principle. The theory of this literary style has been admirably expounded by De Quincey, himself no mean master of the art, but, unfortunately, far blinder than M. Taine to the merits of styles differing from his own. De Quincey is as unable to see the art of Swift as M. Taine to perceive the art of Burke. To have a fair account of English literature we should combine the two modes of judgment. To the writers of whom Swift is the most eminent type, M. Taine really does justice. Though we may differ from some of his opinions about Swift, Burns, and Byron, we must admit that his essay upon each of them is instructive and appreciative. They possess in common a quality which, though emphatically English, belongs to that side of English character with which a Frenchman can sympathise. That masculine vigour confined by sturdy common sense, which animates the style of Hobbes and Chillingworth in the seventeenth century, of Swift and Defoe in Queen Anne's days, and which was transmitted through Cobbett to some of our best modern periodical writing, is thoroughly English, and yet has an analogy to the French sparkle and clearness. A critic to whom Voltaire is the type of literary excellence, can admire the more clumsy, less brilliant, but richer and more impassioned style of Swift. The Berserker energy fires a mind, not indeed bound by rigid rules, but concentrated by its own passion upon a distinct purpose. The eloquence pours along a narrow channel, instead of spreading itself like a deluge over a wide surface. The imagination is not indulged in the apparently arbitrary freaks of the lawless Berserker, because it is in the service of a masterful emotion. And under such conditions, M. Taine can heartily admit its force without being shocked by its capriciousness. This is what he really admires in Byron, whose love of the classical school expressed, as M. Taine truly says, a genuine tendency of his nature. The glowing and concentrated passion atones for his occasional affectations and his wayward humour. Though not polished after the French model, his vigour spontaneously produces the unity of effect which is wanting in less passionate natures.

What, however, M. Taine thinks of the genuine Berserker may be discovered from his account of the greatest name in our literature. It is not at the fag-end of an article that one can do justice to his elaborate and brilliant study of Shakespeare, but I may briefly indicate the ground of my dissent from his judgment. It is a representative case, and gives the pith of M. Taine's view of the English character. Stripping M. Taine's remarks of their epigrammatic surroundings, his criticism may be summed up by saying that Shakespeare, like Carlyle, was a madman. It was in no mere figure of speech that his eye rolled in poetic frenzy, whilst his pen swarmed with images from heaven and earth, heaped together with incongruous profusion. His style is a "compound of furious expressions." "Raving exaggerations . . . the whole fury of the ode, inversion of ideas, accumulation of images, the horrible and the divine, are jumbled into one line." He "never writes a word without shouting it." Hamlet talks in "the style of frenzy." His vehemence will be explained by the fact that he was half-mad; but the truth is that he was Shakespeare. Now Shakespeare "never sees things tranquilly"; his "convulsive metaphors" seem to "have been written by a fevered hand in a night's delirium," and so on through pages in which the same criticism is presented to us in a hundred different forms. The doctrine is summed up in a passage where M. Taine says that Racine and Corneille would have agreed with Descartes in regarding the world as ruled by reason: whereas Shakespeare would have agreed with Esquirol in substantially regarding it as a vast lunatic asylum. This inspired madman can have no art; for he crowds together, without discrimination, all that he sees, and allows the grotesque to jostle the sublime; he has no decorum, for he calls things by their dirty names, and his "words are too indecent to be translated"; he has no sense of social proprieties, for his nobles, such as Coriolanus, use the language of modern coalheavers; he cares nothing for virtue, for he sympathises with the ribaldry of Falstaff and the cynicism of Iago. The purity of his women is a mere matter of organisation, not of principle. He has no sense of religion, for to him the future life is merely a scene where the gloomy forebodings of Claudio will be fulfilled, or at best the sleep which perchance may be broken by fearful dreams. If Shakespeare indulges in the sweet fancies of *As You Like It*, or the *Midsummer Night's Dream*, it is but to seek a relief from the terrible strain of his habitual mood; his "delicate soul, bruised by the shocks of social life, took refuge in contemplations of solitary life." His personal history, chiefly constructed from the sonnets, confirms these theories. M. Taine is good enough to express the hope, rather than the belief, that he succeeded like Goethe in discharging the "perilous stuff" of his imagination through his poetry rather than through his life, but it is only credible by help of a theory that in those days the human machine was more firmly constructed than at present. The full head of the bust encourages him to entertain this consolatory fancy.

I do not wish to argue for a moment that Shakespeare was much given to preaching moral truths. M. Taine's judgment, though exaggerated, gives one side of the truth. Shakespeare's characters do as a rule act by overpowering impulses, and are not calculating utilitarians. What morality he actually preaches does not take the form of concrete maxims, but is diffused through the general spirit of his writing. He is a moral writer in this sense, that he was (as I venture to say in spite of M. Taine's theories) one of the sanest and healthiest of men. He produces a moral effect, not because he lectures us, but because in reading him we feel that we are in contact with a mind erring in tolerance rather than rigidity, sensuous rather than ascetic, but still blessed with superabundant health. Nothing is more characteristic of him than that intense delight in all natural beauty which appears in so many of the most exquisitely poetic passages in his writing and in our language. To consider his love of the "meanest flower that blows," of the moonlight forest, and the enchanted island, as a mere reaction from overstrained excitement, is to distort his whole character. This marvellous tenderness is part of the very groundwork of his nature, and could exist only in a mind unpoisoned by the vices which he contemplates. What we know of Shakespeare's life (putting aside strained inferences from uncertain interpretations of the sonnets) is clearly in harmony with this view. M. Taine makes it a kind of miracle that Shakespeare, unlike so many of his brother dramatists, made money like a good man of business, and retired to enjoy a country life. The miracle is only that it contradicts M. Taine's theories. The best illustration of the argument may be drawn from a comparison suggested by M. Taine himself. We Englishmen, he says, in our vanity, refuse to separate an artist from his conscience. "We will never consent to see that such is the leading feature of our Shakespeare; we will not recognise that he, like Balzac, brings his heroes to crime and monomania; and that, like him, he lives in a land of pure logic and imagination." The reference to logic must surely be an oversight, but the comparison is significant. What is the difference between the characteristic moods of Balzac and Shakespeare? To sum it up in one word, it is that the imagination of Shakespeare is pre-eminently healthy, and the imagination of Balzac pre-eminently morbid. In every page of Balzac we have a whiff from the odures of Paris, in every page of Shakespeare a breath from the free forest and the ocean. Balzac writes in the glare of the street-lamps, Shakespeare under the sunlight in the air of heaven; and therefore we are constantly saying, as we read Balzac, that is false, and in reading Shakespeare, that is eternally true. Shakespeare's pure women may be pure from instinct, but they have never been sullied by dwelling upon vice. Balzac's pure women are pure by instinct also, but the instinct which has saved them from vice has not prevented them from poring over it and tampering with it. Shakespeare's characters go mad, it is true, but in their madness they show, like King Lear, the wrecks of a noble mind. Balzac's characters are monomaniacs and their mania renders them like the Père Goriot, almost too contemptible to be pathetic. The English readers of Balzac may be unjust in calling him immoral in the sense that he actually approves of vice, but he is immoral in the sense that he enjoys gloating over morbid products of a corrupt civilisation. M. Taine calls this scientific psychology. I will not argue the point, but I confess that this appears to me to be a degradation of the name. Shakespeare's psychology is not scientific, but it is the spontaneous sympathy of a marvellously endowed mind, with passions which have not been distorted into unnatural shapes, though they may have been pushed to excess. Shakespeare, according to M. Taine, is irreligious, because he holds that our little lives are rounded with a sleep. Shakespeare, no doubt, was potentially a Prospero and a Hamlet, and could feel their despair and the awe with which they looked upon the gloom of the surrounding universe. But Shakespeare was of necessity something more than any one of his characters. He was not essentially gloomy because he could feel that mysterious awe which comes upon every noble and imaginative nature looking out upon this little island in the infinite. As M. Taine remarks, Mr. Carlyle shares the awe and is fond of repeating that our lives are such stuff as dreams are made of. The fact is sufficient to prove that the sentiment is not incompatible with a deep religious feeling. That Shakespeare was not a professed theologian is true enough, but I think that M. Taine, of all people, should scarcely cast it in his teeth, and infer that he is speaking in his own character, when for dramatic purposes he makes a coward express a slavish fear of hell. The temper expressed in such utterances as those which Mr. Carlyle delights to repeat, is indicative, not of mere gloom or sordid cowardice, but of the solemn sense of the visionary and transitory nature of the world which must be in the background of every grand imagination. And therefore I venture to conclude that here, too, M. Taine's confidence in certain *a priori* theories about Berserkers, and other types of national character, has led him to overcharge one side of his portrait so strongly that we cannot accept it for a faithful representation of our greatest literary celebrity.

(The Fortnightly Review, 1873)

# The Late Lord Lytton as a Novelist

THE eulogies which are very rightly pronounced over the graves of distinguished men have this inconvenience—that they are apt to make an impartial estimate of the dead sound like a protest. To speak generously and tenderly of those whom we have recently lost is only becoming; and it follows that we should touch lightly upon their faults, and linger with some emphasis upon their merits; but it does not follow that we should invent imaginary merits. If there were no other reason, it would be sufficient to say that such over-charged panegyric is in fact the bitterest of satires. Can you not praise the dead man sufficiently, unless you tell lies about him? Do you not then implicity assert that the plain truth is not complimentary? Some illustrations of these obvious remarks—more pertinent than that which we are about to produce—might be drawn, were it desirable, from some recent events. They have, however, been immediately suggested by the case of Lord Lytton. Of the many articles devoted to his memory, some were judicious, and some generous, and some at once generous and judicious; but many were in that modern style of highly-spiced writing which has added a new terror to death. A poor human creature cannot now retire to his grave, humbly hoping that he has done rather more good than harm in the world—a frame of mind which is surely confident enough for most, even of those whom we call eminent men—without a discharge of fulsome rhetoric, which would have disgusted him in his lifetime, and sounds terribly hollow in the solemn presence of death. The memory of Lord Lytton was honoured or insulted by some estimates of his literary eminence, limited only by the writer's command of epithets. Yet, as a poet, he was not equal to Milton; nor as an orator, to Burke; nor as a dramatist, to Sheridan; nor as an essayist, to Addison. Such parallels are foolish; and, in fact, we need not hesitate to admit at once that Lord Lytton's real claims to posthumous reputation must rest upon his novels. A most versatile, laborious, and cultivated intellect enabled him to play his part very creditably, and with a certain air of scholar-like polish, in many capacities for which he had no special aptitude. His poetry, for example, is not of the inspired, but of the skilfully manufactured variety; his facility in verse-making was a graceful accomplishment, not a heaven-born instinct—and a critic, whilst receiving such poetry with all due courtesy, should not do it the complimentary injustice of comparing it to really great works of art.

Let us attempt, then, to make a fair estimate of the value of his novels. That they deserve to stand far above the great mass of fictitious literature of the day needs no demonstration. Lord Lytton deserved—as every critic has admitted— one praise which has a value in proportion to its rarity. He was a thoroughly good workman. Whatever faults may be imputed to him, are not the faults of a man who despises his art, or is slovenly in his execution. He resisted, that is, temptations which have been not a little injurious to some greater writers and have ruined many smaller ones. The temptation to turn popularity to account by writing as much as possible, and to win it on the easiest terms, by writing down to the level of an audience which only asks for amusement, has been too often found irresistible. Lord Lytton, during a career of some forty-five years, never sought for easy successes whilst relaxing his exertions. And, doubtless it is for this reason that he is one of the few men who have written so much without writing themselves out. The success with which he opened an entirely new vein in *The Caxtons*, at an age when the style of most men has long been definitely fixed; and the success which he so recently gained in the *Coming Race*, whilst declining to use the prestige of his name, are remarkable proofs of his continued vigour. Beyond all cavil, he was a man of remarkable powers; and, indeed, to deny him praise of a very high kind would be to run in the teeth of that general verdict of public opinion which, if not infallible, possesses an authority superior to that of any individual. But a further question still remains open. Great success may be won, and deservedly won, by writers who are essentially in the second rank. There are two races of men—the mortals and the immortals. Swift's *Struldbrugs* bore upon them from their birth the signs of the awful destiny which divided them from their kind; but that is by no means the case with the heirs of literary immortality. Their prerogative often fails to make itself recognised until it is actually asserted. Not till we see that their vitality persists, whilst others, who once seemed to be their equals, are dropping off around them, do we recognise their surpassing value. Gradually it turns out that the work of some few men in a century has something about it which defies corruption. Perhaps it may be some trifling fragment of prose or poetry, which lives upon men's lips, when other works, to all appearance of equal merit, have sunk into eternal silence; and even whilst we admit the fact, we are unable to analyse the cause, of its survival. Only when we find such a fragment, we know that another immortal has been amongst us, not recognised, and it may be, taken for a fool in his lifetime. To discover the indefinable essence which constitutes genius, before it has revealed itself to the world at large, should be the highest triumph of criticism; but such discoveries are generally made by the multitudinous judgment of public opinion before the professional critic has awaked to them. Whether the possession of genius, even in an imperfect form, places a man at once in a class above his fellows —whether, for example, the author of a song which lives for centuries should be by that fact alone ranked above the writer of an epic which secures the applause of a generation, and then sinks into darkness—is a question probably insoluble, and certainly not to be solved here. Would one rather have written Southey's respectable, but unmistakably mortal poems, or the stanzas on the burial of Sir John Moore, which alone preserve the memory of their author?

Perhaps an ingenious person might suggest some reasons on behalf of the wider, though less enduring reputation. It is, however, plain that to entitle any man to be placed in the first class of writers, even into the lowest rank of that class, he must come of the strain of the immortals. Even to admit that such a question is an open one, in regard to almost any author, is to pay him a high compliment; and we venture to ask it in regard to Lord Lytton. Was he in any true sense a man of genius, or only a man of very great talent? Is he one of the originators, or only one of the transmitters of the great contemporary impulses—a creative artist, or a skilful manipulator of the materials given by others?

Some memories would lead one to answer in favour of the loftier claim. There is a certain force and freshness about some of his writings, *Pelham* for instance, which has a close resemblance to genius. There is one at least of his novels upon which we are unable to express a distinct opinion, for a reason which will probably be appreciated by many readers. It happens that his *Last Days of Pompeii* is sanctified for us by schoolday associations. Glaucus exposed to the lions stands in our memory beside Charles O'Malley in his Peninsular adventures, and Ivanhoe in the castle of Front de Bœuf and Robinson Crusoe discovering the footprint in the sand. We can no more reason about the merits of the story than we can seriously entertain the question whether the captain of the boats in those days was the biggest, strongest, and most active of men since the days of Achilles. Its excellence is with us an article of faith, not of reason. And we therefore decline, even in the discharge of a critical duty, ever again to consult its pages. The eruption of Vesuvius may have been very sublime, and the fights in the circus very spirited, and the Egyptian magician very imposing; but it is impossible that they should ever again be so imposing and so spirited as they appeared to us at the time. There is a kind of irreverence in returning in the colder spirit of mature life to the haunts of one's boyhood, to discover that our mountains have shrunk to hills and our palaces to commonplace houses. We should preserve soundly those early illusions which, once dispelled, can never be restored. Why should an elderly person ever return to a pantomime to discover that the actresses are painted women instead of *bona fide* fairies? Let there be still a sanctuary to which we can retire by the help of memory, where the toys of childhood retain the ancient glow of the imagination and are not pulled to pieces by the colder reasoning faculty. As to the enduring value of the great bulk, however, of Lord Lytton's novels we can judge more dispassionately. Most of them belong to that class of literature which presupposes a certain amount of experience in the writer. They are, even ostentatiously, the productions of a man of the world, who has taken his part in serious business and is familiar with all the wheels of the great machinery of life. The peculiarity, indeed, is only too prominent. The most palpable defect of his novels is their extreme self-consciousness. The writer is evidently determined that we shall not overlook his claims to be a teacher of mankind. He is always philosophising in good set terms, which is a very different thing from writing philo-sophically. His moral is not embodied in his work, but exhibi-ted with all the emphasis of sententious aphorisms. He aims at the Ideal, and very rightly, but the Ideal and the True and the Beautiful need not always be presenting them-selves with the pomp of capital letters. And though we honour him for not despising his art, we should be glad if he could oc-casionally forget his art in his instincts. As it is, we are always asking whether he is not rather artificial than truly artistic. Ex-treme cleverness is the word which suggests itself much oftener than genius; we exclaim how ingenious! rather than how true! and are more impressed by the judicious balancing of his scenes than by their genuine beauty. In short, Lord Lytton is wanting in that spontaneity and vigour which is the surest mark of genius. We do not meet, in his pages, with those sudden electric flashes which thrill us as we study the really great men; and we have an uncomfortable sensation that there is something stagey and unreal about the whole performance.

In some of his earlier novels, these faults are the most painfully conspicuous. The thoroughness of his work shows itself in the careful construction of his plots; but that very carefulness is indicative of a certain weakness. Far be it from us to say that a plot should not be well put together! Undoubtedly that is one of the demands which a reader is fairly entitled to make of his author; for it contributes infinitely to the satisfaction of reading a story. But ingenuity in constructing complicated series of events, fitting into each other as neatly as the parts of a Chinese puzzle, is a very dangerous talent. Lord Lytton did not sink to the level of merely appealing to his reader's curiosity, and making a novel a conundrum to be guessed at the last page, and then to lose all interest. He always has some central idea to present, and the story is designed to illustrate some moral or psychological or artistic theory. And yet, the mechanical perfection of his devices is apt to interfere with their higher meaning. Let us take for example, though it is not a favourable specimen of his style, the novel of *Eugene Aram*. He speaks with considerable complacency of the merits of his story. None of his books, he says, have been so much attacked, and none so completely triumphed over attack. The attacks, indeed, were chiefly directed against its morality; and we may fully admit that no homicidal mania was produced, or was likely to be produced, by the history of this remarkable murder. But the merits which he claims of excellence in style and in construction are more doubtful. The problem to be considered was worthy of his powers. Eugene Aram, as at once an inoffensive student, a man of singular kindness to animals, and a murderer, is certainly an interesting subject for speculation. The subject might be treated artistically in various ways. As a study of character, or of the tendencies of certain social or religious theories, or of the terrible passions which preceded and followed the crime, there is abundant room for a pathetic or speculative writer. A very similar subject has been treated in the singularly impressive novel of *Caleb Williams*, to which Lord

Lytton refers. In spite of some obvious faults, *Caleb Williams* has the distinct mark of genius; and the difference in the mode of treatment is characteristic. Godwin's hero, Falkland, like Eugene Aram, has committed a murder, although a man of highly cultivated mind and an excessively delicate sense of honour. Caleb Williams, being a dependent of Falkland's, discovers his patron's crime; and Falkland persecutes the possessor of the secret, succeeds in fixing a false imputation of theft upon him, and then makes his life a burden to him; Falkland at last breaks down under the tortures of his own conscience, and dies after confessing his guilt. Godwin's purpose was, of course, to illustrate his own eccentric social theories; but the picture which he draws is interesting for its own sake. The proud man, conscious of hideous guilt—for he has allowed two other men to be hanged in his place, and yet resolved to wade through any amount of crime rather than part with his honour—is opposed to the miserable victim of his tyranny, innocent of any crime and yet shunned by all honest men, and entangled in a net woven with diabolical ingenuity. Those two figures, with a few subsidiary actors, are constantly before us, and though the plot is awkward and even absurd in details, the force of the conception is unmistakable. Lord Lytton's mode of dealing with Aram is curiously different. We can see how the story was put together. Aram must fall in love with a beautiful young lady, to make his fate more disagreeable. The young lady is contrasted with a sister, after the conventional fashion of Minna and Brenda or the inevitable pair of young women in *Fenimore Cooper;* and is provided with an admirer to act as rival and counterpoise to Aram. Having got thus far, the plot is worked with infinite dexterity. Aram's rival is also, as it ultimately turns out, the son of the man whom Aram murdered. And thus, in hunting up the traces of his father's death, he is at the same time unmasking the villain who has supplanted him with his mistress. Nothing can be more ingenious than the gradual development of events; Aram is kept judiciously balancing between the altar and the gallows; the mystery is unveiled by carefully measured degrees; we change imperceptibly from curiosity as to the lonely scholar to dark suspicions of his character, and finally to conviction of his guilt. All the persons concerned come together in the most natural way for an affecting tableau at the conclusion; and there is abundant opportunity for heart-rending displays of sentiment.

Lord Lytton's complacency is entirely justified; for no French dramatist could have worked out the problem more neatly; and the contrast with Godwin's clumsy devices for convicting Falkland and torturing his victim is triumphant. And yet *Eugene Aram* has become barely readable by anyone who seeks for more than clever manipulation of complicated threads of intrigue. The reason is simple. In the first place, all this ingenious byplay distracts our attention from the murderer. A number of irrelevant characters have to be introduced; such as a comic servant, of the Andrew Fairservice variety, but as wooden as that excellent Scotchman is full of life; a conventional crone who rejoices in funerals; and two or three elderly gentlemen, who are butts for rather commonplace satire. The humour is, of course, poor; but the worst is, that so much pains is bestowed on showing how the murder was found out that our attention is distracted from the murder itself. All the rules of art have been observed; the light and shade is most carefully distributed, and the composition elaborately balanced; and when it is done, the central figure has become merely one in a crowd instead of absorbing our whole attention. For, besides this, poor Eugene Aram himself is one of Lord Lytton's most palpable failures. Our wonder is, not that such a good man should have had the heart but that such a prig should have had the courage to commit a murder. The extraordinary delight with which he pours out his pinchbeck philosophy upon his father-in-law, and his mistress, and his accomplice, may be venial in a man who has long led a solitary life; but one cannot be seriously annoyed at his execution. Hanging is too good for a man who could address the lady to whom he has just become engaged after this fashion: "Oh, Madeline! methinks there is nothing under heaven like the feeling which puts us apart from all that agitates and fevers and degrades the herd of men: which grants us to control the tenor of our future life, because it annihilates our dependence upon others; and while the rest of earth are hurried on, blind, and unconscious, by the hand of fate, leaves us the sole lords of our destiny; and able, from the past, which we have governed, to become the prophets of our future!" If society were arranged on ideal principles, a human being capable of such a monstrosity would be sentenced to solitary confinement for life. The character of Eugene Aram corresponds to a favourite type of Lord Lytton's. In almost all his novels there are one or more gentlemen with a morbid propensity for apostrophising the heavenly bodies, and talking sham philosophy about the true and beautiful. Often, however, they are subsidiary personages, and are something more than mere talking machines. The misfortune is that in *Eugene Aram*, the central figure—the character whose passions and sufferings should be the moving power of the story—is a mere windbag, and a windbag of the most pretentious kind. The problem is, given a man of intellect and amiable temper, to account for his committing a murder. Lord Lytton's answer would suggest, not that he was driven to desperation by poverty or jealousy or sense of unrequited merit, but that his mind had run to seed owing to an unfortunate habit of talking twaddle, till he had lost all sense of reality and fancied that a few fine words would convert a murder into a noble action. And yet the creator of this mere wooden dummy in philosophical robes takes him for a living human being.

In *Eugene Aram* we see proofs of remarkable technical skill; but we also see the very weakest side of his art. No writer could afford to be judged by his failures, and we turn gladly to a story which, to many readers, appears to be his best. *The Caxtons* is, beyond all doubt, an admirable novel.

Whatever its defects, it carries one along with it. The characters are skilfully contrived, if not vividly conceived; they harmonise with the scenery; and, except an irrelevant pamphlet on colonisation intruded in the disguise of fiction, the whole story is worked out with great force and abundant dexterity. If not a work of real genius, it resembles a work of genius so closely that only a rigid examination will detect the difference. To decide whether it belongs to one or the other category, we may examine the principles on which it was constructed. Lord Lytton had resolved to strike out a new line. The interest of his story was to turn upon domestic life, and an element of the humorous was to be introduced. There is something curiously characteristic in this preconceived determination to appeal to new motives of interest. In nine cases out of ten such a purpose would be fatal to an author's success, because it would imply a total absence of that spontaneity to which all genuine art owes its charm. Lord Lytton, however, succeeded beyond expectation, though his success had very definite limits. To write a domestic novel was comparatively easy; but how could any man, and especially a man of forty-five, with no previous success of the kind to give him confidence, say, I will be humorous? Humour is the last quality to be acquired of *malice prepense* or at a time of life when the animal spirits have grown weak. Lord Lytton, however, set about his task systematically. He went to one of the best masters in that department of literature, and engaged at one blow a whole dramatic company. Sterne's Tristram Shandy became Pisistratus Caxton; the pedantic father and the chivalrous uncle appeared with little change as the two elder Caxtons; and the wife, the doctor, and the corporal, accepted their old parts. There could be, of course, no plagiarism in adopting children whose paternity was so notorious; and, although the first idea is palpably taken from Sterne, the subsequent development of character is characteristically different. The Shandy family have changed in the course of their transmigration. They have become far more decent and perhaps more coherent; but to

say the truth, they have pretty well lost their humour. The
essence of humorous writing of any high order is the power
of thoroughly fusing into a harmonious whole the ludicrous
and the pathetic elements of character. Sterne, with all his
faults—and they are many—has effectually performed that
feat. The foibles of the Shandys are absolutely inseparable
from their virtues; you cannot think of the one without the
other. But the foibles of the Caxtons appear only in the first
chapter. Caxton *père* begins as a pedant, so absorbed in his
books as to forget that a child is being born in his house;
and when the child has forced itself upon his attention, he
evolves the ingenious theory of the influence of names upon
character which was his characteristic opinion in his previous avatar. But Mr. Caxton, unlike Mr. Shandy, forgets
his foibles after he has once introduced himself to the reader,
and becomes a respectable old scholar, with a full share of
that worldly wisdom which is so predominant in all Lord
Lytton's heroes. In the same way Roland Caxton begins
with a set of crotchets worthy of Uncle Toby; but he devel-
ops almost at once into the old Peninsular officer, with a
rather Quixotic sense of honour, but still able to pass muster
in good society without any taint of decided eccentricity. In
fact, it must be said that both of these excellent old men,
though amiable and excellent in their way, descend with
great alacrity into the regions of commonplace. The purely
humorous element, if it does not exactly disappear, is so
softened as to be scarcely perceptible, and adds at most a
slight provincial flavour like the faint suspicion of a Scotch
accent in the mouth of a pretty woman. They are still most
serviceable characters in a novel; we like and even admire
them; but the change which has passed over them is not the
less a change destructive of their perfect originality. The
difference may be expressed in scientific language by saying
that the combination of the odd and the lovable is with
Sterne a stable combination, whereas with Lord Lytton it is
unstable in the highest degree. The intensity of the truly
imaginative writer forms a new and delightful compound;

where the skilful literary artist is able at most to give a slight
tinge of oddity to his performers, but not to make it an
essential element in their character. Mr. Caxton, in fact, and
Uncle Roland, very soon begin to use the same dialect which
we have noticed in the case of the distinguished Eugene
Aram. It is materially altered and improved. Mr. Caxton's
declamations are ornamented by classical quotations instead of references to abstract qualities. We have quotations
from Horace or Strabo instead of platitudes about the True
and the Beautiful. The doctrine has been skilfully adapted
to the tastes of the British public. Nothing flatters that respectable body so much as to hear a man of the world testify-
ing that, after familiarity with the most refined cookery at
the Clubs and the tables of the aristocracy, he has come to
the conclusion that nothing is so good as plain bread and
butter. Such teaching satisfies the two strongest impulses of
our nature, the snobbish and the self-satisfied—the tendency
to worship our nobility and to worship ourselves. Lord
Lytton was a profound believer in the existence of what is
called knowledge of the world, or knowledge of human
nature. He held that there was a body of sound maxims
familiar to men who combine literary and philosophical
tastes with an intimate acquaintance with the worlds of
literature and politics. We by no means deny that such persons acquire a shrewd practical instinct which has its value,
and the lessons of which may be judiciously compressed into
pithy aphorisms. We are inclined, indeed, to doubt whether
they are really much wiser than their neighbours; but it was at
least natural that Lord Lytton should believe in the surpassing
value of a body of doctrine which he was admirably qualified,
both by temperament and by circumstances, for acquiring.
And when he gives us frankly and unaffectedly the results of
his observations, he utters much shrewd sense of which we
should be very sorry to underrate the value. Unluckily, it is
seldom that he is quite unaffected. His characters are generally too self-conscious, and are apt to think that a very
obvious platitude can be made philosophical by giving it a

sententious turn, and sprinkling it with a few adjectives beginning with capital letters. To this tendency we owe those portentous statesmen, who appear in *The Caxtons* and *My Novel*, and who are intended to represent the essence of worldly wisdom. To people who are not quite imposed upon by their dogmatic airs, they appear more frequently to be the very incarnation of red tape. We cannot conceive two greater bores than Mr. Trevanion and Audley Egerton. They might be taken as model specimens of Mr. Carlyle's "miserable creatures having-the-honour-to-be." We altogether decline to fall down and worship them as their creator expects us to do. They may be strangely familiar with blue-books, full of parliamentary experience, and crammed with "knowledge of human nature"; but to us they are intolerable prigs, and remain so to the end of the chapter. A characteristic peculiarity of a prig is a profound belief in the omnipotence of good advice; and this is one of the most marked peculiarities of Lord Lytton's great men. We all remember, for example, the lecture delivered by Parson Dale and Riccabocca to Leonard Fairfield, on the aphorism "Knowledge is power," attributed to Bacon. It is not a bad sermon, but it is terribly commonplace; and, at the end of it, we are just as much convinced as before that knowledge, after all, is power; though it is quite true, as those worthy gentlemen take infinite pains to prove, that other things are also power, and that knowledge by itself is not everything. Nobody ever asserted that it was. But few things are more characteristic of would-be originality than delight in pulling to pieces an aphorism—as if it was not the essence of aphorism to be a partial truth. One of the most characteristic passages in *The Caxtons*, is that where the amiable old pedant converts the youthful scapegrace by a little good advice, by telling him stories of his virtuous cousin. The same excellent adviser—whose advice on paper is so admirable—converts a young infidel by making him read Tucker's *Light of Nature*, some scraps of Scotch metaphysics, and a little German transcendentalism. It is all very well; but is it not marvellously unreal? Are scapegraces and infidels converted on such easy terms in real life? Are they not much more likely to be bored than edified by the infliction of a few commonplaces by an elderly gentleman given to preach sermons composed of pedantic quotations and second-hand metaphysics? We might wish, perhaps, that the real world were more like the world of fiction; and that vice and rash speculation could be eradicated so summarily by a few sententious aphorisms. Unluckily it is not so; and to represent things as carried on in this fashion is to show a want of that penetrative imagination which goes down to the roots of character, and appreciates at their true value the forces of human passions.

This element of portentous platitude—we know not what else to call it—very much interferes with our enjoyment of the Caxtons. A little genuine vigour of mind would dissipate this atmosphere of sham philosophy. Old Mr. Caxton, in fact, is a bore; and his brother—though there is much that is affecting about him—is a sentimentalist; and young Caxton is a prig; and Mr. Trevanion is unconscionably fond of red tape. A writer with a firmer grasp of real life, that is to say, of more imaginative intensity, would have detected this feeble side of his character, and would have made him more interesting because presenting him with less parade of profound wisdom. And yet, in spite of these obvious defects, we repeat that *The Caxtons* is an admirable novel. It is a book which we can read for a second and even for a third time with increased pleasure. There is abundant vigour about it; though not many symptoms of high imaginative power. And, in short, it is as clever as a book can be of which we nevertheless come to be perfectly clear that cleverness is the highest epithet that can be fairly applied to it. Compared with the ordinary run of novels, it is to be placed in a class by itself; compared with the few novels of which we can say that they bear unmistakable marks of genius, it is as distinctly in the second rank. There is not in it one really living and moving character; but there are a large number of characters, who live and move as much as most of the persons who pass themselves off for real human beings in the course of our daily lives.

We have spoken at much length of one of Lord Lytton's worst and of one of his best performances. If we were to examine his others, the historical novels, such as *Rienzi*, *The Last of the Barons*, and *Harold*; or of the sentimental novels, such as *Ernest Maltravers*; or of the wilder romances, such as *Zanoni* and *A Strange Story*, we should exceed our limits, and perhaps we should not find any material additions to our means of forming an opinion of his merits. It would be instructive, indeed, to compare such a novel as *Zanoni* with the writings of a man of genuine genius such as Hawthorne. We should see how the man of second-rate ability takes refuge in a mere accumulation of wonder, where the more imaginative artist is able to cause a deeper thrill by a far slighter tinge of the mysterious. But we do not wish to attempt anything like an exhaustive account of Lord Lytton's versatile performances. The same characteristics, in fact, meet us everywhere. So far as industrious labour can take a man of great ability and of studiously cultivated literary skill, Lord Lytton is an admirable model. Nobody could combine his materials more judiciously, or turn to better account the results of much laborious thought guided by excellent taste. But we always feel the want of that vivifying power which is possessed in its perfection only by a few men in the course of ages, and in an inferior degree by a large number of writers whose works show greater faults but are also by fits more impressive than any of Lord Lytton's. He can put together all the elements of a story or a character according to the most approved rules of art; he can discourse to us with abundant felicity and fertility of illustration upon philosophy and morality; but then he cannot send through his creations that electric current which makes them start into reality, or give to his reflections that force which can be drawn from the deepest emotions of a powerful nature. He is not a creator of new types, but is so ingenious in restoring the old that to a careless observer they are almost as good as the originals. And, therefore, whilst we willingly concede to him a very high place amongst the mortals, we cannot admit his claims to a loftier place.

(*The Cornhill Magazine*, 1873)

# Biography

THE most amusing book in the language is *The Dictionary of National Biography*. If anyone doubts what appears to me to be a self-evident proposition, he has only to buy the work and to dip into it at odd moments. He must be hard to please if he is not interested in a collection of all that is known about our countrymen of all ages, including the dim personages who "flourished" in an uncertain century and the last M or N whose obituary notice is in last year's newspapers. Many volumes full of interesting anecdotes, every word of which is true, must surely fascinate every intelligent reader. As I had the fortune to be closely connected with this undertaking for some years, and was bound therefore to read every article, I ought to speak with some authority, as I can now speak with impartiality. An excellent friend of mine, who inferred that I must be overflowing with the knowledge so imbibed, asked me the other day whether I had not become a profound psychologist. Possibly I ought to have acquired what is called "a knowledge of the human heart." But, in the first place, I find that I forget all about the A's before I have got well into the C's. In the next place, the chief part of an editor's duties consists in acting as Dryasdust. Questions as to whether a date is given in the old style or the new, or as to whether two different titles refer to the same book or to two different books, or to two different modifications of the same book, cannot be said to throw much light upon problems of psychology. And, finally, to say nothing else, one has to study not life at first hand, but what has been said about lives by biographers, which is a very different thing. A study of biographies by the dozen, though it often leaves one pretty much in the dark as to the people biographised, ought perhaps to give one some views as to the art of biography. It is difficult, indeed, to say much that is true and that is not perfectly obvious about any art whatever, and I feel that the few remarks which my experience has taught me will be neither original nor profound.

Biography in the dictionary form has certain peculiarities of its own. The dictionary-maker stands in awe of Dryasdust. He must try to satisfy the genealogist and the bibliographer. He must, therefore, give a number of details which often have little bearing upon the life of his hero. It is impossible to say what minute fact may not have some incidental interest for the historian, and a good deal of dry information must be recorded which the reader for amusement must be trusted to skip. Still more has the dictionary-maker to trust to the reader to supply the flesh and blood to his dry bones. He must restrain his rhetoric and sentiment and philosophical reflection within the narrowest bounds. Our critics—it is the only fault I can find with them—sometimes do us too much honour by comparing us with literature of a more ambitious class. They take the show-lives—the Shakespeare or William the Conqueror—and ask whether they have been adequately written, and whether the writers show a sound judgment in their literary or historical theories. Now, we cannot afford to expatiate about Shakespeare: we have to make room for the less conspicuous people, about whom it is hard to get information elsewhere. The real test of the value of the book is in the adequacy of these timid and third-rate lives. Nor, again, will a reader of sense look to a dictionary to tell him (if he wants to be told) what he ought to think of Shakespeare's plays, or of William's position in the world's history. There are plenty of philosophers who will gladly supply him with ideas on those subjects. The dictionary-maker can at most give a brief indication of the opinions held by good authorities and a reference to the books where they are discussed; and, possibly, may intimate summarily his own conclusions. But to discuss or expound those conclusions at length is impossible, and the critic, if he chooses to take the article as a peg on which to hang his own theories, must not complain if it pretends to be no more than a peg.

I have given these hints because they may indicate the true nature of the problem to be solved. The dictionary-maker writes under the strictest limitations. But art, as is often observed, may show itself best under such limitations. The writer of a sonnet, if the comparison be not too ambitious, knows that his success is due to the difficulties which he has surmounted. His gems are imperishable if he has fitted his thought precisely to the prescribed form. Now, the writer of an ideal dictionary life would achieve a somewhat similar task. He would manage to say everything while apparently saying nothing; to give all the facts demanded from him; to give nothing but the facts; and yet to make the facts tell their own story. If he is not allowed to comment or to criticise, he may put the narrative so that the comment or criticism is tacitly insinuated into the mind of his reader. By skilful arrangement of his story, by condensation of the less important parts, by laying due stress on the most essential, he should set the little drama of a human life in the right point of view and reveal its most important aspects. A smart journalist knows how to beat out a single remark into a column of epigrams and illustrations. The dictionary-maker should aim at the reverse process: he should coax the column of smoke back into the original vase; he should give the very pith and essence of the case, and, like the skilful advocate, appear to be simply relating a plain narrative, when he is really dictating the verdict. "Thou hast convinced me," as Rasselas says, that nobody can write such an article. That is perfectly true; but to produce such an article may be the dream of the writer, however conscious he may be that ideals are rarely attainable in this world.

I say this from the dictionary-maker's point of view; but it applies to biographers in general, and now more than ever. The modern biographer is not content to be silent when there is nothing to be said. If facts are wanting, he fills up the gap with might-have-beens. He tells us that

when Robinson was born Brown was on his deathbed and
Jones prime minister, and speculates upon what would
have happened if they had all been contemporaries. What the
poor dictionary-maker has to say briefly is, "John Smith was
educated at the grammar school of his native town"; the
writer of a graphic biography talks of the Renaissance and
the early system of scholastic training, and Dr. Bushy and
corporal punishment, and the influence of classical culture
upon the human mind in general as well as upon Smith in
particular. The dictionary-maker must trust that his reader
will see all this between the lines; take the philosophy and
the pathos for granted, and make his own picture of the
small Shakespeare creeping like a snail to the Stratford
school, instead of repeating the well-known paragraph which
begins, "The imagination loves to dwell." When I have had
to read some of these exuberant biographies I have wished
that I could have had the writer under my charge for a
time. Firmly, if benevolently, I would have drilled him;
cut out all his fine things, condensed his sentiment by a
little cold water, and squeezed his half-dozen pages into
half-a-column. I have tried the experiment, and it should
be recorded, for the credit of human nature, that a writer
was once good enough to express gratitude for my surgery.
Others mildly remonstrated; yet surely, if I did not use the
knife very clumsily, the discipline was a good one. In these
days, when we have decided, as it seems, that nothing is to
be forgotten, two things are rapidly becoming essential—
some literary condensing machine, and a system of indexing.
Our knowledge, that is, requires to be concentrated and to
be arranged. When I have been in the library of the British
Museum I have been struck with a not wholly pleasing awe.
I went one day to the manuscript-room, and there was
invited to regale myself with three thick volumes of closely-
written letters by the London agent of certain foreign book-
sellers, filled, in an illegible hand, with the smallest literary
gossip of the days of George II. I extracted from it, after
much pains, the name of the University at which Des-

maizeaux had taken his degree, for which I hope my readers will be thankful. I went to the reading-room, and discovered there a college exercise printed in the seventeenth century at Leyden, which enabled me to reveal to an inquisitive world the name of Bernard Mandeville's father. It is bewildering to think that a lad cannot print a declamation in Holland without the thing being preserved for the benefit of Englishmen two centuries later. The mass of matter preserved on the shelves of that invaluable Museum is the externalised memory of the race. There is nothing too petty or contemptible to be preserved. When one thinks of all the records preserved up and down Europe in the archives of various States, of all the materials in private hands, of the infinitesimal portion which any reader could get through in a lifetime, and then of the enormously ac-celerated rate at which information is now being compiled and amassed in safe repositories, one stands aghast. If a fire should take place at the Record Office or the British Museum I would give all the strength I possess to working the engines. But if fire were a discreet element, which could be trusted to burn only the rubbish, I could find it in my heart to applaud a conflagration.

This is a digression; but it gives the reflection which is constantly before the dictionary-maker. He is a toiler among those gigantic piles of "shot rubbish" of which Carlyle complained so bitterly when he too was a slave of Dryasdust. He is trying to bring into some sort of order, alphabetical at least, the chaos of materials which is already so vast and so rapidly accumulating. To write a life is to collect the particular heap of rubbish in which his material is contained, to sift the relevant from the superincumbent mass, and then try to smelt it and cast it into its natural mould. His first operation is, of course, to take the lives already written, and to boil them down into the necessary limits. Many lives must contain as much history as biog-raphy, and of the historical aspects I do not propose to speak. The life with which I am concerned is the record of

what happened to a single human being between his birth
and his death; and the purpose of the narrator is to show what
he was and how he came to be what he was. It is only in a
few cases that these questions can be said to have been
adequately treated. The most really interesting problem—
that of the development of the human character—is generally
the most inscrutable. If, as has been frequently said, any man,
even the most commonplace, could be adequately explained;
if we could be told with what qualities he started, and what
influences really moulded and developed them, we should
have a book of unsurpassable interest. But it is rare to find
any approach to such an account. Few facts are preserved
till a man has become well-known, and by that time his
character is generally formed. Nothing is more striking to
the biographer than the rapidity with which all possibility
of satisfactory portraiture vanishes. Nobody, as Johnson
somewhere says, could write a satisfactory life of a man who
had not lived in habits of intimacy with him. Now, it is rare
for a man to preserve the intimates of his early years; school
friendships are transitory, and schoolboys are not generally
keen psychologists. All they can generally remember is the best
score made in a cricket-match or the prize at an examination.
They generally see nothing of their schoolfellow's real life,
and they are divided between the wish to show that they
recognised genius early, and the pleasure of supporting the
paradox that the genius was originally stupid. If the father
or mother or schoolmaster survive, the schoolmaster has an
eye to the merits of his school; the father probably thought
more of the school-bills than of the boy's work; and the
mother—was a mother. The friends who survive are generally
those who have been attracted in later years; and even if
they are keen of penetration and of power of telling what
they have perceived—both rare qualities and frequently
disjoined—they only tell us of the finished product. The
few biographies which give a really instructive account of
mental and moral growth are autobiographies. After making
obvious allowances, they are always instructive, and they

generally dwell with natural fondness upon the early years, in which the critical process was undergone. Without such a narrative or letters or diaries which are in some respects a better, because a more unconscious and less modified, autobiography, the life of a famous man is often an insoluble problem even at his death. I could mention men whom I have known, who were known to very wide circles, and who were survived by many contemporaries, whose early history, except so far as the bare external facts are concerned, must remain purely conjectural, simply because no competent witness has survived them. Those who were in a position to know were unobservant, or stupid, or dull, or forgetful.

We can now generally ascertain—it is a rather melancholy reflection—all the external facts; but whatever cannot be inferred from them vanishes "like the smoke of the guns on a wind-swept hill!" School registers and the like will supply us with an ample framework of dates; but the history of the mind and character evaporates, and is vaguely supplied by conjecture. Do we even remember our own history, or did we even know at the time what was really happening to us? Some people with powerful memories seem to preserve a detailed map of the past; but in my own case, which is, I suspect, the commonest, I should be reduced to mere guessing as to my motives and the influences which affected me almost as much as though I were writing of a stranger. And yet, with all such necessary imperfections, biographies have a fascination, even when they are of the scantiest. They stimulate the imagination to realise one of the hardest of all truths to accept—that the existence of a *Hamlet* now proves that there must actually have once been a William Shakespeare. The lives written in that period, indeed, seem to leave the case almost doubtful. They are so vague, perfunctory, and unsubstantial, that we are half inclined to regard the heroes as mere phantoms, vague X's and Y's who never trod the solid earth. The actors upon the great stage of politics here, of course, come down to us with sufficient vividness. A man who has cut off other men's heads, or had his own cut off, has impressed his reality upon the world; but the mere author, philosopher, or poet, has vanished, like Aubrey's famous spirit, leaving nothing behind but a "twang" and a sweet, or perhaps, not sweet, savour. The biographers at most were content to amplify the conventional epitaph; or at times, like the excellent Izaak Walton, they wrote most charming little idylls, beautiful to read, but curiously empty of facts, and tinged with a rose-colour calculated to rouse suspicions. For some biographies the main authority is a funeral sermon; and the typical funeral sermon is one which an eloquent divine constructed out of an elaborate parallel between the characters of Kind David and George II. If we had only known of George the points in which he resembled the Hebrew monarch, our information would obviously have been defective. A writer to whom all readers of seventeenth-century biography often owe their fullest knowledge is Anthony à Wood, one of the most thorough and satisfactory of antiquaries. His inestimable collection is charming not only from its good workmanship within its own limits, but also for the delightful growls of disgust extracted from the old High-Church don at every mention of a Nonconformist or a Whig—especially if the wretch claims to possess any virtues. But Wood can only give, and only professes to give, data for lives, not the finished product. As time goes on we get the biography which serves as a preface to collective works. The author is haunted by the modest conviction that his readers are anxious to get at the author's own writings, and is content with pronouncing a graceful *éloge*, without defiling his elegant phrases by the earthy material of facts. Toland wrote a life of Milton, when a dozen people were extant who could have described for him the domestic life of his hero. He felt, however, that to go into such details would compromise his dignity, and leave no room for his judicious observations upon epic poetry. Of Toland himself we are told by a biographer that he was forced to leave the Court at Berlin "by an incident too ludicrous to mention." We vainly feel that we would give more for that incident than for all the other facts mentioned. This dignified style survived till the end of the last century, and we have a grudge against Dugald Stewart, otherwise an excellent person, for writing a life of Adam Smith in the spirit of a continuous rebuff to impertinent curiosity. The main purpose of such biographies seems to be to prevent posterity from knowing anything about a man which they could not discover from other sources. There is a biography famous for not giving a single date, and an autobiography in which the hero apologises for once using the word "I." The biographer of modern times may be often indiscreet in his revelations; but so far as the interest of the book goes the opposite pole is certainly the most repulsive. We want the man in his ordinary dress, if not stripped naked; and these dignified persons will only show him in a full-bottomed wig and a professor's robes. Johnson changed all this as author and subject of biography.

In the *Lives of the Poets*, we have at least a terse record of the essential facts seen through a medium of shrewd masculine observation. The writer is really interested in life, not simply recording dates or taking a text for exhibiting his own skill in perorating. He is investigating character, and, with obvious limitations, investigating it with remarkable insight. Of the immortal Boswell, it is happily needless to speak. Since his book, no writer has been at a loss for a model; and many most delightful books are its descendants, though none has eclipsed its ancestor. Boswell founded biography in England as much as Gibbon founded history and Adam Smith political economy. He produces that effect of which Carlyle often made such powerful use, the sudden thrill which comes to us when we find ourselves in direct communication with human feeling in the arid wastes of conventional history; when we perceive that a real voice is speaking out of "the dark backward and abysm" of the past, and a little island of light, with moving and feeling figures, still standing out amidst the gathering shades of oblivion. Perhaps there are no books in which the imagination is so often stimulated in that way as in Carlyle's own *Cromwell* and Spedding's *Bacon*. The *Bacon* is to me a singularly attractive book, to which, indeed, the only objection is that it is not properly a book, but a collection of documents. It is therefore the mass of raw material from which I hope that a book may some day be constructed. Such a book might be a masterpiece of applied psychology. It would give the portrait of a man of marvellous and most versatile intellect, full of the noblest ambitions and the most extensive sympathies, combined with all the weaknesses which we are accustomed to class as "human nature." Spedding's hero-worship led him to apologise for all Bacon's errors; and, though the very ingenuity of the pretexts is characteristic both of the hero and his biographer, we are sensible that a more disengaged attitude would have enabled Spedding to produce a more genuine portrait. He has provoked later writers to air their virtuous indignation a little too freely. We want the writer capable of developing the character in the Shakespearian spirit; showing the facts with absolute impartiality, not displaying his moral sense, if that be really the way to display a moral sense, by blackening the devil and whitening the angel. We should then have a pendant to Hamlet with the advantage of reality; the true state of a man of the highest genius, but without enough moral ballast for his vast spread of intellectual sail.

This case represents the great crux of the biographer. Is he to give a pure narrative of his own, or to let his hero talk to us face to face? In some cases the raw material is better than any comment. No biographer could supersede the necessity of reading Pepys's own diary. The effect is only producible by following Pepys to his own closet and overhearing all his most intimate confessions to himself. Indeed, if we had time, we should generally get a far more perfect picture by studying all a man's papers than by reading his life. But that means that we are to cook our own dinners and write the life for ourselves. I say nothing of the vast rubbish heaps which would have to be sifted. Many such collections,

again, Walpole's letters, for example, are really interesting
for the side-lights thrown upon other persons or the general
illustrations of the period; and a life which only showed us
Walpole himself would miss the interest of all that Walpole
saw. Everything must, of course, depend on the particular
circumstances, the nature of the hero's career, and of the
materials which he has left. The life proper, however, is
that in which the main interest is the development of the
man's own character and fortunes. Now, as a fairly working
principle, I should say that the main purpose of the writer
should be the construction of an autobiography. Boswell's
felicity in being able to make Johnson talk to us is, of course,
almost unique. Only the rarest combination of circumstances
can produce anything approaching to such material. But
the next best thing is the autobiography contained in letters.
The question of whether a really satisfactory life can be
written is essentially the question of whether letters have
been preserved. It is a general belief that the art of letter-
writing has been killed by the penny post. Your correspond-
ent, you know, will pick up all the gossip from the papers,
and a Horace Walpole is therefore an anachronism. Cowper's
delightful letters, again, presuppose an amount of lesiure, a
power of sitting down quietly to compose playful nothings
for a friend, which has now almost vanished. Your author
can put his good things, if he has any, to better account.
But the general statement is, I think, disputable. The letters
of the day must always appear to be bad, simply because
few are yet published. Our grandsons will first be in a
position to judge of us. Many of the best letters of the last
generation were written by busy men, already exposed to
many of our difficulties, and yet were, I think, equal to any
of the past. I do not know a much pleasanter course of
reading than is to be found in the letters of Scott, Southey,
Byron, Macaulay, and Carlyle, to mention no others. The
very fact that we have not to act as newswriters often gives
us a better opportunity of expressing our feelings about the
events of the day. We may take for granted that our corre-

spondent has read the debates, and may confine ourselves to blessing or cursing Mr. Gladstone or Mr. Balfour. One can hardly bless or curse without displaying one's own nature. While letters become less important as records of events, they preserve their full significance as revelations of character; and that is what the biographer chiefly requires. It should therefore be regarded as a duty (it is one which I systematically transgress) to keep all letters written by a possible biographee; and I think that we shall be surprised, not that they have so little merit, but rather that the amount of passion and feeling with which they are throbbing has allowed them to lie quiet in their dusty receptacles.

Be this as it may, letters in the main are the one essential to a thoroughly satisfactory life. From them, in nine cases out of ten, is to be drawn all that gives it real vividness of colouring. Everybody knows the strange sensation of turning over an old bundle of letters, written in the distant days when you were at college, or falling in love. Your memory has ever since been letting facts drop, and remoulding others, and colouring the whole with a strangely delusive mist. You have unconsciously given yourself credit for deliberately intending what came about by mere accident; and, in giving up youthful opinions, have come to forget that you ever held them. I found out once from an old letter that I had taken a decision, of great importance for me, upon grounds which I had utterly forgotten, and of which I had unconsciously devised a totally different (and very creditable) account. I burnt the letter and forgot its contents, and I now only know that my own story of my own life is somehow altogether wrong. A writer of an interesting autobiography tells us how he refused a certain office from a chivalrous motive; and then adds, with charming candour, that, though he has always told the story in this way, he has found from a contemporary letter that one of his motives was certain natural but not chivalrous fears as to his own health. His memory had kept only the agreeable recollection. Such incidents represent the ease with which the common

legend of a life grows up; and the sole corrective for good or
for bad is the contemporary document. To know what a man
said at the moment is of primary importance, even if he was
lying or acting a part. The letter which shows what a man
wished to appear generally tells a good deal as to what he
was. Even if we take a hero in active life, one of Nelson's
letters or phrases shows more of the man than the clearest
narrative of the battle of Trafalgar. His signals enlighten us
as much as they appealed to his crews, and show what lay
behind the skilful tactics and the heroic daring. A biographer has, of course, to lay down his framework, to settle
all the dates and the skeleton of facts; but to breathe real
life into it he must put us into direct communication with the
man himself; not tell us simply where he was or what he was
seen to do, but put him at one end of a literary telephone
and the reader at the other. The author should, as often as
possible, be merely the conducting wire. Some biographies
are partly intended to show the merits of the biographer;
but even the most undeniable hero-worship is often self-
defeating. The writer shows his zeal for a friend's memory
by treating him as the antiquaries treat Shakespeare. It is
pardonable, in our dearth of information about Shakespeare,
that, no real biography being possible, we should hunt up all
the trivial details which are still accessible. We cannot know
what he thought of his wife or his tragedies, or what realities,
if any realities, are indicated by the sonnets; and we may
therefore be thankful for a beggarly account of facts from a
few legal documents and registers. But when a man's
memory is still fresh and vivid, when the really essential
documents are at hand, biographers display their zeal too
often by preserving what would be useful only in the
absence of the genuine article. There is some interest now in
reading Goldsmith's tailors' bills and noting the famous
bloom-coloured garment; but a biographer need not infer
that the tailors' bills of his own hero should also be published
at length. We have to learn the art of forgetting—of
suppressing all the multitudinous details which threaten to

overburthen the human memory. Our aim should be to present the human soul, not all its irrelevant bodily trappings. The last new terror of life is the habit of "reminiscing." A gentleman will write a page to tell us that he once saw Carlyle get into an omnibus; and the conscientious biographer of the future will think it a duty to add this fact to his exhaustive museum.

The ideal biographer should in the first place write of someone who is thoroughly sympathetic to him. Excessive admiration, though a fault, is a fault on the right side. As Arbuthnot observes in the *Recipe for an Epic Poem*, the fire is apt to cool down wonderfully when it is spread on paper. Readers will make deductions enough in any case; and nothing can compensate for a want of enthusiasm about your subject. He should then consider how much space his hero undeniably deserves, divide that by two (to make a modest denominator), and let nothing in the world tempt him to exceed the narrower limits. Sam Weller's definition of good letter-writing applies equally to biography. The reader should ask for more and should not get it. The scrapings and remnants of a man's life should be charitably left to the harmless race of bookmakers, as we give our crumbs to the sparrows in winter. If there are any incidental facts with which the hero is connected, but which have no bearing upon his character, consign them to an appendix or put them into notes. I have myself a prejudice against notes, and think that a biography should be as independent of such appendages as a new poem. But there are people, perhaps, of better taste than mine, who like such trimmings, and have a fancy for trifling with them in the intervals of reading. The book itself should, I hold, be a portrait in which not a single touch should be admitted which is not relevant to the purpose of producing a speaking likeness. The biographer should sternly confine himself to his functions as introducer; and should give no more discussion than is clearly necessary for making the book an independent whole. A little analysis of motive may be necessary here and there: when, for example, your hero has put his hand in somebody's pocket and you have to demonstrate that his conduct was due to sheer absence of mind. But you must always remember that a single concrete fact, or a saying into which a man has put his whole soul, is worth pages of psychological analysis. We may argue till Doomsday about Swift's character: his single phrase about "dying like a poisoned rat in a hole" tells us more than all the commentators. The book should be the man himself speaking or acting, and nothing but the man. It should be such a portrait as reveals the essence of character; and the writer who gives anything that does not tell upon the general effect is like the portrait-painter who allows the chairs and tables, or even the coat and cravat, to distract attention from the face. The really significant anecdote is often all that survives of a life; and such anecdotes must be made to tell properly, instead of being hidden away in a wilderness of the commonplace; they should be a focus of interest, instead of a fallible extract for a book of miscellanies. How much would be lost of Johnson if we suppress the incident of the penance at Uttoxeter! It is such incidents that in books, as often in life, suddenly reveal to us whole regions of sentiment but never rise to the surface in the ordinary routine of our day. Authors of biographies come to praise Cæsar, not to bury him; but too often the burial, under a mass of irrelevance, is all that they really achieve. It requires, indeed, a fine tact to know what is in fact essential. A dexterous use of trivialities often gives a certain reality to the whole. St. Paul's cloak at Troas, I fancy, has often interested readers by a suggestion of certain human realities; though commentators hesitate about its inspiration of the allusion. Mason, who deserves credit for being the first (or one of the first) to see what use could be made of letters, thought himself at liberty to manipulate Gray's correspondence so as to make it suit his notions of literary art. The stricter canons of later times have led us to condemn the falsification of facts which was involved. But too many modern authors

seem to think that Mason's fault consisted not in attributing
to Gray things which he did not write, but in omitting anything that he did write. Mason would have been fully
justified in making a selection, with a clear statement that it
was a selection. Even so admirable a letter-writer as Gray
wrote of necessity a good deal which the world could perfectly well spare. In these days many men write several
volumes annually, of which nine-tenths is insignificant, and
the remainder consists in great part of repetitions. To choose
what is characteristic, with just enough of the trifling matter
in which it is embedded to make it natural; to avoid the
impression that the writer was always at the highest point of
tension, is the problem. I wish that more writers achieved the
solution.

Every life, even the life of Dr. Parr, has its interest. We
want to know what was under the famous wig. Many modern
lives are especially charming in spite of excesses; and in the
briefest and driest of dictionary lives I have always found
something worth reading. I have only ventured a mild protest against a weakness which naturally grows upon us. My
protest comes simply to suggesting that a biography should
again be considered as a work of art; the aim should be the
revelation, and, as much as possible, the self-revelation, of
a character. Everything not strictly relevant to that purpose
should be put aside. Some of our ancestors were so anxious
to be artistic that they wrote mere novels and mere essays,
with occasional allusions to the chief events of their hero's
life. We are too apt to fall into the opposite error of simply
tumbling out all the materials, valuable or worthless, upon
which we can lay our hands; and making even of a life,
which has a most natural and obvious principle of unity, a
chaotic jumble of incoherent information. The ideal of
such writers seems to be a blue-book in which all the evidence bearing upon the subject can be piled like a huge
prehistoric cairn over the remains of the deceased, with no
more apparent order and constructive purpose than the
laws of gravitation enforce spontaneously. Let us have neither

the blue-book nor the funeral oration, but something, with a beginning, middle, and end, which can cheat us for the time into the belief that we are really in the presence of a living contemporary.

(*The National Review*, 1893)

# Thoughts of an Outsider: International Prejudices

WHEN General Grant delivered an address the other day upon the opening of the Exhibition at Philadelphia, we courteously expressed our surprise that he had not talked greater nonsense. He indulged in pretty good common sense instead of soaring into the regions of bombast upon the wings of the American eagle. He even admitted that Americans might have something to learn from Europe; and that the inevitable struggle with material obstacles had distracted their attention from the pursuits more immediately interesting to the intellect and the imagination. This, doubtless, was all as it should be. A certain lowering of the old tone of patriotic bluster is perceptible just now throughout the world. It is curious to notice the great waves of sentiment which sweep at intervals across whole nations. Popular fits of depression and exultation seem to propagate themselves like the cholera. At one period in the life of a people everything seems to be rose-coloured. A great chorus of self-satisfaction goes up from the whole civilised world. We believe—as people believed at the opening of the French revolution—in the perfectibility of mankind: war was about to disappear; reason was then to take the place of blind prejudice; social wrongs were all to be redressed; man was about to become omnipotent over matter; and all human wants to be supplied by the labours of half an hour in every day. Then came a change in our anticipations. The dawn was overcast. The old spectres of tyranny, cruelty, and superstition stalked abroad; we learnt anew the old lesson that the cause of our evils lies deep in the hearts and heads of mankind; and that stupid heads cannot be cleared nor corrupt hearts purified by any political catastrophe. A gloom settled over our spirits, and instead of expecting the millennium, we sought for analogies to our position in the periods of decaying empires and declining faith.

The external causes of this revulsion of sentiment are sometimes palpable; sometimes they must be sought for in some obscure morbid tendency. They represent the dim forecasts of

*the prophetic soul*
*Of the wide world dreaming on things to come.*

Nobody can fully explain his own moods, and tell why one hour of his own life is tinged with a mystic glory and the next wrapped in darkness; and still less can we unravel all the symptoms of widespread social disquiet. The race, like the individual, has strange presentiments of coming good or evil, which help perhaps to fulfil themselves. Just now, it may be said, the spiritual barometer is low. We are tormented by a vague unrest. The enigmas of life torment us more than usual; and we know not whether our constitutional twinges forebode a coming attack or are destined to pass away like a bad dream. Men are not disposed either in England or America to indulge in that extravagant exhilaration which greeted the first great show a quarter of a century ago; an exhilaration which, seen by the light of later history, looks almost like a judicial infatuation. Grave men in all seriousness declared that the opening of a large bazaar was equivalent to the proclamation of a gospel of peace. We cannot think of such utterances without a cynical smile. We are looking rather at the seamy side of things; we ask whether the old order has vitality enough to throw off its maladies, and whether the new order promised by the sanguine is anything but a skilful pretext for an attack upon the very bases of society. In such a mood, the pleasant old confident formulæ are out of place. We are tired of calculating the number of miles of railway and yards of cotton turned out of factories and looms; and we cannot speak of the boundless stores of mineral wealth in the American continent without thinking of some mining enterprises which have redistributed rather than augmented the aggregate wealth of mankind. Instead of purple and fine raiment we are disposed to fancy that sackcloth and ashes might be the most appropriate fashion of the day.

Why, indeed, should we not return to the good old custom of days of fasting and humiliation? The practice may have been wholesome in the main, when it did not mean that every man was lamenting his neighbour's sins. A Liberal would humble himself with great complacency for the shortcomings of a Conservative ministry; and the Conservative would groan over the long arrears of mischief bequeathed by the supremacy of his antagonists. But if for once we could make up our minds to apply the lash to our own backs heartily and sincerely, some good might be done. The press sometimes affects to discharge the duty; but the affectation is not very successful. When its lamentations get beyond mere party squabbling, they are apt to ring hollow. Even the platitudes about modern luxury and over-excitement—the most popular text of the would-be satirist—do not seem to imply sincere indignation so much as a thinly disguised satisfaction in dwelling upon the vicious splendours described. When a man really quarrels with the world and strikes with all his force at its vulnerable points, he soon finds as of old that the world takes him for a madman. We are melancholy just now; but we have not got so far as to admit that our sins are of a deep dye.

Englishmen indeed boast themselves to be grumblers by profession. We confess, it is said, and even exaggerate our own shortcomings. Surely of all our national boasts this is about the emptiest. I have known a sincerely religious person rather confounded by the discovery that somebody had taken in downright earnest his confession that he was a miserable sinner. He was forced to explain with some awkwardness that though, on proper occasions, he admitted the utter vileness of his heart, yet, as a matter of fact, he was not more in the habit of breaking the Ten Commandments than his most respectable neighbours. The admission that they do things better in France means just as much or as little as this confession of the ordinary Pharisee. Nations differ widely in their mode of expressing their self-satisfaction, but hardly in the degree of complacency. A German, perhaps, is the most priggish in his consciousness of merit. He expounds his theory of world-history with the airs of a professor, and lays down his superiority to all mankind as the latest discovery of scientific thought. French vanity is the most childlike and therefore at once the least offensive and the most extravagant. American brag is often the noisiest; but it has a certain frankness which is not without its attraction. If you meet an English and an American snob together in a picture gallery, they may be equally indifferent to the fine arts; but the American will frankly confess that he never heard of Raphael before, and dislikes what he now sees; whereas your true Briton puts on a sheepish affectation of good taste and hopes that you will mistake his stupidity for pride. If English patriotism is not pedantic, nor vain, nor bombastic, it has a tinge of sulkiness beneath its apparent self-depreciation which is almost peculiar to itself, and can therefore be more offensively vulgar than that of any other race.

There is, however, little to choose in reality between the varying manifestations of the feeling. A profound conviction that everyone is a barbarian who does not wear clothes of our pattern is common to all mankind. Whether it takes this or that colouring, whether it is frank or reserved, directly or indirectly boastful, is a secondary consideration. And, moreover, the reason is obvious enough; namely, that the conviction does not, properly speaking, represent any intellectual conviction whatever, but is simply the reverse side of the universal instinct of self-satisfaction. When Johnson said, "foreigners are fools," he expressed a belief as universal as the belief that two and two make four. Like that valuable proposition, it may be regarded as really an identical proposition. It means simply, foreigners are foreigners. A man is a foreigner in so far as he differs in some degree from my ways of thinking; that is, as I think that he thinks wrong; but thinking wrong is the mark of folly: therefore, I think that he is a fool. No mathematical demonstration can be more practically convincing, though, from the point of view of universal reason, it may be possible to detect some error in the chain of reasoning.

So long as we remain in generalities, most people will admit that there is an ugly side to all patriotism. Patriotism is one of the great virtues, and the mainspring of the noblest human actions; but a monstrous brood of mean and ugly prejudices shelters itself under this venerable name. The people of whom we are most ashamed naturally brag the most of our acquaintance; and, on the same principle, the least admirable of Britons are apt to flaunt the silliest British prejudices most annoyingly in the eyes of the civilised world. We often have to blush for the pride of our countrymen. If, however, we were to try to go a step farther and to settle which Britons are offensive and which British prejudices are silly, we should no longer meet with the same agreement. Some people, for example, would begin by condemning all our military self-glorification from the days of Crécy and Agincourt down to the Balaclava charge. At the outside, a battle should be remembered as long as we love to pay pensions to those who took part in it. But this doctrine is a little premature.

There is another question more relevant at the present moment, which will bear a few words—would that they could be the last ever devoted to it! Englishmen and Americans have had various uncomfortable relations and seem to be endowed with special power for irritating each other's vanity. The Americans, as we fancy, act like the perverse sailor who excited the boatswain's wrath. "A plague on thee!" exclaimed that official as he flourished the cat, "wherever I hit thee there is no pleasing thee!" We have laid on the lash in every possible way: sometimes it comes down with a stinging satire; sometimes with a lofty moral reproof;

and sometimes with profound political reasoning. Then, to make things pleasant, we rub in a good unctuous compound of flattery and philanthropy, and to our surprise and disgust our attentions are scornfully rejected. If we condemn, we are prejudiced; if we praise, we are silly flatterers; if we speak calmly, we are treating our cousins like children; if warmly, like rivals; if we say nothing, we show a brutal indifference to their claims; if we say anything, we show our profound ignorance at every word. We are like people examining some queer chemical compound, which, for anything they can say, will explode if it is touched, or heated, or chilled, or rubbed, or taken up, or set down, or let alone. We only know that our words are pretty sure to be taken the wrong way and our silence to be misinterpreted. That the fault is not entirely our own may be guessed from the remarks of intelligent Americans; but there may be some force also in their statement that we have spoken of their countrymen in every way but one, namely, as ordinary human beings with much the same faults and virtues as ourselves. If we could manage to hit off the mean between the patronising and the sycophantic attitude, we should perhaps succeed better. But it is not surprising that the failure of many attempts to make ourselves pleasant, and our signal success in attempts of the reverse kind, have produced a certain nervousness in our mutual relations.

After all, matters have improved. Americans have become more independent and less sensitive; and Englishmen perhaps have outlived some foolish prejudices. Let us reflect for a moment how a further advance of good feeling may be secured. A century of separation should have taught us to accept our mutual relations with a good grace. Why do, or why did, Americans and Englishmen dislike each other? One fact is plain. It was not because they knew anything of each other. If so, the question occurs whether it can be accurately said that they did in fact dislike each other. Each nation disliked a certain imaginary entity which it chose to label with the name of its antagonist, but which had of necessity the vaguest possible relation to realities. Suppose, to imagine an impossible case, that Guy Faux was still alive and living in some English village; suppose further that he was in reality one of those highly respectable and immaculate personages who have been made scapegoats by historians to be rehabilitated in later days; suppose that, so far from wishing to blow up the king and the parliament, the true Guy Faux was really a devout Protestant, who occupied the vault for legitimate purposes of business, and that all the rest of the story was a lie contrived by politicians;—if, then, the genuine Faux, being now some 300 years ago, should walk abroad on November 5, and see a hideous image of himself paraded, with a turnip for a head, an old pipe in its mouth, and old rags on its back, and then assist at the conflagration of the said image amidst a discharge of crackers, general exultation, and vows to remember for ever something that never happened, and in regard of which the performers had no conceivable means of judging whether it happened or not—would the respectable Faux be justified in saying that he was hated, or in resenting the hatred? He might be excusably annoyed at the reflection that his Christian name had been converted into a new term of abuse, and regret the fallibility of mankind; but, if he was of a logical turn, he would console himself by thinking that the true object of popular contempt was a mere figment, accidentally connected with his name, and he would admit that the rioters were not responsible for the illusion which they had no means of testing. He would have no more cause for wrath or for a sense of martyrdom than if one of his old hats had fallen into the hands of a tribe of savages and been converted by them into a fetish, which might be accidentally worshipped or regarded as a symbol of diabolical power.

Now the ideal John Bull or Brother Jonathan is to the real Englishman or American what the factitious dummy is to our supposed Guy Faux. He is made up of vague scraps and tatters which have somehow floated across the Atlantic. The steeple-crowned hat of Guy Faux is, perhaps, a traditional portrait of the genuine original; and so the top-boots and knee-breeches of John Bull, and the lantern-jaws and bowie-knife of Jonathan, as they figure in our conventional caricatures, have no doubt a foundation in fact. But what is the substance clothed in this external form? In the case of Guy, it may be supposed, if we are charitable, that the ceremonial partly reflects a horror of dark conspiracy, which is a respectable if not a virtuous sentiment; or a love of Protestantism, with which we may or may not sympathise, but which is at least not intrinsically a vicious sentiment; and whatever the ostensible pretext, the chief constituent of the popular emotion is clearly a love of noise. What are the analogous elements in the absurd fetish which we call by the name of a nation? He is made up partly of vague antipathy—the dislike of a fat man for a thin, or of the man who shaves his chin instead of the upper lip for the man who shaves on the inverse principle; partly, again, of the pure spirit of combativeness—a very excellent ingredient in national character, though sometimes developed in excess; but chiefly, of course, of what we call patriotic feeling. To an American, John Bull represents simply the outside world; England being the only country with which he has sensibly come in contact. England meant little more than not America; and the hatred of England was merely the shadow cast by his own self-esteem. The English sentiment is, of course, a little more complex. We have been knocked about enough in the world to distinguish between foreigners and foreigners; and the American dummy might be chiefly the reflection of that most sensitive part of national feeling which was bound up with pride in the British Empire. It is not simply dislike to the non-English world, but dislike to that part of it which had most humiliated England. That is to say, it is the reverse side of the vague but keen sentiment produced by a consciousness of our colonial greatness. To hate the foreign nation is, therefore, at bottom to think with complacency of ourselves. The feeling is of course natural. Not long ago I heard some farm-labourers chanting an old song which ended by a vigorous defiance hurled at "the Pope and the King of Spain." How the poor King of Spain came in for this denunciation I know not. Perhaps it was a tradition from the times of the Armada, or possibly from the more recent excitement in the days of Walpole. Anyhow it was highly probable that the singers did not know whether Spain was nearer to England or Australia, whether Spaniards talked Hebrew or Japanese, or worshipped Mumbo-jumbo or the Virgin Mary. They would doubtless have cheered the monarch whom they denounced if he had presented himself in flesh and blood. But, in any case, their hatred of Spaniards might just as well have been called hatred of the Chinese or love of ourselves. It implied no sort of opinion about the real Spain, bad or good. The ordinary English judgment of Americans is not much more valuable. In the lower classes it means a vague impression that America is the land of promise for labourers; in the higher a vague impression that America is a bad place for people of artistic tendencies or conservative politics. But in any case it would be ludicrous to consider it as a serious judgment formed upon sufficient evidence.

If, indeed, we consider for a moment what it implies to make any decently satisfactory judgment of thirty or forty millions of human beings; how difficult it is for the imagination to realise different conditions of country and climate and social development; what ludicrous mistakes are committed by the most acute and impartial foreign travellers; how little we know even of our own country; how little an ordinary cockney, for example, knows of the farm-labourer or of the factory hand; how little he knows even of nine-tenths of his fellow-townsmen in this wilderness of brick and mortar; what miscalculations are made even by statesmen whose business in life is to understand their fellows as to the real currents of national sentiment on the most important matters; how hopelessly different are the estimates formed by intelligent persons as to the religion, the morality, the cultivation of classes with whom they are in daily contact; how confidently one man will decide, say, that intoxication is visibly increasing and another that it is diminishing;—we may form some estimate of the utter inadequacy of nine-tenths of our hasty verdicts about nations. We could easily mention writers of great ability who have studied English literature and English characteristics for years, and yet make errors in every page palpable to the most ordinary Englishman. Our judgment of our neighbours is very unlikely to be as near the mark as (say) M. Taine's judgment of us. And yet what Englishman thinks that he can really learn from M. Taine? We think ourselves entitled, indeed, to form opinions by a very expeditious process. Most people reason by particular instances. An American ruffian plots the destruction of a ship, or a Frenchman cuts half-a-dozen throats, and we assume that they represent typical instances of national development. An international antipathy means a healthy instinct combined with a logical fallacy. The instinct flourishes in proportion as a nation is contented and happy. It is developed when the sentiments of which all the bonds of society are ultimately composed are in a thoroughly healthy state; its decay would mean the approach of revolution or national dissolution. Its vigour means that the social order is moulded upon the strongest popular convictions. But this most desirable passion gives strength incidentally to a mass of silly prejudices. It encourages us to hate or despise people of whom we know nothing but the name and the fact that they differ from ourselves. We should be ashamed in any matter of daily life to frame any opinion upon grounds so slight as those which determine our judgment of a foreign nation. Those grounds are vague traditions, trifling observations of the external peculiarities of an infinitesimal fraction of the phenomena in question, or hasty surmises of incompetent judges passed through a dozen intermediate stages. But when a proposition falls in with a vigorous instinct, it acquires a strength utterly dispropor-tionate to its logical value, and may produce serious mischief.

Does it really produce such mischief? Are these groundless prejudices really more than a harmless amusement? The mutual dislike of Americans and Englishmen has been lamented, but has it done much harm? So far as it has in fact envenomed diplomatic quarrels it has, of course, been objectionable. It may have made the preservation of peace more difficult, or produced discreditable diplomacy. Of that I can here say nothing; but there is an allowance or two to be made before we can judge rightly. Nothing, in the first place, is so transitory as a sentiment of this kind. Nations behave to each other like a pair of fickle lovers. They kiss one day, and curse the next. When the Northern States were angry with us during the war, some of their papers vowed eternal vengeance. The eternity has not lasted for ten years. The vows were pretty well forgotten before the ink was dry; and the same writers are as ready to talk the regular series of "Anglo-Saxon" platitudes. The reason is, doubtless, that the antipathy lies on the surface of men's minds, and, owing nothing to logic, may disappear without logic. Washington told his countrymen very sensibly in his last message that the national policy could not be determined by sentimental considerations. It is a cardinal virtue in a nation to guide itself by an exclusive regard to its own interest short of absolute injury to others. The French Government did not help the American patriots because it loved them, but because it thought that it could strike at its great rival with their help. Therefore the French had no real claims upon American gratitude. Sympathy or antipathy between two races does not bring them into alliance or collision, but is caused by their collision or alliance. Frenchmen and Germans hate each other because they have been opposed; they have been opposed by force of geography and by tangible religious or political considerations. The hatred is merely the heat developed by the friction of two neighbouring powers. We hated the French as long as we were in the habit of fighting them. Since we have fortunately been at peace for two generations, the hatred has died out, and the desire to avenge Waterloo, which some people thought so dangerous, has calmly gone to sleep.

Men are foolish enough and wicked enough in all conscience. But, foolish and wicked as they may be, they are not generally so bad as to cut each other's throats simply because they dislike each other. Some mistaken view of very solid interests generally brings them into hostile contact, and then the hatred developes itself, and may sometimes pass itself off as the pretext. But the more we look at the history of past wars, the less force we shall be inclined to attribute to this superficial feeling, however ugly it may look and however awkward may be the complications which it sometimes introduces. Desire of wealth or of power, religious or political propagandism has caused innumerable wars, but when has a war been caused by antipathy?

Doubtless, it does not follow that the evil is a trifling one. A better mutual understanding would be an important step towards many good things. It would facilitate the disappearance of the countless fallacies arising from our narrow views of national greatness and our inclination to believe that the gain of one people must be the loss of another. It would, therefore, be desirable, if it were possible, to bring reason to bear upon some of the fallacies involved. What, for example, do we mean when we speak of the faults of rival people? Do we mean that the average American, or a Frenchman, is made of intrinsically worse materials than ourselves—that he belongs to a distinctly lower type of the race? Surely not, for then we should not hate him in any sense. Nobody despises a child because it cannot talk, or a woman because she has not the muscular strength of a man. We seldom hate a negro; and that is just because we sincerely hold him to belong to a lower order of development. We don't hate a monkey for his want of a moral sense. Many people have, it is true, a certain prejudice against the monkeys, just in so far as they seem to be caricatures of men. We can pardon the ill behaviour of a pig, because he clearly belongs to a different genus from our own; but we are more or less offended when a beast of semi-human appearance behaves himself after a fashion totally inconsistent with human dignity. That is, our antipathies become strong just in proportion as we recognise the essential similarity of the offender to ourselves. We should feel the absurdity of hating an insect because it had six legs; but we should be disgusted by a creature, otherwise like ourselves, which so far diverged from the common style.

Thus, antipathy is avowedly based upon an admission of similarity. It is not proportioned to the difference between ourselves and its object; but to the superficial difference, combined with underlying identity. We are startled by a kind of logical contradiction. Different conclusions seem to follow from the same premises. This man is just like me, yet he acts differently from me. That is the very cause and justification of my offence. To be reasonable, then, we must take account of the implied resemblance as much as of the observed difference. If we really thought that Americans had an inferior nature to our own, we should not blame them, but nature; or rather, we should regard them as an odd phenomenon, not as a standing insult. The very ground of our dislike is that they are about as good as ourselves.

The French, the Germans, and the other European races differ from our own. Nobody will dare to say that any one of these races is intrinsically inferior to its neighbours. Each has its own special aptitudes and deficiencies: but even in the height of national vanity, we don't explicitly hold that an Englishman differs from a Frenchman simply as a superior from an inferior. Americans, again, are descended —the majority within a generation or two—from the European races. Any differences which may appear must therefore be due, not to a radical difference of nature, but to circumstances of climate, social condition, religious persuasion, and so on. We may regard the whole nation, therefore, as the embodiment of a vast and most interesting experiment. We may trace back their characteristics to the circumstances which gave them birth. We have planted offshoots from our own stem in a new and vast territory within historical times. We have poured out these enormous masses of population of our own blood, or of blood closely allied to ours. The existing order of the United States represents the effect of the resulting processes, carried on under conditions all of which are tolerably ascertainable. There cannot be a more interesting field of inquiry; and the philosophical remarks of such a man as de Tocqueville, for example, are of the highest possible interest. Even de Tocqueville made many blunders, as a foreigner was certain to do; but his conclusions, though they may apply as much to France as to America, marked a distinct stage in political speculation, and indicate the true spirit of the inquirer. He began by admitting that American flesh and blood was like his own. Unluckily, very few writers have shown de Tocqueville's impartiality or acuteness. They have tried to justify their prejudices, good or bad, instead of trying to form their judgments; and it is here that Americans have some ground of complaint. If it should be proved that this vast operation in national chemistry has had an unfortunate result, we might be justified in disliking the race. If, for example, the Americans turned out to be rogues, the plea that their roguery was the result of natural causes would not be valid against our antipathy. I have a strong prejudice against the late Mr. Palmer, though I may hold that Palmer's wickedness was caused by temptations acting upon hereditary predispositions. Metaphysicians may settle the free-will question as they please; however they settle it, hatred of evil propensities will be as natural and rightful as before. If we suppose—purely for the sake of argument—that Americans are greater cheats than Europeans, I should take the liberty of disliking Americans in consequence, though it might be proved by the most invincible logic that their knavery was the inevitable result of their democracy, and that again of their social condition, and that of the conditions of their growth. Trace back the chain of cause and effect as far as you please, and a knave remains a knave, and ought to be a hateful person to the end of the chapter. Scientific observation may to some extent unravel the causes of moral deformity, and thereby teach us very useful lessons, but it certainly should not diminish our disgust at such deformity.

The fact, however, that American vices, whatever they may be, are thus traceable to assignable causes suggests some cautions, though it would not justify indifference. The first is that on which I have already insisted—namely, the utter futility of 999 judgments out of 1,000. To say deliberately that the moral standard of a nation is distinctly lower or higher than that of its neighbours requires an amount of careful observation and candid reasoning which hardly anybody can give. It is said, for example, that American politicians are more corrupt than our own. What is the legitimate inference, supposing the fact to be proved? One man is content to infer that Americans generally have a low standard of honour. Another explains it as a general incident of democracy. A third excuses it by the universal excuse—which indeed asserts an undeniable fact—that America is a new country. A fourth sets it down to the unprecedented emigration of ignorant foreigners. A Roman Catholic, perhaps, traces it to the demoralising influences of Protestantism. A Protestant retorts that it is due to the influence of priests upon an ignorant population. A profound philosopher shows his ingenuity by connecting it somehow with the influence of climate. A radical thinks that it is part of the legacy left by slavery. A constitution-monger considers it to be clearly produced by the absence of a system for representing minorities. A sound English constitutionalist remarks upon the want of a House of Lords. An educational reformer thinks that the school system is defective. A believer in race puts it down to Celtic or Teutonic tendencies. A lover of the past says it is caused by the growth of luxury. A "nihilist" says that it is owing to the growth of centralisation. An historian says that we were once equally corrupt in England, and regards the disease as a kind of measles incident to all races in certain stages of development. Each of these and a dozen other causes may have something to do with the phenomenon. I only observe that to consider any one of them fully involves a whole series of complicated observations, and to allow to each its due share would be the work of a philosophic lifetime. The connection, for example, between the standard of honour accepted in private life and that recognised in political life suggests innumerable curious questions, upon which volumes might be written. In some cases, the morality of a nation is very high in particular directions—as, for example, in regard to domestic virtues—whilst it is very low in regard to politics; whilst the reverse is constantly illustrated. One nation, like one man, is more given to drink than its neighbours, or more given to one particular form of drinking, and at the same time less inclined to crimes of violence or to offences against property. To sum up all the lines of inquiry which converge upon such problems is a task of the utmost nicety, for which, perhaps, nobody is fully competent. It implies a combination of the imagination which can see through the eyes of a strange race, with the power of accumulating knowledge which can swallow whole libraries of statistics, and the power of reasoning which can digest them.

When, therefore, a hasty traveller brings out his pat explanation, ascribes the evil to the influence which he happens to dislike, and then ascribes the influence to a natural defect in the character of the people, and further, infers that we ought to hate them instead of pitying, he is guilty of a whole series of doubtful assumptions. So far from seeing this, he probably gives himself the airs of a philosopher, and henceforward takes his little theory for granted, as though it were a proposition in Euclid. The true moral is surely different. We should blame any vices and praise any virtues proved to exist as heartily as if they were our own. We should sympathise with efforts to reform and denounce the fallacies by which errors are defended. On all such matters we should speak without fear or favour. We are on safe ground, and may treat with contempt any resentment that we may excite. Unluckily, this is just the course which we generally decline. Either we make a show of shutting our eyes to evils, and are despised as insincere sycophants; or we proceed to make hasty inferences as to cases which are as obscure as the consequences are palpable. Bribery and corruption are abominable—that is an undeniable truth. A or B is convicted of corruption; that is often equally clear, and so is the inference that A or B ought to be punished. It is another and quite a different thing to assume that the forty millions of men represented by A or B must all share his faults, and are therefore corrupt by nature or perverted by that particular influence on which we happen to pitch as most offensive to our own tastes. It is by this error in logic and feeling that we give legitimate ground for complaint, and manage to oscillate dexterously between administering unworthy flattery and unprovable imputations.

This or that, we may most properly say, is bad. As to its causes, we can only form some general conjectures, entitled to more or less respect, but always requiring to be carefully tested by experience. Most of us have no right to any opinion whatever. Our rash conjectures about Americans have often little more claims to respect than a schoolboy's fancies about the ancient Trojans. They are founded upon evidence, so far as they have any connection with evidence at all, which is ludicrously insufficient to justify any distinct conclusion, favourable or the reverse. Conversely, we have no right to be angry when people form utterly absurd opinions about ourselves. They do not really hate us, but a figment which happens to be called by our name. Their error is not in judging wrongly, but in judging at all; but that offence is so universal that it does not deserve to be condemned severely. So long as we take advantage of the liberty common to all men of forming opinions without knowledge of the facts, we must not be angry if other people use the same privilege, and fall into similar blunders.

The argument, it may be replied, would justify a mischievous scepticism. Are we to admit that no judgment can be formed about national character? Are we to assume that all nations, or all civilised nations, are equally good? And are we therefore to love our neighbours as well as ourselves, and to regard patriotism as a vice instead of a virtue? None of these terrible conclusions really follow; but some things follow which we do not admit so willingly as we ought, because we find it hard to resign pretensions to supernatural sagacity. Judgments can be formed about national character, and certain conclusions established which are of the highest value in political and historical reasoning. We can assign with great confidence certain distinctions between the great varieties of the human race. We can define with some accuracy the peculiar qualities of temperament which separate the Teuton from the Celt, and the Englishman from the American. But what few people can do with any show of reason, and probably no one can do with any approach to certainty, is to effect a sound analysis of national character, to decide upon the intensity as well as the general tendency of the various constituent impulses, and then to determine the resultant value of the amazingly complex forces which result when these elements are brought together to form the whole which we call a nation. A few acute critics or political reasoners can say pretty accurately in what directions French modes of thought and action diverge from English, and can infer which is best on a given occasion. Even such men will be the first to confess their utter inability to say which type is on the whole the best. But as the overwhelming majority of the race are utterly incapable of taking the first steps in this difficult process; as their hasty conclusions are not even based indirectly upon rational judgment, but reflect a number of utterly irrational prejudices, it may perhaps be said that modesty in expressing their opinions is distinctly desirable. Nor, again, need we assume that all nations, and still less the institutions of all nations, are equally good. To learn in what respects and why one is better than another is precisely the great problem of the philosophical observer.

We should be foolish indeed not to take warning by the breakdown of some constitutions or be encouraged by the success of others. A national calamity should be a warning to others besides the persons directly affected. The objectionable practice in this case is the common tendency of jumping at the conclusions which flatter our preconceived prejudices. The action which takes place is so complex that every party has some excuse for attributing all the evils which arise to its own pet object of detestation. It you had all believed in my creed, we exclaim, this would not have happened; and the retort is easy—neither would it have happened if we had all disbelieved. Both remarks may be right. When two parties are struggling, many evils happen which would not occur if either had converted its antagonist; but that does not show which conversion is desirable. Nothing is easier than to devise taunts to vex your opponents from any historical incident that ever happened. You have only to read it by the light of your own theories. The true reason is that the extreme intricacy of all such problems makes all inferences precarious. Whether the ultramontanes or the unbelievers, the absolutists or the democrats, are most to blame is a question which may be ultimately decided by experience, but can only be confused by these hasty snatches at an immediate conclusion. The great mass may be content with observing frequent illustrations of the great truth that moral enormities bring round their punishment in time. The old maxims that honesty is the best policy, and oppression an evil both to tyrant and slave, are worth hearing afresh because incessantly forgotten. When, not content with those simple truths, we try to pronounce specific verdicts upon the conduct of people of whose motives, designs, characters, and difficulties we know next to nothing, we are apt to make disgraceful blunders and indirectly to flatter our own faults. The chief use of these national prejudices is to blind ourselves to the reflection that, if we had been in the same position, we should probably have done the same thing. The epithet "French" or "American" is easily made to account for everything, and flatters us into the generally erroneous assumption that we are not as those Publicans.

Is not this to preach a futile cosmopolitanism? We are proud of our English descent, and we won't admit that our pride can be wrong, for it is that pride which has made us do things to be proud of. But how can we be proud if we don't hold that we are better than our neighbours? This is, no doubt, the final difficulty which perplexes us, and yet the answer seems to be very simple. A man, for example, may respect himself without holding that he is of more value than his neighbours. He may take an honest pride in doing his duty and exerting his talents without holding that he ought to be Prime Minister, or that he is the intellectual equal of Shakespeare and Newton. Or, to come nearer to the point, a man may love his wife and children; he may be ready to fight for them to the death, to work himself to the bone, to prefer their society to that of the best people in the land, and may yet be quite ready to admit that they are not far removed from the average standard. Undoubtedly it is difficult to keep our affections from prejudicing our reason; to judge things by their intrinsic value, and yet to value them in practice by their importance to ourselves; and, in short, to refrain from declaring our own favourite geese to be swans. But that is just one of the lessons which we all have to learn in our private relations, on peril of bitter disappointment to ourselves and serious injury to those we love. A man who is capable of learning by experience finds out that the face of one whom he loves need not be the most beautiful in the world in order to be the most delightful to his eyes; and that he may admit that the maternal instinct which proportions affection to the weakness of its object instead of to its abstract merit is so far from being irrational that it represents the great condition of domestic happiness. The paradox of patriotism is precisely the same. A man may hold that Frenchmen or Americans are every whit as good as Englishmen in all essentials; that virtue and wisdom are fortunately not confined by the four seas or the horizon visible from his parish steeple; and he may yet be as ready as his neighbours to die for his country, to do his best to carry the English flag to the North Pole or Timbuctoo, or to give his whole strength to remedy the many evils which threaten our social welfare. In this sense, indeed, the worse his country may be, the greater its demands upon him; and the more convinced he is that it is behind its neighbours, the greater should be his efforts to bring it up to their level.

The whole difficulty, in fact, lies in this persistent assumption that because I love a country or person I must logically hold it to be the best of all countries or persons. That is the temptation, not the legitimate inference. My country is or ought to be dear to me, because I am tied down to it by a thousand bonds of birth, connection, and tradition; because it is that part of the world in which I can labour to most purpose; because my affections are governed by all kinds of associations which have no connection whatever with my intellectual estimate of its value. But this is just what people in general refuse to see. They insist upon my drawing an illogical inference. If I am forced to admit by evidence that another race is in any respect better than my own, they declare that I am unpatriotic. They do not condescend to inquire whether my recognition of that fault leads me to love my country less. That is taken for granted; and therefore the test of patriotism is taken to be my persuasion of the truth of certain conclusions about matters of which, in ninety-nine cases out of one hundred, I am an utterly incompetent judge. It is sought to make patriotism rational by insisting that my emotions shall have a logical basis which may or may not exist. The only result is that I make a factitious basis by inventing the proposition which gratifies my vicarious vanity, and then assuming that it is the cause instead of the effect of the vanity.

I must, for my part, decline to stake my patriotism upon any such test whatever. Something may prove to-morrow morning that another nation is better than mine, and then I must either believe a lie or cease to be patriotic. I claim the right, on the contrary, of expressing such opinions as I can form, with absolute freedom, and without admitting any inference as to my sentiment. I believe that Englishmen are in many and important respects at the rear instead of being in the van of civilised races. As a mere matter of taste I generally prefer the society of intelligent Americans, because they are not hidebound by British prejudice. I never go to Paris or travel in Germany or Italy without being impressed by the great superiority of foreigners in many respects—intellectually, artistically, and socially. But, for all that, I may be just as patriotic as the Briton who makes his first trip to the Continent when he is already soaked to the core with native prejudices, and swears that all foreigners are filthy barbarians because he does not find soap in his basin in the first hotel. Why not? A man may love his children better than all the world, and yet know that they are short, ugly, stupid, and far from being models of all the Christian virtues.

And, therefore, I shall be perfectly happy on the next 4th of July. I shall admit most cheerfully that we made a dreadful mess of things a century ago, and that we shall probably make other messes for centuries to come. I shall admit that the United States have a larger territory than the British Islands; that they have more coal and iron, and bigger rivers, mountains and prairies; nay, I would admit, if it were proved, that their system of government is in some ways better than ours, that they have better schools, less intoxication, and a greater diffusion of general intelligence. On all these points, and many others, I am perfectly open to conviction. Only I shall look with extreme suspicion upon any attempts to sum up the merits of their national character, and proclaim, as examiners do after a competition, that England deserves only ninety-nine marks whilst America has earned one hundred, or *vice versa*. I have a strong conviction that in such matters our confidence generally increases in proportion to our ignorance; and that the chief result of expressing it is to set up an irritation mischievous as far as it goes, though luckily it does not go so far as we think. And meanwhile I shall be quite content to be in ignorance about most of these problems, which nobody has yet solved, and shall, with Johnson and Savage, "stick by my country" so long as it does not insist upon my telling lies or doing dirty actions on its behalf.

(*The Cornhill Magazine*, 1876)

# Vacations

M<small>R</small>. C<small>REECH</small>, it is said, wrote on the margin of the *Lucretius* which he was translating, "Mem.—When I have finished my book, I must kill myself," and he carried out his resolution. This story, true or false, is reported by Voltaire as characteristic of English manners, and represents a current French theory as to our national tastes. Life in England, if we may venture to draw the moral of the anecdote, is a dreary vista of monotonous toil, at the end of which there is nothing but death, natural, if it so happen, but if not, voluntary, without even a preliminary interval of idleness. To live without work is not supposed to enter into our conceptions. We are nothing but machines employed to execute a particular duty; and when that duty is done, we think it better to break up the machine than to allow it to rust into gradual decay. In this opinion we may, if we please, see nothing but French prejudice, or rather nothing but a particular case of that utter want of appreciation with which rival nations regard each other. Each people can understand the more serious occupations of its neighbour, but finds it hard to enter into its amusements. Everybody wants to eat and drink and sleep, but everyone has his own peculiar notion of pleasure. Seeing the spare time of foreigners employed on purposes for which we care little, we fancy that they must be intolerably bored. A sporting man imagines that life must be unendurable in a country where there are no horse-races, no prize-fights, and no *Bell's Life* to chronicle the glories of the turf or the cricket-ground. Yet, unreasonable as all such prejudices are said to be, we can sympathise to some extent with the feelings of the Frenchman in England. We can guess at the horror which overwhelms him if he has arrived on a Saturday night, and turns out for a Sunday walk along the streets of London. Imagining, as he would naturally

168

imagine, that he is witnessing our mode of employing a day set apart for relaxation, he would shudder on picturing to himself the more serious moments of a nation whose pleasure so strongly resembles the settled gloom of other races. On holidays, we are just capable, it would seem, of creeping along our streets in funereal processions, and relieving our woes by draughts of gin and "porter-beer." How is his imagination to paint the horrors of our working days? and is it strange if suicide seems to him to be the most fitting termination of such melancholy lives?

Let us suppose, however, that our friend recovers from this shock to his nerves, and penetrates the rough outside of English life. Will that domestic hearth, whose pleasures we are accustomed to celebrate, strike him as compensating by its glowing warmth for the chill fog without? If, for example, he is fortunate enough to receive an invitation to one of those cheerful entertainments called evening parties, is he likely to be raised to an almost unbearable pitch of exhilaration? The theory on which they are constructed seems to imply the existence of an amazing faculty for amusement. We apparently consider it sufficient to cram into a room twice as many people as it will comfortably hold, to make them all happy. We love each other so much that we can't pack too tight. By squeezing a number of apples into a press we can produce cider; and it is apparently believed that in a sufficiently crowded mass of humanity, raised to the proper temperature, there takes place a kind of social fermentation, possessing a certain spiritually intoxicating influence. There is so much brotherly love, I suppose, permeating our constitutions, that it only requires pressure to bring it out. And therefore it may be from some peculiar moral perversion that in my case, and some others which I know, the fermentation somehow takes place the wrong way; it all turns sour; and besides detesting the gentleman who stands on my toes, and the other one whose bony framework is imprinted in my back, I suffer from a general misanthropy on such occasions, and receive awful revelations of the depths of

169

human folly. That some persons are happy is perhaps probable; flirtations, for example, may take place at evening parties, as they certainly do in shipwrecks, in hospitals, in the interior of omnibuses, and other scenes of almost universal misery: but when I look round, with the conventional compromise between a scowl and a simper, I fancy that I catch many answering symptoms of disgust on the faces of fellow-sufferers. The true final cause of evening parties, it may be urged, is not pleasure, but business; they are frequented, as the Stock Exchange is frequented, with a view to ulterior profit, rather than with any expectation of immediate returns in the shape of amusement. They are the markets at which we extend our social connections; and, perhaps, if Mr. Mill be right, do a little in the way of slave-dealing. That people should hypocritically continue to express pleasure in attending them, if melancholy, is only in accordance with our usual practice in social grievances. We could not get on without a little lying; and, so long as music is not added to the other torments provided, I am ready to bear my part of the suffering with such stolid indifference as I can command.

We may suppose, however, that our foreigner is ready to extend his researches a little further. If he believes as implicitly as a man ought to believe in the thorough trustworthiness of the British press, he will learn that the Derby is the true national holiday. Its pleasures are so great that even our legislators relax in its favour their habitual regard to the duties of their station. It illustrates all our best qualities; our manly spirit of play, our power of self-government, our wonderful facility for keeping order without the presence of the military, our genuine politeness and felicitous combination of boisterous good-humour with freedom from anything like horseplay, and so on. And yet, I think, a sensible man will mentally ask himself, on his return, what on earth so many thousands of people went out to see? That some answer must be found follows from the well-attested though melancholy fact that many persons have been to see the Derby

twice; but what that answer is, I have never been able to
discover. I do not speak of gamblers or professional persons; their motive is plain enough; though it may be observed, by the way, that nothing is so strong a proof of utter
mental vacuity as a love of gambling; it is the pursuit of
excitement pure and simple by a man who is capable of no
nobler interest, and accordingly it is found to exist most
strongly in savages, who, having nothing to do, will play for
their scalps, and in those classes which most nearly approach
the savage type in modern society and are forced to find a
field for energies running to waste in field-sports, betting,
and other such barbarous amusements. We can, however,
dimly understand why a man should frequent a place where
he is winning or losing thousands of pounds. But we may
fairly assume that ninety out of a hundred attendants on
Epsom Downs have no serious pecuniary interest, that they
only know a horse as a four-legged animal generally forming
part of a cab, and consequently that the mere sight of twenty
such animals galloping for two or three minutes is not very
exhilarating. Yet for this, at any rate, ostensible reason, they
undergo a day of pushing and squeezing in railways and
carriages, they are assailed by all manner of predatory
humans, they stand for hours in rain, wind, and dust, and a
large minority find their only intelligible pleasure in getting
drunk. That, however, they might do at home; and it is not
the motive of ladies or of many other persons who expose
themselves to the inflictions of the day. I can understand the
pleasure of a prize-fight or a bull-fight; I can believe that a
gladiatorial show, when you had suppressed all humane
feeling, must have been one of the most absorbing, if one of
the most horrible, of amusements. I can even appreciate,
though I have never shared, the pleasure of going to see a man
hanged, or still more of seeing martyrs burnt. In all these
there is a real spectacle of human suffering, and when they
are properly managed, of human heroism, which may properly affect our sympathies. Athletic sports of all kinds are
worth seeing, when we understand anything about them, as

they possess something of the same interest without the counterbalancing horrors; but to see horses pass you like a flash of lightning gives to the mass of the crowd no pleasure that would not come equally from witnessing the throwing of dice or the drawing of a lottery. It is merely a question of whether a red or a blue jacket is first at a certain post. And, to be short, in accordance with the celebrated precedent of Artemus Ward, I treat the inquiry into the causes of this strange pleasure as a conundrum and give it up.

One conclusion, however, may be drawn, which is tolerably evident from other considerations. When a student is learning to paint, one of the great difficulties is to teach him what it is that he really sees. When he sits down before a landscape, it is twenty to one that he will try to represent, not the image of which he is supposed to be immediately conscious, but something which other people have persuaded him that he ought to see and must see. He does not copy the direct impression on his senses, but some imaginary object, which, without knowing it, he has constructed partly from observation and partly from a long series of traditions and inferences and arbitrary associations. In the same way, one of the most difficult of things is to know what we really enjoy. We do something which we have been always taught to consider as a convivial proceeding, and fancy that we are in a high state of enjoyment. Nothing is easier in practice, though in theory nothing should be more difficult, than to deceive people about their own emotions, and to cheat them into a belief of their own happiness. This is the difficulty which lies at the bottom of all our conventional modes of enjoyment, and till somebody has the courage to unravel the complex web of associations which conceals us from ourselves, we go on stupidly suffering, in the sincere conviction that sixty minutes of weariness and vexation of spirits make up an hour of happiness. Many thousands of persons at the present moment are enjoying, or pretending to themselves that they are enjoying, a holiday. They will come back almost tired to death of their pleasures, and delighting to return to their business, and yet they will persuade themselves and others that they have passed an inconceivably agreeable vacation. To convince oneself of their mistake, it is enough to watch the British tourist at his so-called amusement. Of all the dreary places in this world, none, perhaps, is more depressing to a philanthropic mind than the ordinary English watering-place. That the lodging-house is a torment has become notorious. A workhouse or a gaol is bad enough; but their inmates are scarcely in more melancholy quarters than those gloomy rooms, at once bare and frowzy, with a large shell and a china shepherdess on the mantelpiece, a picture of the lord-lieutenant of the county on the walls, a slatternly landlady downstairs, and a select party of parasitical insects in the bedrooms, in which the English pater-familias consumes uneatable food, and tries to recall London to his imagination by reading the *Daily Telegraph*, from its glowing leaders to its interesting advertisements. Mariana found the moated grange bad enough; but she was not tormented, so far as we know, with barrel-organs. Sailors confined through the winter to their ships in the Arctic seas are generally pitied; but they have a greater variety of amusements than the visitor of some miniature of London *super mare*. An ocean steamer appears to its passengers for the time as about the culminating point of human weariness; yet even there, if there is more sea-sickness, there is also more society and more excitement in the incidents of the voyage. A grown-up man cannot make mud-pies, or build castles in the sand with wooden spades, and he is not, as a rule, passionately devoted to donkey-riding. Yet, so far as I have been able to discover, either from personal observation or from a careful perusal of the pages of contemporary novels and newspapers, these seem to be the main amusements provided for an intellectual public. It is true that some persons are brutal enough to amuse themselves by shooting gulls, in the spirit, I suppose, of the lady who, in one of Mr. Browning's poems, smashes a beetle, because, being wretched herself, she dislikes witnessing the enjoyment of other living beings. I rejoice that their cruelty is to be checked; but one cannot but ask oneself, what then are they to do?

Following the Briton abroad, we find him scarcely the better off for powers of enjoyment. Let any intelligent person strike into the tracks of a party of Mr. Cook's tourists and study their modes of passing their time. Watch them in picture-galleries, at churches, or in celebrated scenery, and try to determine whether their enjoyment be genuine, or a mere conventional parade. Two or three painfully notorious facts are enough to settle the question. The ordinary tourist has no independent judgment; he admires what the infallible Murray orders him to admire; or, in other words, he does not admire at all. The tourist never diverges one hair's breadth from the beaten track of his predecessors, and within a few miles of the best-known routes in Europe leaves nooks and corners as unsophisticated as they were fifty years ago; which proves that he has not sufficient interest in his route to exert his own freedom of will. The tourist, again, is intensely gregarious; he shrinks from foreigners even in their own land, and likes to have a conversation with his fellows about cotton-prints or the rate of discount in the shadow of Mont Blanc: that is, when he imagines himself to be taking his pleasures abroad, his real delight consists in returning in imagination to his native shop. The tourist, in short, is notoriously a person who follows blindly a certain hackneyed round; who never stops long enough before a picture or a view to admire it or to fix it in his memory; and who seizes every opportunity of transplanting little bits of London to the districts which he visits. Though all this has been said a thousand times, the same thing is done more systematically every year, until one is inclined to reverse the old aphorism, and declare that every man is a hypocrite in his pleasures. We are supposed to travel mainly in search of the beautiful and the picturesque; and yet the faculty which takes pleasure in such things is frequently in a state of almost complete atrophy. Writers of poetry and florid prose have now for many years been singing the praises of lovely scenery, and it is considered disgraceful to be unmoved by mountains, lakes, and forests: but I suspect that four people out of five share Dr. Johnson's preference of the view at Charing Cross to the most charming of rural landscapes. Why, indeed, should it be otherwise? At Charing Cross there is that peculiar manufactory in which Mr. Matthew Arnold delights; there are omnibuses, and cabs, and beggars, and policemen, and shop-windows, and newspaper placards; and every one of these objects has a certain interest for the intelligent cockney. There is a long succession of little dramas, which appeal in one way or another to his sympathies, and a gratuitous exhibition of all the articles which are supposed to be suitable for his wants. Why should he go to look at a variety of green objects whose names and uses are a mystery to him, or to stare at a big cliff with a mass of ice on top of it, whose very size he is unable to appreciate? I believe that the appreciation of scenery, like that of art, requires careful study, and that a man must familiarise himself with natural objects and their various properties before he can understand the charms which they have for those who have grown up amongst them. To take a raw Londoner and, with no previous training of mind or eye, to place him in the midst of the finest scenery, is to subject him to an unfair trial. He has not acquired the inward sense to which it appeals; he has passed a life in a wilderness of dingy bricks and mortar, and regards the sun chiefly as a substitute for gas-lights; it is no wonder if he feels as bewildered and awkward as the countryman transplanted from the fields to Cheapside; and turns from the real beauties to congenial talk with his fellows, or at best, to admire some freak of nature which he can partly understand—a cliff that seems to be tumbling over, or a rock shaped like a human head. It is said that a man who has grown up amongst the "great unwashed" feels the first ablution to be a species of ingenious torture; and we cannot expect that the accumulated grime and soot of London streets will fall off at once on our immersion in the country. Indeed, to be honest, I think that there is something strained in our assumed love of scenery. For a change, it is well enough; Switzerland is an admirable relief to the Strand, for those who have a touch of true mountain fire: but even they would, I think, if they were honest, generally agree that in the long run the Strand is a pleasanter view than the Rhone Valley, and human nature a better ingredient in a picture than hills and woods. Both Lamb and Wordsworth, in the opinion of most people, went to extremes; but Lamb showed, to my mind, a healthier and more genuine taste in his love of London than Wordsworth in his love of the Lakes.

This, however, is beside the point. I care not what people's tastes may be, so long as they express them candidly and gratify them sincerely. But how are we ever to persuade people to enjoy themselves rationally, when they are in a secret conspiracy to hide their real likings from themselves and the world? And how are people to be made sincere? How am I to persuade a man that he sees what is before his eyes—that he likes the tastes which really please his palate—that he is comfortable, when his senses are all gratified, and not when somebody else tells him that they ought to be gratified? We suffer from such an inveterate habit of self-deception on all these points, that the task is almost hopeless. A lad may often be seen smoking a cigar, whilst turning green in the face and qualmish in the stomach, and not only declaring that he likes it, which is intelligible, but even proving it to his own entire satisfaction. If it were not for this strange faculty of self-imposition, I doubt whether anybody would ever learn to smoke; it accompanies us through life; grown-up men may often be observed who affect a dislike—supposed, for some strange reason, to be creditable—to anything sweet, and who as soon as the ladies have disappeared fall upon preserved fruits and bonbons with a marvellous appetite. How many similar practices are common in more serious matters need hardly be pointed out. How would managers of concerts get on, or preachers of sermons draw congregations, or artists sell their pictures, if we did not

spontaneously conspire to impose upon ourselves in regard
to our own likings? But it is useless to point out how many of
the arrangements by which society is knit together depend
upon this tacit consent to the manufacture of factitious
pleasures.

Let us, however, ask this one question. Assuming that a
man is so eccentric as to really wish to enjoy himself, and not
to persuade other persons that he is enjoying himself, how
may he best set about it? And it may be admitted, in spite of
the general rule, that there are in fact many persons who
really like evening parties, and horse-races, and watering-
places, and foreign tours, and that, without a certain sub-
stantial foundation of genuine enjoyment, the mere figment,
the empty simulacrum of pleasure, would not be so permanent as it is. One great element of the satisfaction derived is,
of course, the merely negative pleasure of indolence. We
like to obtain a good background of utter inertia with which
to contrast the ordinary activity of our lives. It may, however, be doubted whether any European nations are capable
of doing nothing to perfection; and the English, next to the
Americans, are probably the most incapable race in the
world. The Eastern can placidly reduce himself to a state of
temporary absorption into the infinite, or allow visions to
float before his imagination as formless and transitory as the
smoke from his narghile. At rare moments we may enter
that elysium far enough to guess at its pleasures. Our blood
may be charmed into "pleasing heaviness,"

> *Making such difference 'twixt wake and sleep,*
> *As is the difference betwixt day and night,*
> *The hour before the heavenly harnessed team*
> *Begins his golden progress in the east.*

But the waking comes quickly; and the dreams are not altogether easy. They are crossed by figures savouring un-
pleasantly of reality, and bringing with them disagreeable
whiffs from the outer life. The nearest approximation that I
have ever observed in holiday-makers to this blissful state of

dreaminess is in those harmless enthusiasts who sit in punts on the Thames under some transparent pretence of fishing. The rush of the cool waters, the swaying of the weeds in the deep stream, the soft beauty of the quiet gardens and woods that slope to the bank, produce a mesmeric influence; the monotonous bobbing of the float is designed, as I imagine, to discharge a similar function to that of the metal disk which "electro-biologists" used to place in the hands of their victims; the act of gazing at it dazzles the eye and helps to distract the attention from outward things. The dim legends which still float about that at some former periods a punt-fisher has been known to have a bite, or even to catch a gudgeon, serve partly as an excuse, but chiefly to make the repose more delectable by the faint suggestion of a barely possible activity. It soothes without exciting the patient, as the distant plunge of the surf helped the lotus-eater to enjoy his indolence by a half-formed reminiscence of his long-past labour "in the deep mid-ocean."

It is given to few persons to enjoy such repose for long. We cannot lower our vital powers like the animals which lie torpid through the winter. There is a certain amount of energy always being generated within, and we are forced to discover some kind of channel into which it may be directed. That channel should be as different as possible from our ordinary walks in life; for rest means to us, not a simple repose, but the use of a different set of activities. The fault of our tourists is, that they have about as much ingenuity in discovering an outlet for their energies, as a man who, after ploughing in the fields all day, should at night take a turn on the treadmill by way of relaxation. And it must be confessed that, if a man has no love of art, does not care about nature, is thoroughly indifferent to books, and is fitted for no society except that in which he was born, it is rather difficult to supply him with a satisfactory object of amusement. A very large number of Englishmen (and I dare say of other persons) are fit only to be human mill-horses, plodding along one weary round. When you turn them out for a

run in the fields, they instinctively fall into the same mechanical circling, and prove that they are cramped in nature as
well as by physical constraint. They resemble that fabulous
animal the "brock," whose two right legs were half the length
of his left legs; and who could, consequently, only live
on the side of a conical hill, which he was obliged to be perpetually perambulating in the same direction. Yet few men
are so stupefied that they cannot, by a little care, select some,
more or less satisfactory, hobby—a selection in which the
whole secret of judicious holiday-making may be said to
consist. And here is one counterbalancing benefit in the
lamentable natural deficiency of which I have been speaking.
Our pleasures, I have said, are as artificial as a lady's hair is
sometimes asserted to be; we live by rule instead of my instinct, and fashion our amusements after some arbitrary
model. Yet it is also true that almost any amusement may in
time become amusing. We smoke, as boys, purely out of
imitation; but the acquired habit becomes as strong as a
primary instinct. A man who will take up any special pursuit, from whatever motives, will end by loving it, if he only
acts his part with sufficient vigour. The real misfortune is,
that not only do people deceive themselves as to their pleasures, but that they only half-deceive themselves. They have
a suppressed consciousness of their own hypocrisy, and
therefore their occupation never generates a genuine passion.
My first rule would be, take up some amusement for which
you have a natural taste; and my second, act in any case as
energetically as if you had one, and in time a very satisfactory artificial taste will be generated. It should, of course,
give as much scope as possible for varied and long-contin-
ued pursuit; but devotion to any hobby whatever is prefer-
able to a cold-blooded dawdling in obedience to general
fashion after nothing in particular. Thus, for example, I
remember reading the adventures of a gentleman who had
made it the object of his spare hours to see big trees. Why he
had hit upon that particular fancy did not appear; he was
not a botanist, nor a timber merchant, nor in any other pur-

suit which had any particular reference to trees. So far as I remember he was, at his normal state, a hard-working clergyman. But he had trees on the brain. He dreamt, at his spare moments, of trees hundreds of feet in height, and covering acres with their shade; when he had a day or two to spare, he visited the finest trees in England; when he had a longer holiday, he travelled through the Continent in search of big trees. On one happy occasion he crossed the Atlantic, sailed up the Amazon, and penetrated the tropical forests of South America in the hope of finding some worthy object of his idolatry. Before this he had doubtless reached California by the Pacific Railway, and paid his respects to the gigantic pines in the Yosemite Valley. It is easy to imagine, not to play upon words, how this topic would branch out into all kinds of minor inquiries; how he would collect books on trees, pictures of trees, and statistical facts about trees; how, at moments when the composition of sermons was heavy upon his hands, the vision of some monster of the forest would float before his eyes, and enable him to return with fresh vigour to his work; how he would gradually acquire the pleasure of being the greatest living authority on one particular subject; and how he would look down from the heights of a genuine passion upon some miserable creatures who wander aimlessly and hobbilessly through the world, in obedience to the arbitrary dictates of the British traveller's bible.

The happy man who has selected his hobby always excites my admiration; whether it is sporting, or art, or athletic pursuits, or antiquarianism, or what not, he is at least able to boast of a genuine enjoyment. To be perfect, it should be happily contrasted with the regular pursuits of his life, so as to give a proper relaxation to his faculties. We are all more or less in the position of those artisans whose physical frames are distorted by one special kind of labour, and like them, are in want of something to call a different set of muscles, physical or spiritual, into play. But some energetic pursuit is at all events a blessing, and nothing seems less wise than to ridicule those who have hit upon some pleasure, however unintelligible to the rest of mankind, which may fill their leisure hours.

Unluckily most people are stupid. Every genuine hobby is speedily surrounded by a crowd of mock articles. The man who hunts and likes it, as Mr. Trollope has told us, is counterfeited by numbers who hunt and don't like it. One enthusiast goes to a picture gallery because he loves art, and fifty because they have succeeded in persuading themselves that they love it. Half the accepted creeds in the world are not what people believe, but what they believe that they believe. Other feasts than the theatrical are made off pasteboard dishes, with guests quaffing deep draughts of emptiness from tinsel cups. Vacations are less a time of enjoyment than a time of general consent to be bored under a hollow show of enjoyment. The best hope for many of us is that by pretending very hard, the pretence may come to have a sort of secondary reality; and as a large part of the pleasure derived from any pursuit consists in the recollection of our performances, and in the stories which they enable us to repeat to our friends, that satisfaction is open to those who never really enjoy the original pleasure, but believe in their own assertions after they have made them half-a-dozen times. There comes a time when the past sham is almost as good as the past reality, and a man persuades himself that his report of his own ecstasies is more or less founded on facts. Meanwhile a little more sincerity would be a good thing, for it would at least deliver many devotees of the genuine pleasures of foreign travel from those worst of bores—their own countrymen.

(The Cornhill Magazine, 1869)

# Round Mont Blanc[*]

SOME time ago I ventured to write an article, called the "Regrets of a Mountaineer." In it I endeavoured to express the sentiments which might naturally occur to a man who, having once been bitten by the mania of mountain-climbing, and having indeed suffered from a somewhat virulent type of the disease, had been suddenly cut off from indulgence in his favourite pursuits. Following the precedent of dramatic performances, I bade a solemn farewell to the mountains, and—still according to that precedent—I have to confess that the farewell was perhaps a little premature. That which ought to have been was not, in fact, my positively last appearance in the character of an assailant of the High Alps. Should the announcement be made in the spirit of a penitent, or of a sinner returning to the true fold? Must I speak like a dipsomaniac who has, after a temporary course of teetotalism, once more fallen a victim to the charms of brandy-and-water, or like a deserter begging for re-admission to the army from which he has prematurely withdrawn himself? Members of the Alpine Club will, of course, be inclined to take the latter view of the question; and I must regard them as receiving the present confession. Perhaps, however, I might make some defence to those who would regard my conduct in a severer light. Good resolutions, I might urge, are made by all sensible men chiefly for the pleasure of breaking them. Or rather, to define the precise state of the case more accurately, I may perhaps put it thus: the advantage of resolving to break off a vicious habit is that you no longer practise it when it is disagreeable; though you need by no means feel bound to refrain when it is only liable to the objection that it is immoral. My position, at any rate in regard to mountaineering, is, that I no longer indulge

*A paper read before the Alpine Club, December 12, 1871.

182

in it as, to say the truth, I once used to indulge in it, even when in the depths of my private consciousness I felt it to be rather a bore; I have cast off that fanaticism which made me regard it as a solemn duty to spend all available moments of leisure in measuring myself against some previously inaccessible peak. I regard mountain-climbing as a weakness instead of a duty, and therefore I only climb when I thoroughly enjoy it; and this is a state of mind which, if not rising to the highest moral strain, has, at any rate, many undeniable comforts.

So much by way of preface to a paper which might perhaps most fitly be entitled the "Relapses of a Mountaineer." And yet I must add that the relapses have not been of a grave character. Indeed, I have so little to communicate to the Club that, but for the barrenness of these latter days upon which fate has cast us, I should scarcely venture to consider that I have the raw materials of a presentable narrative. Such crumbs of remainder biscuit as I have managed to gather may, however, be palatable to appetites doomed to a very scanty diet; and I will venture to chronicle with some minuteness the incidents which produced my recent lapses from the paths of virtue. And, first, let me endeavour to set forth the numerous temptations by which I was surrounded.

I was spending a month at the lovely village of St. Gervais. Though the Chamonix diligences call daily at the baths, few cockneys stop at that repulsive establishment, and still fewer climb the 600 feet which are necessary to reach one of the most beautiful centres of Alpine scenery. The excellent Hôtel du Mont Blanc, in which we took up our quarters, was almost free from the visits of our dear fellow-countrymen, and I was reduced to solitary rambles. St. Gervais can boast of an almost infinite variety of *courses*, great and small, rising by exquisite gradations from the Mont Joly up to the monarch himself. In almost all these walks, I need hardly say, the view of Mont Blanc is the culminating point of the interest. I saw him from many points of view, and meditated much on their respective merits. Mont Blanc is a noble

183

object, when looking across the valley of Montjoie from the
Mont Joly; or when lying in one of the little hollows amongst
the great beds of rhododendrons that cover the undulating
summit of the Prarion; or, still more, for the explorers of a
less hackneyed district, from any of the summits that rise
above the great limestone wall which stretches from the
Aiguille de Varens to the cliffs above the Col d'Anterne.
I climbed that wall at two points; and I will in passing
notice, for the benefit of the lovers of scenery, that one of
the most perfect of Alpine walks may be taken by climbing
the path which leads to the pass of the Portettaz. A very
good path lies beneath the western half of the limestone
range of cliffs which enclose the Plaine Joux. Just where the
forest ceases, a number of streams suddenly burst in full
vigour from beneath huge boulders covered by a dense
growth of underwood. From that point, or a little higher,
Mont Blanc appears, filling up the whole space between the
horns of the great crescent of limestone cliffs. After climbing
a path not unlike that of the Gemmi, the traveller reaches the
edge of that singular stone-glacier—as it appears—called
the Désert de Platé; and from thence he may either climb
the Aiguille de Varens, which lies at some distance from the
edge of the plateau; or, if his time be too short, he may easily
ascend the point known as the Aiguille de Platé. From any
high point in this neighbourhood the view of Mont Blanc is
necessarily superb. I was not sufficiently favoured by the
weather to enjoy it in perfection; but from what I saw and
inferred, I came to a conclusion rather opposed to the
ordinary doctrines about Mont Blanc. If anyone were asked
what is the best single view of the Mont Blanc range, he
would probably reply by naming one of the well-known
belvederes, the Buet, the Brévent, the Mont Joly, or, if he
prefers the southern view of the mountain, the Crammont,
or it may be, the Ruitor. Now, in endeavouring to settle this
question, two or three principles may be laid down. It must,
in the first place, be admitted that a view of the panoramic
kind ought to include as many points of the range as possible,

compatibly with a due picturesque effect. The Mont Joly, for example, must be pronounced a failure, in so far as it affords a very imperfect view of the north-eastern portion of the chain. Secondly, the point of view should be so high and at such a distance as to involve the least possible distortion of the fair proportions of the mountain. The Brévent, for example, and the Mont Chétif near Courmayeur, are perhaps rather too low and too immediately beneath the monarch to enable the spectator to do him justice. And thirdly, it is certainly desirable, if possible, that the whole height of the mountain should be visible, without any intervening range to break the effect of his imposing grandeur. The Buet and the Crammont fail conspicuously in this respect; and I imagine that they owe part of their reputation to fashion, and (in the latter case) to the influence of Saussure. Guides are an unimaginative race, and when a point of view has once obtained a reputation, it is hard to overthrow it. No other reason can be given why the range of the Aiguille de Varens should never have obtained the reputation which is its undoubted due. Admitting the grandeur of the view from the Buet, it is impossible to rate it above, or, in my opinion, on an equality with, that obtained from the cliffs divided only by the deep ravine of the Arve from the majestic snow-fields of the great mountain.

And yet, admirable as is the view from any part of that remarkable plateau, I discovered—and my apology for making these remarks is, that I appear to have been the first person who has made, or at any rate published, the discovery—that there is yet another point of view which combines in the highest degree all the essentials that I have enumerated, and which has yet never been visited by a traveller. If I am right in this assertion, it is a curious proof of how much is overlooked, even in the most familiar portions of the Alps; and I think that the reasons I can allege will at any rate raise some *prima facie* presumption in my favour. Indeed, I regard the matter as almost capable of mathematical demonstration. If anybody will glance at the map of the Mont Blanc range, he will see that, in order to obtain a view of all the chief summits, the spectator must be placed in or near a line drawn from Mont Blanc through the Aiguille du Goûter. Otherwise, the central dome will cut off either the western or eastern end of the chain. We must look for a summit of between (say) 9,000 and 11,000 feet somewhere sufficiently near to this axis. It must be at a distance of, at least, ten or twelve miles from the object, and there must be no intervening range, but, if possible, a level plain in the foreground. It is impossible to state these propositions without at once perceiving that we are describing the celebrated view from Sallanches, as it would be seen by a spectator from a balloon raised some 8,000 feet above the town. The view from Sallanches is, in fact, unique, and the only objection to it is that Mont Blanc is too much foreshortened, owing to his great height above the spectator. The question then occurs whether there is no peak which will serve the purpose of the hypothetical balloon; and I answer by saying that there is such a peak, and that its name is the Mont Fleuri. Looking, in fact, from St. Gervais, the great wall of limestone precipice which forms a background to Sallanches is crowned by a lion-like mass of rock, on which I had frequently looked with curiosity before I made its closer acquaintance. Nobody except chamois-hunters had made the ascent, though it was said to be free from all serious difficulty; and I had the pleasure of ascertaining, by personal observation, that the view of Mont Blanc is all that I have described. Nearly every summit in the chain, from the Col de Balme to the Col du Bonhomme, is visible; the whole 14,000 feet of ascent from Sallanches to the summit is revealed, and made more striking by its contrast with the level intervening plain of the Arve valley; whilst the height and distance of the Mont Fleuri is just sufficient to show the huge mass in its fair proportions, whilst preserving the distinctness of detail. The height, I may observe, is not known to me; but, as the mountain is palpably higher than the Aiguille de Varens, I should put it at between 9,000 and 10,000 feet. And now I am ready to maintain against all comers that, although tourists have been seeking the best point of view for seeing Mont Blanc for at least three generations, nobody except a few chamois-hunters has ever seen that particular aspect of the monarch of the mountains which is demonstrably the best.

Nobody? it will be asked; not even yourself? and I am compelled reluctantly to repeat, nobody! And thereby hangs a tale, which shall be told as briefly as possible, though it is strictly relevant to the main purpose of this paper. The studied ambiguity of a certain sentence in my last paragraph may not have been noticed; but though I satisfied myself by "personal observation" of the surpassing merits of the view in question, I am constrained to add that my observation was taken from a point some distance below the summit. My friend (Mr. J. Birkbeck, jun.) and I took a guide one fine morning from St. Gervais, and walked by moonlight to Sallanches, and thence up the beautiful glen of Cordon to a lofty alp immediately under the Mont Fleuri. It would be hard to find a more exquisite spot than that from which we saw the sunrise, and it is easily accessible, even by those whose delight is in the legs of a mule. A brilliant lawn, studded by groups of beech trees, a mighty wall of cliff rising behind with a really fine waterfall spouting in Staubbach fashion from a ledge midway, a grand view of Mont Blanc and his attendant aiguilles in the distance, put us in the best possible spirits. But our guide—whom, because it is not his name, I will call Russell—was labouring under a singular disease. Its symptoms were a burning thirst, a certain squeamishness like that which the vulgar call "hot coppers," and a decided incapacity for steady pounding uphill. He attributed it partly to an undue consumption of milk at the chalets—which, however probable in itself, scarcely accounted for its coming on a couple of hours before we reached them—and partly to a bullet-wound in his arm, which had been received some months before as he was following the fortunes of Garibaldi. At any rate, it delayed us very much in our ascent, and perhaps had something to do with his decision, when we were very near the top, that the fresh snow made the last rocks too dangerous to be attacked. It is my invariable rule, however, not to press a man to proceed to what he considers to be dangerous, whatever the causes of his nervousness, and I do not regret that I observed it in this instance. Yet if I had had a little more experience of Mr. Russell's character, I should perhaps have been less ready to listen to his appeals for a retreat. For on a subsequent occasion the same singular disorder manifested itself on a start for the Aiguille de Miage, and he became not a little sulky when I positively refused to allow him to treat it by doses of brandy at a tavern. On that occasion also we were forced to retreat from the Aiguille de Miage (and I must add that I think our retreat was no more than prudent) by the state of the snow; and I found that from some cause or other his nerves had been so shattered that from a daring mountaineer, as I am told he had once been, he had sunk to be one of the least satisfactory companions I have ever had for the passage of very moderately difficult rocks. I cannot give his real name; but let travellers at St. Gervais be careful as to their guides.

Before leaving the Mont Fleuri, I must observe that though there appears to be no difficulty in climbing it, some local knowledge would be useful. The last part of the ascent lies through a very deep couloir, which descends into a wild hollow on the southern, or it may be the south-western, side of the arête which the traveller follows so far as it is practicable, in starting from the valley of Cordon. But the discovery of the route may fairly be left to the ingenuity of experienced mountaineers. I will only remark that the experiences thus described ended by sharpening my appetite for the mountains. The constant views of Mont Blanc from various heights and in various directions disturbed my peace of mind; and the irritation produced by useless guides made me long for an expedition more after the old fashion. I groaned at the ineffectual nibblings at second-rate peaks, and I longed

inexpressibly to be once more assaulting with an Anderegg
or a Lauener one of the true race of giants that looked so
invitingly near. Other circumstances speedily heightened
my zeal. We had transferred ourselves to the pleasant little
inn kept by Couttet (dit *Baguette*) at Chamonix. It is an
oasis in the midst of a desert of cockneyism. Looking
towards the great mountain, and having at your back the
huge caravanserais which bring New York and Piccadilly to
the Alps, you may fancy yourself at Zermatt or the Æggischhorn. There my growing desire to climb was strengthened
by the presence of sundry members of the Alpine Club. The
enthusiasm of the younger was contagious; and my own
contemporaries, who have more or less retired from the field
of action, who groaned at grass slopes, poured maledictions
upon zigzags, and appeared to find the Alpine air sufficiently stimulating to their appetites without the aid of rough
exercise; even those respectable verterans, I say, could still
tell stories of youthful prowess, and solaced their post-
prandial hours not more by tobacco and other gentle aids
to digestion than by eloquent exhortations to their friends
to be up and doing. If I—who was the substance of most of
these harangues—measured no more around the waist than
you, my energy would know no bounds, and the lurking
scepticism evoked by such protestations was unable to
quench the effect of the eloquence by which they were
enforced. Moreover, those pleasant tobacco parliaments
were joined by an honorary member of our club, who is in
danger of becoming one of the recognised attractions to
Chamonix. M. Loppé, who may be described as court
painter to the monarch of mountains, has, as my readers
know, or ought to know, opened a gallery of Alpine paint-
ings at Chamonix, and there spends most of the summer. He
is always ready to give the friendliest advice to the tourists
who have the good fortune to make his acquaintance; and
was the object of incessant, and I fear rather wearisome,
appeals from everyone who wanted anything done. Ladies
taking a mule to the Glacier des Bossons, and travellers on

the look-out for a hitherto untrodden peak, trespassed with equal recklessness and equal impunity upon his good nature. To him I owed a very pleasant walk, which may be indicated to mountaineers, as not yet sufficiently known. Leaving Chamonix in the morning, we ascended the Glacier du Tour, crossed the Col du Tour, thence passed to the Fenêtre de Saleinaz, and crossed by the Col du Chardonnet to the Glacier d'Argentière, returning to Chamonix at night. It is difficult to design a walk which, with an equally small expenditure of fatigue, shall show so much of the very grandest snow-scenery. My appetite for climbing was naturally sharpened; but the final impetus was yet to be given. M. Loppé informed me that there were still two or three untrodden peaks on the Mont Blanc range, and of these the most seductive, because offering the greatest chances of success, was the Mont Mallet. Whilst shaking under this temptation, there appeared another and a most unanswerable cause for action, in the person of my old friend Melchior Anderegg. He came fresh from ascents of the Matterhorn, and I know not what other peaks, in company with Messrs. Mathews and Morshead. I had engaged him for a week, more for the sake of old acquaintance than with a design for work, and destined him chiefly to the occupation of carrying a certain young lady of eight months old to such heights as were appropriate to her time of life. But the combination of circumstances just enumerated was too powerful for me. Mont Blanc had been appealing to me for weeks with eloquent silence; M. Loppé, not only by his pictorial and verbal exhortations, but by his guidance on the glacier expedition I have noticed, made my mouth water for higher things. The youthful enthusiasts who said "Come," and the decayed veterans who said with equal emphasis "Go," urged me in the same direction; the weather was perfect, the snow in first-rate order; a new mountain was waiting for the first comer, and here was Melchior Anderegg promising to compensate me by his unsurpassable skill for the annoyances suffered from inferior guides. If Adam had been able to produce equally good reasons for eating the apple, his justification, to human eyes at least, would have been amply sufficient; and what was I that I should be better than my remote progenitor? If that precedent be somewhat doubtful, we live at any rate in days when the rulers of our country have laboured to erase the word "irrevocable" from the political dictionary as actively as the Alpine Club to get rid of another objectionable epithet. Is this a time for being over-scrupulous as to pledges or consistency? Leaving my good resolutions to pave any place that may be in want of such materials, I agreed once more to gird up my loins and start in search of glory.

What was the precise task before us requires a few words of explanation. The tourist who climbs the giddy heights of the Montanvert sees before him, apparently closing the valley of the Mer de Glace, a mass of mountains upon which the unsophisticated taste of an earlier race of peasants conferred the name Mont Mallet—*mallet* being the patois for *mauvais*. The great block conspicuous from Chamonix itself, and including Mont Blanc, was called the Mont Maudit. In a free translation they might, I presume, be called Mount Hell and Mount Purgatory. By degrees the name of Mont Maudit has been confined to one peak in the higher mass; and by a similar process Mont Mallet has become the name of a single summit, and indeed has almost disappeared from popular usage; for the Mont Mallet, so called in the official map, is more generally known as the Aiguille Noire (though this name again is affixed in Mr. Reilly's map to a subordinate summit). If the Dent du Géant be regarded as a canine tooth in a monstrous jaw, from which all the incisors have been extracted, the jaw itself will be represented by a wild ridge sweeping round the head of the glacier, and the opposite canine tooth will be the Mont Mallet. It is of nearly equal height with the Géant, and may also be regarded as the highest point in the wild range called *les Périades*. A huge glacier descends from the northern side of this range, and joins the Glacier de

Léchaud some distance above its confluence with the Glacier du Talèfre on the opposite bank. Few travellers have ever ascended this (apparently) nameless glacier; and the completeness with which, in spite of its vast dimensions, it is withdrawn from the observation of tourists, few of whom would even suspect its existence, is a striking proof of the immense extent of the Mont Blanc snow-fields. A few crystal-hunters had rambled among the Périades, and Mr. Wills had climbed the glacier in his attempt to cross the Col des Grandes Jorasses. A short inspection and the testimony of M. Loppé convinced us that the most promising route was to ascend this glacier and to reach, if possible, a col lying, as it were, at the back of the Mont Mallet, and forming the watershed between the French and Italian valley, and thence to attack our mountain from the east, i.e. from the side opposite to that visible from the Montenvers. And this led to a remarkable incident, which I commend to the consideration of the Alpine Club. My friend Mr. Wallroth had joined forces with me, and proposed to bring with him a very eminent Chamonix guide, with whom he had attempted just before to ascend the Aiguille de Blaitière. They had been repulsed by showers of stones in a couloir of such unprepossessing aspect that the bare attempt to ascend it became a standing joke with our party. The guide—he shall be nameless—has a high character for courage and skill, and we were not a little amazed when he came to Mr. Wallroth with a story of a venerable father who had begged him not to attempt the glacier of the Mont Mallet. This venerable person declared, on what grounds it did not appear, that it was the most frightfully dangerous of all Alpine glaciers; it was a nightmare of a glacier; a collection of all horrible crevasses, seracs swept by avalanches, falling stones, and I know not what else, defying the skill of the bravest of guides. This hypothetical father—for I confess to classing him in my own mind with Mrs. Harris—was impregnable to argument; and the guide, taking refuge under the touching veil of filial piety, turned a deaf ear to our remonstrances. Nor was this all. After we had good reason to know by personal experience that the glacier was a glacier of the most domestic and pacific character, a glacier so mild that, as somebody said of a small earthquake, "you might stroke it"; a glacier which we traversed from top to bottom at a jog-trot, and which barely deserved the ceremony of a rope; after we could make our affidavits to all this, the most fearful reports continued to circulate in Chamonix, and induced another guide to bring forward a venerable mother in the same character as his colleague's father. Other benevolent persons endeavoured to bring female influence to bear upon the travellers themselves, by informing a lady that her husband was moving to almost certain destruction. Luckily the said lady possessed more strength of mind than had been expected, and the final result was simply to intensify our desire for success. Different opinions were expressed as to the secret of this singular reluctance of some of the best men in Chamonix even to look at a glacier, whose supposed terrors a single look would have sufficiently dissipated. Those who like it may believe in an epidemic terror affecting the venerable relations of our guides. M. Loppé inclined to the opinion that the nerves of the Chamoniards had been shaken by the accidents of the previous year. My own belief is that it was simply a case of jealousy, and that the objection was not so much to a glacier as to a Swiss guide.

It may be right to mention that, since returning, I have referred to Mr. Milman's interesting account of his expedition to the Col des Grandes Jorasses, and I there find that one at least of the guides who refused to accompany us had been with Mr. Milman on that occasion. This being so, it would appear that the fiction about the difficult glacier was even less excusable than one would have supposed, for the guide knew from personal experience that the glacier was perfectly practicable. It is true that Wills and Milman found, as I infer from their narrative, far greater difficulties than we encountered; and it appears to be generally the case that the high snow-fields were this year unusually easy, in consequence, it would seem, of the quantity of snow which fell during the previous winter. Still it is utterly impossible to justify a good guide for shrinking from the danger, if danger it can be called, of finding a passage through a series of seracs which would not at the worst be more troublesome than those of the Col du Géant. On the whole, therefore, I think that this fact tends to strengthen the theory that jealousy of a foreign guide was at the bottom of the reluctance exhibited.

On the night of Friday, September 1, we slept at the Montenvers, and I prided myself not a little on the obstinacy with which I had resisted an insane proposal to sleep in the hut at the Pierre à Bérenger. It is my opinion—and I state it in defiance of the zealots who love to torture themselves at lairs combining cold bad air and general discomfort in the highest degree—that no policy is worse than that of gaining an hour in the morning at the expense of a bad night. Indeed, as a rule, nothing is gained; because it is generally possible to reach the said lairs over the easier ground below by the time at which it would in any case be possible to start for the more difficult climb above. But, right or wrong, I have done with sleeping in anything but beds, always excepting fresh hay. A mountain which involves a night on the rocks is a mountain which my sense of duty to my family imperatively forbids me to undertake. When we started from the Montenvers at one o'clock, by the light of a waning moon, I was in a thoroughly peaceful frame of mind. Quiet slumber had come to me in a decently good bed, and its calming influence still rested over me as I moved in a half-doze along the well-known track up the Mer de Glace. The night was one of those questionable ones in which the mountains seem as if they had been painted against the sky in moist colours which had "run"; they were surrounded by a faint misty halo, which blurred their sharp outlines; light clouds drew an occasional veil across the moon, and even when it shone out the rays were feeble and uncertain. I ought, I suppose, to have been annoyed by the prospect of indifferent weather, and perhaps in more enthusiastic days I might have been restless; as it was, I seemed to be continuing a peaceful dream; the moon was nothing but a dim night-light; the clouds were muslin curtains swaying sleepily in front of her; the little party silently plodding in front of me were such figures as one watches in a half-dream, moving monotonously yet never seeming to advance; and the huge glacier itself lay ice-bound in a slumber almost death-like, except that the booming sound of a distant moulin suggested that the monster was peacefully snoring. Brilliant moonshine on the mountains is crisp, frosty, and stimulating; but in such a night as this Nature has that watery, tremulous, and rather shambling aspect, which she sometimes wears to a gentleman lurching homewards under London gaslights just before dawn; only here the change was without and not within us; the moon herself, not our little party, was in the state so vividly described by the poet as "no that fou, but just a drappie in her ee"; and the stern voice of the mountains was for once sentimental, not to say maudlin. Gradually daylight straggled down to us, but through ever-increasing masses of cloud. Far overhead, a faint flush upon the loftiest vapours showed that the sun was rising, but the lower strata only grew more black and angry as the lights and shadows became more pronounced. The Aiguille Verte, in particular, was shrouded in vast masses of gloomy vapour, which clung throughout the day to his grim cliffs; another body of cloud, of even more threatening aspect, was suspended in mid-air across the Mer de Glace. So dismal was the prospect, that after our first meal in a crevasse I threw out a suggestion that we were only wasting our time by perseverance. Luckily, a sterner sense of duty prevailed, and we toiled up the glacier till, about eight o'clock, we were seated on its highest plateau. Close above us, as we knew, rose the final rock-tower of the Mont Mallet, and we also knew vaguely that the col of which I have spoken was in our immediate neighbourhood. But we were now in the position of men who, having climbed a long ladder, find that they are only knocking their heads against the ceiling—a ceiling composed, in our case, of the dense masses which were hanging in that painfully uniform formation "the under-roof of doleful grey," so well known to luckless mountaineers, and cutting off the heads of all the peaks at a height of about 11,000 feet. There was nothing to be done but to eat and then to smoke, and then to discuss the length of time during which we were bound in honour to wait. A few shifts in the gathering vapours permitted occasional glimpses upwards, and forbade us entirely to despair. Suddenly, the keen-eyed Wallroth exclaimed "Chamois!" and pointed upwards towards the rocks of the Mallet. There, in fact, through a gap in the clouds, appeared a chamois, prancing down towards us, and giving his shrill whistle of alarm. The vapours instantly drifted back again, and Melchior was ready with an ingenious theory. We, he said, had frightened the chamois upwards; the animal had tried the rocks, and finding them impassable, was coming downwards and reconnoitring the enemy. The inference was that the rocks which had frightened the chamois would probably be impracticable for us. Having uttered this gloomy opinion with an air of considerable satisfaction, Melchior sat down, and cheerfully observed that he had foreseen, from the time we started, that we should be stopped by the weather. Rather annoyed at this application of the "I told you so" formula, I was just about to retort, when the wind took the words out of my mouth. Puffing aside the vapour-curtain, it revealed a lovely little glacier rising at a gentle slope towards the col which we had marked from below as the stepping-stone to the summit. We sprang hastily to our feet, and pushed forwards. Climbing an easy snow-slope, and cutting a few steps, we found ourselves well on the glacier, and scarcely a hundred feet lower than the col. Ten minutes more, and we should have won the day. The cup, so despairingly regarded, was suddenly presented to our lips;

two steps more, and it was as suddenly dashed away; for the glacier was rent from side to side by a monster crevasse; and a wall of ice varying in height from (at a guess) twenty to a hundred feet fairly blocked all further progress. Without a ladder all direct assault was hopeless, and the fearfully steep cliffs of ice by which the glacier was bounded on both sides seemed to make it impossible to turn the obstacle. Melchior was furious, and tried to force a way up a very nasty mixture of smooth rock and ice on our left. He hacked away vigorously for a time, and finally announced to me his opinion that an ascent was possible, but that the descent would be dangerous. It was, in fact, one of those places where it was impossible to make satisfactory progress in consequence of the underlying rock; and, of course, the danger would be increased when we could not see to place our feet. In other words, it was not a place for one who had long ago forsworn dangerous expeditions. Accordingly, I gave the word for retreat with a complacency which rather disgusted my more sanguine friends; but the comfort with which one can consult safety rather than glory is the great advantage of a *blasé* state of mind. For Melchior it was a bitter fate: to be beaten by a second-rate peak; to be beaten when at the very verge of success; and to be beaten in accordance with the predictions of Chamonix was a triple vexation. More than once he returned to the assault, but only to find it worse than before; and indeed the precautions which even he had to use in returning were such as forcibly to suggest the impropriety of an attack by less experienced performers. We retired at length sulkily and grimly, and discussing the possibility of some other route; when suddenly, as we reached once more the scene of our last meal, another puff of wind revealed the rocks on which we had seen the chamois. As seen from the Glacier de Léchaud, this face of the Mont Mallet has somewhat the appearance of a small model of the Matterhorn, and it scarcely required Melchior's ingenious argument from the chamois to convince us of the hopelessness of its rocks. But now, to our surprise and delight, it became at once evident that, as in so many other cases, the rocks looked worse from below than above, and, in short, that there was a fair prospect of climbing them with ease. The hour, however, was late, and the weather doubtful, and a night on the glacier would have been a probable result of an attempt to finish our mountain off-hand. We returned to Chamonix by about 3.30, and reported the result of our operations. M. Loppé, to our great pleasure, agreed to accompany us in another attack; and here occurred the second difficulty about guides, to which I have referred above. A jovial porter, one Alexandre Tournier agreed to join us; and after attending a concert at Chamonix on Sunday evening, started at 11 p.m., and reached the Montenvers a little before 1, just in time to join us. He walked all day pluckily and cheerfully, and I commend him to future travellers. The moon still favoured us, and the night was clearer and frostier, and far more promising. The deep rosy hue of a few lofty clouds at sunrise induced the weatherwise to prophesy bad weather for the next day—a prophecy which was of course utterly wrong—but for the present our prospects were good. We reached the foot of the rocks earlier than before, after much chaff about the supposed horrors of the glacier, and immediately addressed ourselves to the climb. It will be a sufficient indication of our route to anyone who may care to follow our steps, that if the face of Mont Mallet be compared to the north-east face of the Matterhorn—and I have already noticed the faint resemblance— our route would correspond to a climb by the Hörnli arête till near the summit; when we crossed diagonally the face analogous to that visible from the Riffel, and then, almost immediately below the summit, crossed still another face, and thus found ourselves on a ridge analogous to the Breuil arête. The rocks were rotten, but nowhere seriously difficult; and part of the lowest arête was composed of ice, which delayed us by the necessity of step-cutting. This might perhaps have been avoided, but it is useless to give indications which cannot be made plain without much detail, and which would be superfluous to anyone standing with a good guide at the foot of the rocks. I will only say that the spiral motion which we adopted at the top was caused by the fact that the highest pinnacle is apparently inaccessible from the arête, which would have led us straight to its base. When we had crossed the first face of the rock, Melchior had detached himself from the line, and went on to examine the route. It was long before he returned; though avalanches of stones testified to the fact that he was clambering somewhere amongst the disintegrated rocks of the summit. When at length he reappeared, he was more excited than usual. "It will be very difficult," he announced, "but go we must." Wallroth enthusiastically seconded the remark, whilst I showed my philosophic spirit by announcing that I would not risk my valuable neck for two Mont Mallets. A short climb, however, revealed the true nature of the case, and proved that Melchior's words required interpretation. There was difficulty, it is true, but there was no danger, and the difficulty concerned Melchior far more than anybody else. The ridge on which we stood was interrupted by a huge rock, "literally overhanging," viciously smooth, and about fifteen feet in height. Melchior paid to it the unusual respect of taking off his coat, which he solemnly deposited on the rocks. Then he somehow fastened himself to the opposing rock, and helped by a shove from Cachat's axe, executed a singular caper in mid-air, which placed him in the right line of ascent; and finally, by a dexterous wriggle, reached the summit of the cliff. It was my fate to follow; and though expecting to need assistance, I expected also to do something towards raising my own weight. Never was expectation more signally falsified. In a second I was as helpless a bundle as ever was hoisted on board ship by ropes and pulleys. My companions, I rejoiced to see, were equally incapable; and the means by which my old friend had surmounted the force of gravity remained to me, as to them, an inexplicable mystery. This difficulty once surmounted, a couple of steps placed us on the top of the mountain in a state of more than usual excitement and satisfaction. We shook hands heartily, indulged in frantic howls, scrupulously ascended the very highest fragment of stone, and then, whilst the guides erected a cairn, I lighted the inevitable pipe and proceeded to contemplate the view. Light clouds hid the more distant ranges, and revealed only one glimpse of Mont Blanc; his proportions are perhaps more magnificent from this than from any other side, and we saw them to the highest advantage above the great snow-fields which feed the Glacier du Géant. The point of view is indeed one of singular merit, as giving perhaps the most complete panorama of all the mighty ice-streams which combine to form the Mer de Glace. So much may be readily understood by the maps; but one special object absorbed most of our attention, and I will venture to say that, in its way, it is one of the most striking in the Alps. From our feet a terrible precipice plunged down abruptly to the wild Glacier du Tacul; whilst just across the head of the glacier rose the astonishing pinnacle of the Dent du Géant. Some mountaineers had been prowling round its base with a view to an assault; and their verdict, as reported to me by Christian Lauener, was to the effect that an ascent might be possible with the help of rockets and a sufficient allowance of rope. How that may be I know not; but the first thought that occurred to all of us as we looked at our tremendous neighbour was "Nobody will ever get up that peak by fair means." Of course it is impossible to say, after the Mont Cenis tunnel, what may not be within the resources of the engineer's art; but without stooping to some of those artifices which the mountaineer regards with the horror aroused in regard to other pursuits by the epithet "unsportsmanlike," no one, I venture to say with unusual confidence, will ever climb the Dent du Géant. Seen from the Montenvers, it looks precipitous enough; but one may cherish the belief that it is approachable from the rear. The view from the Mont Mallet at once dispels that pleasing illusion. At the time it reminded me of one of those quaint flint implements which suggests to

us that our remote ancestors were not altogether unac-
quainted with the miseries of shaving. Take the sharpest of
those flakes, which served the purposes of a razor or a
knife, magnify it till it is some 200 feet in height, and then
place it almost vertically but, if anything, rather leaning over
towards the Italian side, and you have some notion of the
Dent du Géant as seen from the Mont Mallet. The Aiguille
du Dru may, for aught I know, be climbed; the Charmoz
and the Aiguille de Blaitière are perhaps accessible; but if
anybody, by fair climbing, ever reaches the summit of the
Dent du Géant, I can only say that my ideas of the capacities
of human nature will be materially enlarged. I have not, it is
true, examined the peak from all possible points of view, and
some mysterious couloir may have escaped me; but I feel
little hesitation in ascerting that "inaccessible" ought still
to remain in the dictionary till that strange obelisk has
mouldered away to its base.

It is time, however, to turn to our descent; and yet I have
little to say except that the range of Périades presents a
dozen or two of minor pinnacles, each of them as inaccessible as the Dent du Géant, though not of such colossal
proportions. With a passing glance at their grotesque shapes,
we rapidly descended the glacier; and finally, if my memory
serves me rightly, reached Chamonix, drenched to the skin
by a thunderstorm, about 7 p.m. The zeal which formerly
induced me to make a note of the precise time, "including
halts," occupied in the expedition, has disappeared; but I
seem to recollect that the ascent took about ten hours.
Probably, it might be done rather more quickly, if anybody
cares to repeat it; and the walk has many merits to those who
wish really to appreciate the grandeur of the noble glacier
system which we traversed.

And here my task must cease. I should wish, indeed, if so
humble a performance were still regarded as worth description, to recount our subsequent ascent of Mont Blanc—
to utter withering sarcasms against that Chamonix porter
who calmly collapsed about half-an-hour beyond the Grands

Mulets, and left Melchior to take care of two gentlemen alone—of the grand race which took place between a party which ascended by the Bosses and the rival party which followed the old route—of the cutting wind which threatened frost-bites, and made a stay on the summit impossible— and of many other exciting incidents which will never, I fear, find their way into print. They will be cherished not less affectionately by those who enjoyed them; for after all it is a great fact, and one which has of late years been too much forgotten, that there are few more charming expeditions in the Alps than the ascent of Mont Blanc in fine weather; and few, it may be added, more dangerous when the weather is bad. But on these matters I do not presume to speak at length. It is enough to say that, having once lapsed from the paths of virtue, I found the flowery track of vice so agree-able, that I never withdrew more sadly from the glorious Alps, or watched more fondly the last glimpses of cliff and glacier, as we entered the gorge below Sallanches, on our return to London fog. If I have had no thrilling incidents to recount, I feel a kind of senile affection for that child of my old age, if I may so call him, the Mont Mallet, and hope that he may not be found altogether unworthy of the attention of more industrious members of the Alpine Club.

*(The Alpine Journal,* 1872)

# A Substitute for the Alps[*]

THE world was steadily improving till about thirty years
ago. After that period it remained comparatively station-
ary for a long time; but of late it has shown painful symptoms
of deterioration. This truth, which is generally known to men
of my age, is strikingly confirmed by the history of the Alps.
The Alps were once a barbarous and inaccessible region,
fitted only for savages and bears, and even for dragons, the
last of which were still occasionally seen (or heard of) in
the wilder regions a century or two ago. The mountains had
been gradually annexed to the habitable world: Hannibal
and his successors had made roads into their remotest
recesses and across the main passes; William Tell and his
friends had laid the foundation of independent com-
munities; inns had been built to receive travellers, and
guide-books been written to instruct them. A series of poets
and men of science had discovered their beauties, and we had
learnt from the pages of Saussure and Forbes and Ruskin to
visit the shrine in a becoming spirit. And, then, in the fullness
of time arose the Alpine Club. There is, I am told, a fruit
which can only be eaten in perfection at a particular moment;
ten minutes too early it is still sour and ten minutes too late
the flavour has already begun to decline perceptibly. So the
Alps culminated for a few years. The old romantic flavour
was still uninjured. Tourists could be thrilled at the sight
of Tell's chapel; they quoted Byron on the Wengern Alp
and Rousseau on the rocks of Meillerie; the monks of
St. Bernard were picturesque personages of superhuman
devotion, and their dogs showed an amazing instinct in
supplying lost wayfarers with cloaks and brandy. The daring
few who ventured to attack Mont Blanc had their names

* [A review of] *Climbing in the Karakoram-Himalayas.* By W. M.
Conway. London, 1894. T. Fisher Unwin.

203

inscribed in the archives of Chamonix; took a little army of guides and porters, with whom they dined solemnly if they survived the adventure; and repeated legends about mountain-sickness and avalanches which might start anywhere at any moment if the traveller ventured to raise his voice above a whisper. They wrote books when they came home. The guides were daring chamois hunters who loved danger for its own sake, and were (so we understand) invariably doomed to an early death. The innkeeper, in the remote parts, became a friend who only stopped short of such intimacy as would have made it ungraceful to present a modest bill; and you were often lodged by the village priest, who asked with interest about the Thames Tunnel, and had himself imbibed a passion for mountain ascents. We rushed with delight into that enchanted land; climbed peaks and passes; made proselytes in every direction to the new creed; and ended, alas! by rubbing off the bloom of early romance, and laying the whole country open to the incursions of the ordinary tourist. Seiler of Zermatt and Imseng of Saas are dead, and the great Melchior Anderegg is retiring from his profession. The fortunate generation is passing away; and the charm is perishing. Huge caravanserais replace the old hospitable inn; railways creep to the foot of Monte Rosa and the summit of the Wengern Alp and threaten even the summit of the Jungfrau. The tourist despatches Switzerland as rapidly and thoughtlessly as he does Olympia; and the very name of the Alps, so musical in the ears of those who enjoyed their mysterious charm, suggests little more than the hurry and jostling of an average sight-seeing trip. It is sad. The selfish veteran may no doubt say that what has been has been, and he has had his hour. But he has a certain pang when he reflects that such an hour can never come to his children. They can never know the true delight of a first ascent of the Matterhorn, or form one in such a friendly little circle as then had the most delightful of all recreations to itself. While moodily reflecting upon these familiar thoughts, I came upon Mr. Conway's beautiful book upon a still unexhausted region.

Though nothing can bring back the hour of freshness in the Alps, there may be still a chance for other regions. Mr. Whymper, having spoilt the Matterhorn, sought to recompense his fellow creatures by throwing open the Andes. Mr. Conway, who has helped to suppress the Alps, though doomed by unfortunate fate which brought him into the world at a ridiculously modern date, to a narrower range of discovery, has gone to the noblest of all mountain regions. He has penetrated into the marvellous wilderness of gigantic peaks which are the nearest approach made by our planet to the scenery of the moon. We have all lately read Mr. Knight's charming book, *Where Three Empires Meet*. Mr. Knight had the good fortune to see a curious combination of fighting and climbing—the two noblest of human amusements. He assisted at a process which was at once the storming of a fort and the ascent of a precipitous mountain gorge. The wild scene of that daring feat was but the vestibule to the innermost penetralia of the Karakoram mountains, and the gallant robbers who defended the gorge appear to have made their conquerors welcome, and, according to Mr. Conway, need only a little experience to become as good guides as the Balmats and the Andereggs of our own continent. Clearly they will be in no want of materials upon which to practise the art. Mr. Conway naturally compares his new series of peaks to our old favourites; and he has a disagreeable, if conscientious, way of invariably reminding us that the new scenery is on a vastly greater scale. When a literary critic discovers a new light he hesitates a little before declaring, say, that Ibsen is incomparably superior to Shakespeare. Mr. Conway has no such remorse. He roundly declares that this or that upstart is altogether superior to the recognised superlatives. He reminds us of "Dido, a dowdy, Cleopatra, a gipsy, Thisbe, a grey-eye, or so, but not to the purpose." The Jungfrau is all very well, but she is a molehill compared with Masherbrum. The Monte Rosa has some fine snow-slopes, but nothing to put beside the cliffs of Pioneer Peak; and it is no longer Mont Blanc, but

"K2," who must be enthroned as "the monarch of mountains." There is, indeed, one phrase which gives us reason to hope that the Matterhorn in point of form may still hold his own with the Karakoram peaks, but it must be sorrowfully confessed that the merit of a mountain depends greatly upon size; and, in Macaulayan phrase, the Alps apparently bear the same relation to these monsters which Scawfell bears to Mont Blanc or which Primrose Hill bears to Scawfell.

As philanthropists we ought to rejoice for the sake of posterity. We ought not to be grudging on such a subject; to hug ourselves in the thought that we, and we alone, have enjoyed the very cream of mountaineering ecstasy, and that none of our descendants to the end of time can ever enjoy it again. Therefore, though not without reluctance, I have braced myself to consider what is to be said by this devil's advocate —a name which I do not mean to be uncomplimentary, but applicable to any iconoclast who desires me to exchange my cherished superstition for a new, even if a more enlightened creed. In this matter of mere size, it must be confessed at once that Mr. Conway is unanswerable. We used to think a good deal of the Aletsch glacier and the twelve hours' pass which leads from Grindelwald to the Æggischhorn. But what is that to the great Hispar pass, where Mr. Conway's party spent over a fortnight upon the two monstrous glaciers? His guide remarked pathetically upon one occasion that after an hour or two upon a Swiss moraine a man thinks himself entitled to swear, but upon this occasion he felt that he had no right to that relief after a day or two upon the vast wilderness of stones. The mountains are not only gigantic but innumerable. Mr. Conway looks up a lateral gorge and sees a huge glacier tumbling down, one chaotic mass of seracs. He doubts whether a man could cut his way up it in a year. Beyond it opens a new "mass of mountains, unexpected, unexplored, and unnamed." Among these are "three giants, noble in form and fine in grouping." For countless ages they have wasted their beauty on a few wandering bears and ibexes. Indeed, it seems doubtful whether they have had even such semi-conscious spectators of their charms. For these strange monsters, vista opening beyond vista of inaccessible peaks, rise in the region of thin air, to which comes nothing living except some luckless butterfly, carried up by a gale to be frozen in eternal snow, so deserted that Mr. Conway was pleased to get down again to a place where he was once more bitten of mosquitoes. Those insects are at least, in some sense, company. They belong to the world of organised life, though they make a rather objectionable use of their endowments.

It is, indeed, rather pleasant to the ancient Alpine tourist to find that Mr. Conway verifies an old discredited tradition. We used thoughtlessly to mock at Saussure's guide who complained of the stifling air on the insufficiently "aerated" plateau of Mont Blanc. He was right, it seems, after all. At least the upper regions, upon which K2 and his comrades look down, seem for the present to exercise the same influence over their daring assailants. The party took some three weeks in ascending the other monstrous glacier, and painfully forming camp above camp, and lugging themselves up through the thin air to successively higher stations, till at last they stood upon the summit of "Pioneer Peak," some 23,000 feet above the sea, and higher, in all probability, than man has ever climbed before, though their neighbour the "Golden Throne" still rose 1,100 feet higher, and the irrespressible K2 rises another 4,000 feet. That they had perfomed a feat which commands the sympathetic respect of all mountaineers is too obvious to need emphasis. Mr. Conway, though he preserves a proper silence about himself, gives incidentally facts which are significant enough even to the humble Swiss traveller. The Swiss guide Zurbriggen must undoubtedly be a worthy representative of a set of men whose qualities are well enough known. His companions, who had still to learn the art of climbing, showed admirable predispositions. Mr. Bruce, struggling waist-deep through a mountain torrent in flood, with a sheep under each arm, was clearly the man for the emergency; and the gallant Gurkhas whom he led, though not previously experienced upon ice, had the manly qualities of the true mountaineer. They appear especially to have taken everything in the right spirit—that is to say, to regard all the dangers and the toils as part of the fun. Whether they contrive to break each other's heads by butting at each other with the horns of ibexes, or to swing pendulum-like across the face of vast snow-slopes, when their lives depended on the power of their companions to support them by a rope from the unsteady footing of ice-cut steps, they see the performance from the humourist's point of view. And we are grateful to the artist, Mr. McCormick, who, harassed by toothaches and attacks of fever, and in spite of frostbites and sufferings from thin air, managed to preserve speaking portraits of the scenery and the actors.

Then the poor coolies—unlucky porters dragged at the tail of this apparently insane expedition—deserve their word of praise. But here recurs that sentiment which I have endeavoured to mask under an affectation of sympathy. The porter in a Swiss expedition was generally a convenient scapegoat upon whom the unsuccessful traveller could discharge a part of his bile. But what is the mere Swiss traveller to think of an expedition in which the number of porters rises at times to a hundred? It is no longer an expedition, but a campaign. The machinery is becoming too complex for the amusement. Mr. Conway has to be a general rather than a leader. He submits to labours such as are incompatible with the happy thoughtlessness of our simple adventures. He lugs about a horrible instrument called a "plane-table," something, as I dimly conjecture, useful in surveying, and has to spend hours after the day's march in slavery to this monstrous contrivance. He is forced to be scientific, to collect stones and plants and insects, and to keep an elaborate diary recording his observations. He has become a Moltke, toiling at his desk and condensing an elaborate correspondence, instead of a simple-minded barbarian chief rushing out for a day's raid. Mr. Conway, of course, deserves gratitude; but to us of the old-fashioned school, the question will occur whether this is not something quite different from the recreation which we loved so well. In the good old days an Alpine expedition meant a walk from a comfortable inn, a stiff climb or so up a peak of reasonable size, at the outside, perhaps, a night passed in a chalet or possibly on the rocks, and then a return with heightened appetite to a good *table d'hôte*, and a delicious evening talk, in which we recounted our performances with such modesty as we could command to like-minded friends. To travel half around the world (Mr. Conway boasts that you can get to the foot of his mountains in a month from London), to organise a whole army of porters and a system of supplies, to take, in short, almost as much trouble as if you were going to relieve Emin Pasha or discover the remains of Sir John Franklin, may be a good investment of energy; but it does not at present suggest a new sport accessible to the tired barrister or the university don in his vacation. It will be a long time before K2 will be as accessible as Mont Blanc is at present. And this suggests another point. Can K2, or Masherbrum, or any of his nameless compeers, be really as beautiful? The argument in their favour is plausible: they are taller than Mont Blanc; they have bigger precipices; longer ranges of peaked "needles"; they command wider horizons; they send down avalanches by the score, each of them big enough to cover a whole Swiss valley; the sunset lights up their snows, and the clouds wreathe round their ridges in colours as bright and forms as delicate as are ever to be seen nearer home. That proves that if they were in Switzerland they would be beautiful. But can they be beautiful where they are? Mr. Conway laments that his three giants have been "wasting their magnificence" through all the centuries. So we may say that the marble in a quarry or the canvas in a shop have been wasted for want of statuary and painter. What these noble giants want is not simply that somebody should go and look at them. That can be done, as Mr.

Conway has found, at a sufficient cost of time and money, of aching and gasping lungs. But they require also to be enamelled by all that can only come with centuries of civilisation. They want to have picturesque villages and church spires in their valleys; to have zigzag paths traced up their sides by the feet of succeeding generations; to have chalets built on the pastures, and terraced fields creeping up their sides; to be everywhere, in short, made into the framework of a congenial human society. Our ancestors, at whom we sometimes sneer, took their scenery more reasonably perhaps than we do. They loved it as the background of various active pursuits; Izaak Walton loved the gentle flow of the sea, though professedly he was only intent upon the wily carp; and Robin Hood really enjoyed the greenwood, though he affected to be only on the look-out for the Prior of Jervaulx with his sumpter mules. In later years we have learnt to talk as though we cared about Nature for its own sake; as though a hill or a stream could be beautiful not only without suggesting definite thoughts of human life, but when it has absolutely no relation to them. Of course, this is natural enough for a cockney. Eleven months in London qualifies one to enjoy absolute solitude in the twelfth. Our neighbours have been so often in contact with us that the bare sensation of not having our toes trodden and our ribs jogged by other people's elbows appears to be delicious. But it is a delusion to suppose that the mind can permanently take pleasure in the absolute negation of human sympathy, in regions in which you are not only unelbowed by peer or player, but in conditions positively hostile to the human race. I am not one of those persons who are accessible to what are called historical associations: my heart would not beat more quickly on the Field of Marathon; and when I see a place where something has happened, the thing that always occurs to me is its strong resemblance to places where nothing has happened. But, for all that, I like my scenery properly aired; tamed and softened by the labours of my fellows, or at least standing out in harmonious contrast to human works. Mont Blanc never looks so lovely to me as when it shows itself across the Lake of Geneva as the guardian of the dwelling-place of a people; and when I am on the summit I do not feel quite happy without the glimpses of meadow far below, or of the mountain paths winding through the gorges. We are still inclined to regard a railway in the Alps as uncongenial: it is a new, raw, obtrusive phenomenon, suggestive of the intrusive tourist; but nothing adds so much to the beauty of a mountain pass as one of the old carriage-roads, climbing dexterously up the accessible slopes and giving a dramatic interest by its adaptation to the scenery and its suggestion of the many regions which it divides or joins. Savagery, pure and simple, the deathly solitudes of the moon, even the wilderness of the Rocky Mountains or the Karakoram, would, I fear, make me shiver. It is true that Mr. Conway's jovial Gurkhas, to say nothing of Mr. Conway's own party, seem to have kept up their spirits in a marvellous fashion, and even to have made the ridges of K2 echo to strains more familiar in London music-halls. That, I take it, was a tacit confession that they were verging upon homesickness; that these huge, frigid images of death and stagnation were a little too overpowering, and required the stirring of some associations with the land of the living. I love the sea at the Land's End; for if there is the Atlantic in front, there is one's own country, such as it is, behind; but the solitudes of the mid-ocean become a little too appalling in their loneliness; and, on the same principle, Mont Blanc is noble between Chamonix and Courmayeur; but K2, vaguely standing in the wilderness, in a dim region between three distant empires, would, I suspect, suggest the ominous and the monstrous, and even the sublimity would pass into the horrible. Thus, after all, I can find comfort. I shall never see the Karakoram range, unless I become Governor-General of India; but I have persuaded myself for the moment that I don't want to see it. Mr. Conway's account of his life in those regions and Mr. McCormick's pictures of the snows were undoubtedly fascinating; they roused the old man, and I glanced at the ice-axe long suspended peacefully in my study. But I have suppressed the rising emotion and can calmly but decidedly pronounce the Karakoram to be a mistake. I have better reasons for not going there than Wordsworth found for not visiting Yarrow; at any rate, reasons which are much more certain to keep me to my resolution. I will not say that if I am invited there a thousand years hence, I will refuse to go. By that time the mountains may have been got into order. There will be a railway station (if railways should not have been superseded) at Gilgit; there will be pleasant hotels in all the valleys; the Chinaman and the Russian and the Englishman will be meeting on friendly terms, and wondering over the foolish jealousies of long-past centuries; the regions will be swept and garnished, and there will be a proper audience for the heroes who will then be climbing the last untrodden peaks, and lamenting the exhaustion of the last playground of the civilised world. At present I am content to let Mr. Conway go for me. He must forgive the ancients of the Alpine Club if they look with somewhat jaundiced eyes upon the ugly duckling, or, to be more complimentary, let me say the eaglet, whom they have unwittingly hatched. They cannot conceal a certain pride in the monster who has soared beyond their ken; for they claim to have partly implanted in him the impulse which has had such an imposing result. But in private they feel that they really had the best of it; and that these new-fangled monstrosities must not be permitted on the score of mere material magnitude to lord it over the eternal Alps, which have charms never to be rivalled and not even to be quite extinguished by hordes of thoughtless sightseers.

(The National Review, 1894)

# Thoughts on Criticism, by a Critic

PERHAPS the most offensive type of human being in the present day is the young gentleman of brilliant abilities and high moral character who has just taken a good degree. It is his faith that the University is the centre of the universe, and its honours the most conclusive testimonials to genius. His seniors appear to him to be old fogies; his juniors mere children; and women, whatever his theories as to their possible elevation, fitted at present for no better task than the skilful flattery of youthful genius. He is at the true social apex. He is half-afraid, it may be, of men of the world and women of society; but his fear masks itself under a priggish self-satisfaction. A few years in a wider circle will knock the nonsense out of him, unless he is destined to ripen into one of those scholastic pedants now fortunately rarer than of old. But meanwhile it happens that a large part of the critical staff of the nation is formed by fresh recruits from this class of society. The young writer, with the bloom of his achievements still fresh, is prepared to sit in judgment with equal confidence upon the last new novel or theory of the universe. The aim of much University teaching is to produce that kind of readiness which tells in a competitive examination, and is equally applicable to the composition of a smart review. In the schools, a lad of twenty-two is ready with a neat summary of any branch of human knowledge. When he issues into the world, he is prepared to deal with the ripest thinkers of the day, as he dealt with the most eminent philosophers of old. In three hours he can give a history of philosophy from Plato to Hegel. Why waste more time upon Mill or Hamilton?

That much contemporary criticisms represent the views of such writers, will, I think, be admitted by most readers of periodical literature. It is a favourite belief of many sufferers under the critical lash, that it represents scarcely anything else. When an author has spent years, or even months, in elaborating an argument or accumulating knowledge, it is rather annoying to see himself tried and sentenced within a week from his appearance in the world. His critic, it seems, can merely have glanced over his pages, taken down a label at random from some appropriate pigeon-hole, and affixed it with a magisterial air of supercilious contempt. *Là voilà le chameau!* as Mr. Lewes' French philosopher remarks, when composing the natural history of the animal on the strength of half-an-hour in the Jardin des Plantes. The poor history or philosophy, the darling of its author's heart, so long patiently meditated, so delicately and carefully prepared, associated with so much labour, anxiety, and forethought, is put in its proper place as rapidly as Professor Owen could assign a ticket to a fossil tooth. It is not strange if the victim condemns his judge as an ignorant prig, and is tormented by an impotent longing for retaliation. But experience has probably taught him that to argue with a critic in his own columns is like drawing a badger in its den. You may be the strongest outside, but within you have to rush upon a sharp cagework of defensive teeth with your own hands tied. Silence, with as much dignity as may be, is his only course.

All criticism, one may say, is annoying. A wise man should never read criticisms of his own work. It is invariably a painful process; for all blame is obviously unfair, and praise as certainly comes in the wrong place. Moreover, it is a bad habit to be always looking in a glass, and especially in a mirror apt to distort and magnify. If a man is conscious that he has done his best, he should let his work take its chance with such indifference as he can command. Its success will be in the long run what it deserves, or, which comes to much the same thing, will be determined by a tribunal from which there is no appeal. All that criticism does is slightly to retard or hasten the decision, but scarcely to influence it. Every attack is an advertisement, and few authors nowadays have any difficulty in finding the circle really congenial to them. That circle once reached, an author should be satisfied. It may gain him much pecuniary profit but little real influence or fame when he comes to be forced upon those who don't spontaneously care for him. Now, the true author should, of course, be as indifferent to money as to insincere praise, and he is pretty certain to get all that he can really claim, namely, a sufficient hearing. Therefore, authors should burn unread all reviews of themselves, and possess their souls in peace.

Nobody, of course, will take this advice; but at least one may hope that a sense of decency will prevent authors and their admirers from howling too noisily under the lash. Why should the heaven-born poet shriek and rant because his earthborn critic does not do him justice? A true poet is the apostle of a new creed. He reveals hitherto unnoticed aspects of truth or beauty; his originality measures at once his genius and his chance of being misunderstood. It is his special prerogative to give form and colour to the latent thoughts and emotions of his time, and those whom he interprets to themselves will be grateful. But the utterance necessarily shocks all who cling from pedantry or from conservatism to the good old conventions. Their resistance is in proportion to the vigour of his attack, and he should hail their reproaches as compliments in disguise. Bacon or Locke had no right to be angry because the representatives of old scholasticism resented their attacks; nor Wordsworth nor Keats, because the admirers of Pope objected to the new forms of poetry. Wordsworth, with his sublime self-complacency, took hostile criticism as an unconscious confession of stupidity, and declared contemporary unpopularity to be a mark of true genius. The friends of Keats howled, and have been more or less howling ever since, because the old walls of convention did not fall down of themselves to welcome their assailants. Byron's contempt for the soul which let itself be snuffed out by an article is more to the purpose than Shelley's unmanly wailing over the supposed murder. The *Adonais* is an exquisite poem, but to read it with pleasure one must put the facts out of sight.

> *Our Adonais hath drunk poison, oh!*
> *What deaf and viperous murderer could crown*
> *Life's early cup with such a draught of woe!*

Beautiful! but a rather overstrained statement of the fact that Keats had been cut up in the *Quarterly Review*. On the theory that poetry and manliness are incompatible, that a poet is and ought to be a fragile being, ready to

> *Die of a rose in aromatic pain,*

the expressions may be justified. Otherwise Keats's death—if it had really been caused by the review—would certainly provoke nothing but pitying contempt. He that goes to war should count the cost; and one who will break the slumbers of mankind by new strains of poetic fervour must reckon upon the probability that many of the slumberers will resent the intrusion by a growl or an execration. Poets have a pre-scriptive right to be a thin-skinned race; but even they should not be guilty of the ineffable meanness of prostrating themselves before reviewers to receive sentence of life or death. What have these dwellers in the upper sphere to do with the hasty guesses of newspapers? What would a Shake-speare, or a Milton, or a Wordsworth, have said to such wailings? After all, what does it matter? Take it at the worst, and suppose yourself to be crushed for ever by a column of contemptuous language. Will the universe be much the worse for it? Can't we rub along tolerably without another volume or two of graceful rhymes? Is it anything but a pre-posterous vanity which generates the fancy that a rebuff to your ambition is an event in the world's history? If you are but a bubble, pray burst and hold your tongue. The great wheels of the world will grind on, and your shrieks be lost in the more serious chorus of genuine suffering. Whilst millions are starving in soul and body, we can't afford to waste many tears because a poet's toes have been trampled in the crush.

Though criticism may have far less power than our fears and our vanities assign to it, it has its importance; and at a time when all literature is becoming more critical, it is worth while to consider some of the principles which should guide it. We should, if possible, spare needless pangs even to a childish vanity, and we should anxiously promote the growth of a critical spirit such as raises instead of depressing the standard of literary excellence. The historian and the man of science can count upon fairly intelligent and scholarlike critics. Even if they be a little arrogant and prejudiced, they have one great advantage. There is a definite code of accepted principles. A mistake is clearly a mistake; and if the critic and his victim disagree, they have a definite issue and a settled method for decision. The judge may give a wrong decision, but he is administering a recognised code. We can apply scales and balances, and measure the work done with something like arithmetical accuracy.

In æsthetic questions the case is different. There is no available or recognised standard of merit. The ultimate appeal seems to lie to individual taste. I like Wordsworth, you like Pope—which is right? Are both right, or neither, or is it merely a matter of individual taste, as insoluble as a dispute between a man who prefers burgundy and one who prefers claret? The question would be answered if there were ever a science of æsthetics. At present we have got no further towards that consummation than in some other so-called sciences; we have invented a sounding name and a number of technical phrases, and are hopelessly at a loss for any accepted principles. We can, therefore, talk the most delicious jargon with all the airs of profound philosophy, but we cannot convince anyone who differs from us. The result is unfortunate, and oddly illustrates a popular confusion of ideas. There is surely no harm in a man's announcing his individual taste, if he expressly admits that he is not prescribing to the tastes of others. If I say that I dislike Shakespeare, I announce a fact, creditable or otherwise, of which I am the sole judge. So long as I am sincere,

I am no more to be blamed than if I announced myself to be blind or deaf, or expressed an aversion to champagne. But, in practice, nobody is allowed to announce his own taste without being suspected of making it into a universal rule. It is a curious experiment, for example, to say openly that you don't care for music. Many men of good moral character have shared the distaste, and it may mean no more than some trifling physical defect. A thickness in the drum of the ear is not disgraceful, but it makes you necessarily incapable of appreciating Beethoven. One who avows his incapacity is simply revealing the melancholy fact that he is shut out from one great source of innocent pleasure. But no arguments will convince an ordinary hearer that your confession does not carry with it a declaration of belief that delight in music is contemptible and possibly immoral. To disavow so illogical a conclusion is hopeless. Experience, we must presume, has made it into an axiom that a man always hates and despises, and regards as a fit object for universal contempt and hatred, whatever he does not understand.

This is the first great stumbling-block in æsthetic criticism. Both readers and writers confound the enunciation of their own taste with the enunciation of universal and correct principles of taste. There is an instructive story in *Don Quixote* which is much to the purpose. Sancho Panza had two uncles who had an unrivalled taste in wine. One of them asserted that a certain butt of wine had a twang of leather; another detected, with equal confidence, a slight flavour of iron. The assistants laughed; but the laugh was the other way when the butt was drunk out and an old key with a leather thong detected at the bottom. Which things are an allegory. The skilled critic detects a flavour of vulgarity, of foreign style, or of what not, in a new writer. The mob of readers protests or acquiesces. Possibly at some future time the truth is discovered. The critic's palate was vitiated by prejudice, or some biographical fact turns up which justifies his appreciation; or, though no overt fact can be adduced, the coincidence of opinion of other qualified judges or the verdict of posterity confirms or refutes the verdict. We must wait, however, till the butt is drunk out, till time or accident has revealed the truth, and the judge himself has undergone judgment. And meanwhile we have, in the last resort, nothing but an individual expression of opinion, to be valued according to our appreciation of the writer's skill.

We know further that the best of critics is the one who makes fewest mistakes. We laugh at the familiar instances of our ancestors' blindness; but we ourselves are surely not infallible. We plume ourselves on detecting the errors of so many able men; but the very boast should make us modest. Will not the twentieth century laugh at the nineteenth? Will not our grandchildren send some of our modern idols to the dust heaps, and drag out works of genius from the neglect in which we so undeservedly left them? No man's fame, it is said, is secure till he has lived through a century. His children are awed by his reputation; his grandchildren are prejudiced by a reaction; only a third generation pronounces with tolerable impartiality on one so far removed from the daily conflict of opinion. In a century or so, we can see what a man has really done. We can measure the force of his blows. We can see, without reference to our personal likes or dislikes, how far he has moulded the thoughts of his race and become a source of spiritual power. That is a question of facts, as much as any historical question, and criticism which takes it properly into account may claim to be in some sense scientific. To anticipate the verdict of posterity is the great task of the true critic, which is accomplished by about one man in a generation.

The nature of the difficulty is obvious. The critic has to be a prophet without inspiration. The one fact given him is that he is affected in a particular way by a given work of art; the fact to be inferred is, that the work of art indicates such and such qualities in its author, and will produce such and such an effect upon the world. No definite mode of procedure is possible. It is a question of tact and instinctive appreciation; it is not to be settled by logic, but by what Dr.

Newman calls the "illative sense"; the solution of the problem is to be felt out, not reasoned out, and the feeling is necessarily modified by the "personal equation," by that particular modification of the critic's own faculties, which cause him to see things in a light more or less peculiar to himself. He is disgusted by a certain poem; perhaps he dislikes the author, or the author's religious or political school; or he is out of humour, or tried by overwork, or unconsciously biassed by a desire to point some pet moral of his own, or simply to find some excuse for a brilliant article. If he has succeeded in eliminating these disturbing influences, the problem is still intricate. Grant that the author disgusts me, and, further, that I can put my finger on the precise cause of disgust, and discover it to be some tone of sentiment which, in my opinion, is immoral or morbid; how can I be sure, first, that I am right, and, next, that the disgust should be equally felt by my descendants? The greatest errors of judgment have been founded on perfectly correct appreciations. Burke was undeniably right in the opinion that Rousseau's sentiment was often morbid, immoral, and revolutionary. He was wrong in inferring that these blemishes deprived Rousseau's work of all permanent value, so that under the vanity and the disease there was not a deep vein of true and noble passion. Every great writer of the present day is regarded in a similar spirit by the section opposed to him in sentiment, and yet it may be held by the charitable that even the most deadly antagonism is consistent with real co-operation. When we read the great works of a past epoch with due absence of prejudice, we are always astonished by the degree in which those who struck most fiercely really shared the ideas of their opponents.

A critic, it has been inferred, should in all cases speak for himself alone. He is, or ought to be, an infallible judge of his own likes or dislikes; he cannot dictate to his neighbour. For this reason, it has been suggested, all anonymous criticism is bad. A man who calls himself "we" naturally takes airs which the singular "I" would avoid. Whatever the general principles upon this subject, I do not much believe in the remedy. Anonymous criticism may be less responsible, but it is more independent. Why should I not condemn a man's work without telling him that I personally hold him to be a fool? Why should literary differences be embittered by personal feeling? If every man knew his judge, would not the practical result be an increase of bitterness in some cases and adulation in others? The mask may at times conceal an assassin, but it discourages flattery and softens antipathy. I fancy that a man, unjust enough to let his personal feelings colour his criticisms, generally likes to be known to his victim. Spite loses half its flavour when it is forced to be anonymous. Whatever the cause, the open critic differs from his anonymous rival by nothing but a trifling addition of pretentiousness, dogmatism, and severity. A writer is perhaps more modest the first time he has to give his name; but by the twentieth he has rubbed off that amiable weakness. Publicity hardens and generates conceit more decorously than privacy encourages laxity. The most ferocious denunciation, and the most arrogant dogmatism, have, I think, been shown by men whose names were known to everybody, if not actually published.

The fact, however, remains, that after all a criticism is only an expression of individual feeling. The universal formula might be: I, A. B., declare that you, C. D., are a weariness to me, or the reverse. The moral is, that a critic should speak of his author as one gentleman of another, or as a gentleman of a lady; the case being, of course, excepted when the author is palpably not a lady or gentleman, but a male or female blackguard. This maxim may be infringed by brutality or by dogmatism. The slashing reviewer seems to forget that he and his victim are both human beings, and bound by the ordinary decencies of life. The really pathetic case is, not when the heaven-born poet is misunderstood, but when some humble scribbler is scarified by the thoughtless critic. It is not a crime to be stupid, and to be forced to write for bread. Literature is a poor but a fairly honest profession. A widow with a family on her hands, a harmless governess, a clerk disabled by disease, has a pen, ink, and paper, can spell, and write grammar. With that slender provision, he or she tries to eke out a scanty living by some poor little novel. It is, of course, silly and commonplace. It is a third-rate imitation of an inferior author. It will go to the wastepaper heap, in any case, before the year is out, and the only wonder is that it has found a publisher. If the brilliant young prig could see the wretched author in the flesh, and realise the pangs of fear and suspense that have gone to the little venture, he would feel sheer pity, and his hand be attracted to his pockets. But when he sees only the book, and his pen is nearer than his purse, he proceeds to make fun of the miserable sufferer, and sprinkles two columns with sparkling epigrams with the sense of doing a virtuous action. Since the days of the *Dunciad*, it has been clear that nothing is so cruel as a wit. Wits have invented the opposite maxim. Take it for a rule, says Pope, with some truth,

*No creature smarts so little as a fool.*

But even a fool has his natural feelings as clearly as Shylock. When Macaulay jumped upon poor "Satan" Montgomery, and hacked and hewed and slashed him till he had not a whole bone in his body, he tried to prove that the example was demanded in the interests of literature. Surely, Macaulay was deluding himself, and the interest really consulted was his own reputation for smartness. *Satan* (I speak of the poem so-called) would have been dead long ago if Macaulay had never written; and the art of puffery could surely not have been more vigorous.

Such weapons should be kept for immoral writings or for successful imposture. There they are fair enough; and there is not the least danger that, confined to that application, they will rust from disuse. Stupidity enthroned in high places justifies the keenest ridicule. Stupidity on its knees scarcely requires the lash. Some amiable persons seem, indeed, to hold that the lash can never be required. They believe in sympathetic criticism. They would praise the good and leave the bad to decay of itself. The doctrine, however taking, is not more moral, and perhaps is more deleterious than the opposite. No man, says the excellent maxim, has ever been written down except by himself. Hostile criticism gives pain, but does not inflict vital wounds. Many writers, on the other hand, have been spoilt by indiscriminate praise. The temptation to become an imitator of oneself, is the most insidious of all to which an author is exposed. When a man has discovered his true power he should use it, but he should not use it to repeat his old feats in cold blood. The distinction is not always easy to urge, but it is of vital importance. The works of the greatest writers, of the Shakespeares and Goethes, show a process of continuous development. The later display the same faculties as the earlier, but ripened and differently applied. The works of second-rate authors are often like a series of echoes. Each is a feeble repetition of the original which won the reputation. The flattery, now too common, makes this malady commoner than of old. A good writer, like a king, can do no wrong. Wonderful! admirable! faultless! is the cry; give us more of the same, and make it as much the same as possible. Is it wonderful that the poor man's head is turned, and his hold upon the ablest judges weakens whilst his circulation increases.

The michief is intensified when a couple of sympathetic critics get together. They become the nucleus of a clique, and develop into a mutual admiration society. They form a literary sect, with its pet idols and its sacred canons of taste. They are the first persons to whom art has revealed its true secrets. Other cliques have flourished and laid down laws, and passed away; theirs will be eternal. The outside world may sneer, the members of the clique will only draw closer the curtain which excludes the profane vulgar from their meetings. As a rule, such a body contains one or two men of genuine ability, and has some ground for its self-praise, though not so unassailable a ground as it fancies. But genius condemned to lived in such a vapour-bath of perpetually steaming incense, becomes soft of fibre and loses its productive power. It owes more than it would admit to the great world outside, which ridicules its pretensions and is perhaps blind even to its genuine merits. Addison was not the better for giving laws to a little senate; but Addison fortunately mixed in wider circles, and was not always exposed to the adulation of Tickell and "namby-pamby" Philips. Every man should try to form a circle of friends, lest he should be bewildered and isolated in the confused rush of a multitudinous society; but the circle should, so to speak, be constantly aërated by outside elements, or it will generate a mental valetudinarianism. The critic, who can speak the truth and speak out, is therefore of infinite service in keeping the atmosphere healthy.

A critic, then, should speak without fear or favour, so long as he can speak with the courtesy of a gentleman. He should give his opinion for what it is worth, neither more nor less. As the opinion of an individual, it should not be dogmatic; but as the opinion of a presumably cultivated individual, it should give at least a strong presumption as to that definitive verdict which can only be passed by posterity. The first difficulty which he will meet is to know what his opinion really is. No one who has not frankly questioned himself can appreciate the difficulty of performing this apparently simple feat. Every man who has read much has obscured his mind with whole masses of unconscious prejudice. An accomplished critic will declare a book to be fascinating of which he cannot read a page without a yawn, or a sheet without slumber. He will denounce as trashy and foolish a book which rivets his attention for hours. This is the one great advantage of the mob above the connoisseur. The vulgar have bad taste, but it is a sincere taste. They can't be persuaded to read except by real liking; and in some rare cases, where good qualities are accidentally offensive to the prevailing school of criticism, the cultivated reader will reject what is really excellent. The first point, therefore, is to have the rare courage of admitting your own feelings.

> *In poets as true genius is but rare,*
> *True taste as seldom is the critic's share,*

as Pope says; and chiefly for this reason. In all our array of critics, there are scarcely half-a-dozen whose opinions are really valuable, and simply because there are scarcely so many whose opinions are their own. In ninety-nine cases out of a hundred, a so-called critique is a second-hand repetition of what the critic takes for the orthodox view. Whenever we see the expression of genuine feeling, we recognise a valuable contribution to our knowledge. That, for example, is the secret of the singular excellence of Lamb's too scanty fragments of criticism. He only spoke of what he really loved, and therefore almost every sentence he wrote is worth a volume of conventional discussion. He blundered at times; but his worst blunders are worth more than other men's second-hand judgments. Spontaneity is as valuable in the parasitic variety of literature as in the body of literature itself, and even more rare. Could we once distinguish between our own tastes and the taste which we adopt at second-hand, we should have at least materials for sound judgment.

This vivacity and originality of feeling is the first qualification of a critic. Without it no man's judgment is worth having. Almost any judgment really springing from it has a certain value. But the bare fact that an aversion or a liking exists requires interpretation. To find the law by which the antipathy is regulated is to discover the qualities of the antagonistic elements. A good critic can hardly express his feelings without implicitly laying down a principle. When (to take a case at random) Lamb says of certain scenes in Middleton, that the "insipid levelling morality to which the modern stage is tied down, would not admit of such admirable passions," as fill the passages in question, he preaches a doctrine, sound or unsound, of great importance. He says, that is, that certain rules of modern decorum are æsthetically injurious and ethically erroneous. The particular rules infringed are to be discovered from the special instance, and the fact that a man with Lamb's idiosyncrasies denounced them must be taken into account when we would apply them as canons of judgment. The judgments of good critics upon a number of such problems thus form a body of doctrine analogous to what is known to jurists as case-law. The rule for our guidance is not explicitly stated, but it is to be inferred from a number of particular instances, by carefully estimating their resemblance to the fresh instance and assigning due weight to the authority of the various judges.

As competent literary judges are rare, and their decisions conflicting, the task of extricating the general rule is difficult or rather impossible. No general rules perhaps can be laid down with absolute confidence. But the analogy may suggest the mode in which we may hope gradually to approximate to general rules, and to find grounds for reasonable certainty in special cases. Though no single critic is infallible, we may assume that the *vox populi* is infallible if strictly confined to its proper sphere. When many generations have been influenced by an individual, we have demonstrative evidence that he must have been a man of extraordinary power. It is an indisputable fact that Homer and Æschylus delighted all intelligent readers for over 2,000 years. To explain that fact by any other theory than the theory that the authors possessed extraordinary genius is impossible. A man, therefore, who flies in the face of the verdict of generations is self-condemned. The probability that his blindness indicates a defect in his eyesight is incomparably greater than the probability that all other eyes have been somehow under an illusion. The argument applies to less colossal reputations. Not only a critic of the last century who could see nothing in Dante, but a critic in the present who thinks Pope a mere fool, or Voltaire a mere buffoon, puts himself out of court. Let him by all means confess his want of perception if it be necessary; but do not let him go on to criticise men in regard to whom he suffers from a kind of colour-blindness. My palate refuses to distinguish between claret and burgundy, but I never set myself up for a judge of wine.

It may be added that the power of swaying the imaginations of many generations indicates more than mere force. It is a safe indication of some true merit. No religion thrives which does not embody—along with whatever errors—the deepest and most permanent emotions of mankind. No art retains its interest for posterity which does not give permanent expression to something more than the temporary tastes, and, moreover, to something more than the vicious and morbid propensities of mankind. To justify this maxim would lead us too far; but I venture to assume that it could be justified by a sufficient induction. All great writers have their weaknesses; but their true power rests upon their utterance of the ennobling and health-giving emotions.

This doctrine is accepted even too unreservedly by most critics of the past. A slavish care for established reputation is more common than a rash defiance. The way, for example, in which Shakespeare's faults have been idolised along with his surpassing merits is simply a disgrace to literature. Were I writing for students of old authors, I would exhort them rather to attend to the limitations of the doctrine than to the doctrine itself. We are too apt to confound the qualities by which a man has succeeded with those in spite of which he has succeeded. The application of the doctrine to the living is, however, a more pressing problem. Our aim, I have said, is to anticipate the verdict of posterity, and we cannot anticipate infallibly. We cannot even lay down absolute rules of a scientific character. All that we can do is to proceed in a scientific spirit, which may therefore be favourable to the discovery of such rules in the future. If doomed to continual blunders, our blunders may form landmarks for the future, and not be simple exhibitions of profitless folly and prejudice.

The critic who gives a matured expression of his tastes lays down a principle. He should proceed to apply an obvious test. Will his principle fit in with the accepted verdict as to the great men of the past? A simple attention to this rule would dissipate a vast amount of foolish criticism. There has been, for example, a great outcry against a vice known as sensationalism. In one sense, the outcry justifies itself. People have been shocked by overdoses of horror and crime; and the art which has shocked them must be in some sense bad. But when critics proceed to lay down canons which would suppress all literature more exciting than Miss Austen's novels, they are surely forgetting one or two obvious facts. Canons are calmly propounded which would condemn all Greek tragedy, which would condemn Dante, and Milton, and Shakespeare, and the whole school of early English dramatists, and some of Scott's finest novels, to say nothing of Byron, or of Balzac, or Victor Hugo. The simple fact that a poem or a novel deals with crime and suffering cannot be enough to condemn it, or we should be doomed to a diet of bread and butter for all future time. The true question is as to the right mode of dealing with such subjects, and the critic who would condemn all dealing with them is really betraying his cause. He is trying to force an impracticable code upon mankind, and is allowing the true culprits to associate their cause with better men. Moreover, he is talking nonsense.

To keep steadily in mind the verdict of the past, not to break a painted window in anxiety to smash the insect which is crawling over it, is thus the great safeguard of a critic. A more difficult problem is the degree of respect due to modern opinion. The widest popularity may certainly be gained by absolute demerits. We need not give examples of modern charlatans, whose fame has not yet gone to its own place. There are plenty of older examples. The false wit of Cowley and the strained epigrams of Young, the pompous sentimentalism of Hervey, the tinsel of Tom Moore, all won a share of popularity in their own day, which rivalled or eclipsed the fame of Milton and Pope, and Addison and Wordsworth. In two of these cases the fame was partly due to religious associations which superseded a purely literary judgment.

On the other hand, there is a measure of fame which seems sufficiently to anticipate the verdict of posterity. There is perhaps more than one living writer of whom it may be confidently asserted that his influence over the most thoughtful of his contemporaries has been won by such palpable services to truth and lofty sentiment, and has been so independent of the aid of adventitious circumstances, that his fame is as secure, though not as accurately measured, as it will be a century hence. To treat such men with insolence is as monstrous as to insult their predecessors. The burden of proof at least is upon the assailant, and he is bound to explain not merely the cause of his antipathy, but to explain the phenomenon which, on his showing, ought not to exist. A summary *tant pis pour les faits* will not bring him off, tempting as the method may be. When a spiritual movement has acquired a certain impetus and volume, its leader must be a great man. To admit that a mere charlatan can move the world, is to hold with the housemaid that a plate breaks of itself, or, with the Tories in Queen Anne's time, that Marlborough won his battles by sheer cowardice.

How to distinguish between the true and the sham influence is indeed a question not strictly soluble. It is enough to suggest that any man of true force has a sure instinct for recognising force elsewhere. The blindness of patriotic or party rage may sometimes encourage a Frenchman to laugh at Moltke's strategy, or an English politician of one party to call the Pitt or Fox of his opponents an idiot. No man, swayed by such passions, can criticise to any purpose; and the best safeguard against the resulting errors is a constant application of the doctrine that every spiritual impulse requires an adequate moral explanation as well as a physical. Some people are fond of ascribing the success of their antagonists to chance or to diabolic influence. They would be wise if they would remember that either phrase, when analysed, is equivalent to the simple confession of ignorance. It means that the source of evil is in some sphere entirely outside our means of investigation. It is to abandon the problem, whilst masking our ignorance under an abusive epithet. Opponents may be justified if they take language of this kind as a panegyric in disguise.

There is, it is true, a weak side in the appeals often made to critical candour. Politicians sometimes denounce the bigotry of Liberals. The men who pride themselves upon their tolerance are often, it is said, the most dogmatic. But such denunciations, if often just, are apt to confound two very different things. Liberality imposes the duty of giving fair play to our opponents in action as in logic, but it does not command us to have no opinions at all. It is most desirable that every principle should be fully and fairly discussed, but it is certainly not desirable that no principles should ever be definitively established. The pure indifferentist naturally hates faith of all kinds, and tries to impute intolerance to any believer who carries faith into practice. There is, in short, a road to toleration which leads through pure scepticism; if every doctrine is equally true and equally false, there is no reason for ever being in a passion. That is not a desirable solution of the problem. It is very difficult to hold my own opinions and to respect all sincere dissentients —to believe that my doctrines are true and important, and yet to refuse to advance them by unworthy methods. But the only true Liberal is the man who can accomplish that feat, and the tolerance made out of pure incredulity is a mere mockery of the genuine virtue.

The fact that candid people dispute conclusions which seem to me evident is not always a reason for admitting even a scruple of doubt. There are cases in which it may even confirm them. A truth is fully established when it not only explains certain phenomena, but explains the source of erroneous conceptions of the phenomena. The true theory of astronomy shows why false theories were inevitably plausible at certain periods. No doctrine can be quite satisfactory till it helps us to see why other people do not see it. When that is clearly intelligible, the very errors confirm the true theory. In matters of taste there is a similar canon. There are undoubtedly bad tastes as well as good. There are tastes, that is, which imply stupidity, or craving for coarse excitement, or incapacity for distinguishing between rant and true rhetoric, between empty pomp of language and genuine richness and force of imagination. There are tastes which imply a thoroughly corrupt nature, and others which imply vulgarity and coarseness. To admit that all tastes are equally good is to fall into an æsthetic scepticism as erroneous as the philosophical scepticism which should make morality or political principles matters of arbitrary convention. A critic who is tolerant in the sense of admitting this indifference abnegates his true function; for the one great service which a critic can render is to keep vice, vulgarity, or stupidity at bay. He cannot supply genius; but he can preserve the prestige of genius by revealing to duller minds the difference between good work and its imitation.

The sense in which a critic should be liberal is marked out by this consideration. The existence of any artistic school, however much he dislikes its tendency, is a phenomenon to be explained and not to be denounced until it is explained. If it has a wide popularity, or includes many able men, there is a strong presumption that it corresponds in some way to a real want of the time. It embodies a widespread, and presumably, therefore, not a purely objectionable emotional impulse. It proves, at the lowest, that rival forms of expression do not satisfy the wants of contemporaries, and are so far defective. Even if it be, in the critic's eye, a purely reactionary movement, the existence of a reaction proves that something is wanting in that against which it reacts. Some element of feeling is inadequately represented, and therefore the objectionable movement indicates a want, if it does not suggest the true remedy. It may be that, in some cases, the critic will be forced to say that, after taking such considerations into account, he can yet see nothing more in his antagonist than the embodiment of a purely morbid tendency. They represent a disease in the social order which requires caustic and the knife. When a man has deliberately formed such an opinion, he should express it frankly, though as temperately as may be; but it will probably be admitted that such cases are very rare, and that a man who has the power of seeing through his neighbours' eyes will generally discover that they catch at least a distorted aspect of some truths not so clearly revealed to their opponents.

By keeping such rules in mind, the critic will certainly not become infallible. He will not discover any simple mechanical test for the accurate measurement of literary genius. Nor will he or a whole generation of critics succeed in making an exact science out of an art which must always depend upon natural delicacy of perception. But he will be working in the right direction, and undergoing a wholesome discipline. If he does not discover any rigidly correct formulæ, he will be helping towards the establishment of sound methods; and though he will not store his mind with authoritative dogmas, he will encourage the right temper for approaching a most delicate task. In many cases, indeed, the task is easy enough. It would be affectation to deny that there are a good many books which may be summarily classified as rubbish, without much risk of real injustice, though sentence need not be passed in harsh language. But to judge of any serious work requires, besides the natural faculty, possessed by very few, an amount of habitual labour to look from strange points of view which is almost equally rare. There are many poems, for example, which can hardly be criticised to effect till the critic knows them by heart, and a man cannot be expected to do that who has to pronounce judgment within a week. In that case, all that can be recommended is a certain modesty in expression and diffidence in forming opinions which is not universal amongst our authoritative critics.

(*The Cornhill Magazine,* 1876)

# A CHECK-LIST OF WORKS

# A Check-list of Works by
## LESLIE STEPHEN

---

Unless otherwise indicated, all Stephen's books were published in London.

More than one edition of a work is listed whenever no single edition includes all the essays appearing under a given title.

Since Stephen wrote regularly for newspapers and magazines over a period of many years, Section III lists only articles in monthlies, quarterlies, and annuals. In general, his articles elsewhere are much briefer and less important. Within its limits, this list is probably almost complete. Only the first appearance of an article in a periodical is noted. After an article has been collected, its appearance in books by others is not listed.

Most of Stephen's contributions to weekly magazines appeared either in the New York *Nation* (1866–1873) or in the *Saturday Review*. Daniel C. Haskell's *The Nation*, 2 vols., New York, 1951, contains a complete list of Stephen's contributions, and Merle M. Bevington's *The Saturday Review, 1858–68*, New York, 1941, contains a partial list, which may be supplemented by Frederic W. Maitland's *The Life and Letters of Leslie Stephen*, London, 1906, especially p. 163.

All articles in the *Cornhill Magazine* and *Fraser's Magazine* are unsigned unless otherwise noted. All contributions to other periodicals are signed unless marked "anon." or "initialed."

The authorship of the *Cornhill* articles has been checked against the publisher's annotated files. I wish to thank Sir John Murray for his assistance in verifying my list. The unsigned reviews in the *Alpine Journal* have been identified on the basis of what seems to me excellent internal evidence. Maitland is the authority for all other attributions, except for the review of Lecky in *Fraser's*, which markedly resembles one in the *Nation*, VIII (1869), 475–477, identified by Maitland as Stephen's. I have found no reason to doubt any of Maitland's attributions.

The following abbreviations, which appear after some of the titles, indicate the work in which the item was later collected:

*P: The Playground of Europe.*
*F: Essays on Freethinking and Plainspeaking.*
*H: Hours in a Library.*
*S: Studies of a Biographer.*
*A: An Agnostic's Apology.*
*SR: Social Rights and Duties.*
*SEI: Some Early Impressions.*
*B: British Sports and Pastimes. 1868.* Ed. Trollope.

## I. Books

*An Agnostic's Apology and Other Essays.* 1893.

*Alexander Pope.* English Men of Letters. 1880.

*English Literature and Society in the Eighteenth Century.* Ford Lectures, 1903. 1904.

*The English Utilitarians.* 3 vols. 1900.

*Essays on Freethinking and Plainspeaking.* [Collected ed.] 1905.

*George Eliot.* English Men of Letters. 1902.

*History of English Thought in the Eighteenth Century.* 2 vols. 1876.

*Hobbes.* English Men of Letters. 1904.

*Hours in a Library.* [First Series.] 1874.

*Hours in a Library.* Second Series. 1876.

*Hours in a Library.* New ed. with additions. 4 vols. 1907.

*Life of Henry Fawcett.* 1885.

*The Life of Sir James Fitzjames Stephen.* 1895.

*The Playground of Europe.* 1871.

*The Playground of Europe.* Silver Library ed. 1899.

*The Playground of Europe.* Ed. H. E. G. Tyndale. Blackwell's Mountaineering Library. Oxford, 1936.

*The Poll Degree from a Third Point of View.* 1863.

*Samuel Johnson.* English Men of Letters. 1878.

*The Science of Ethics.* 1882.

*Sketches from Cambridge.* 2nd ed. 1832. [1st ed. 1865, by "A Don."]

*Social Rights and Duties.* Addresses to Ethical Societies. The Ethical Library. 2 vols. 1896.

*Some Early Impressions.* 1924.

*Studies of a Biographer.* [Collected ed.] 4 vols. 1907.

*Swift*. English Men of Letters. 1882.

*The "Times" on the American War: A Historical Study*. 1865. [Initialed.]

*What is Materialism?* 1886. [*SR.*]

## II. Contributions to Books, Works Edited or Translated, and Essays Privately Printed

*The Alps or Sketches of Life and Nature in the Mountains*. By H. Berlepsch. Trans. Stephen. 1861.

"The Allelein-Horn," in *Vacation Tourists and Notes of Travel in 1860*. Ed. Francis Galton. 2 vols. 1861. I, 264–281.

"The Ascent of the Schreckhorn," in *Peaks, Passes, and Glaciers*. Second Series. Ed. E. S. Kennedy. 2 vols. 1862. II, 3–14. [*P.*]

"Belief and Evidence," June 12, 1877. [Anon. Privately printed for the Metaphysical Society.]

"Browning, Robert," *Encyclopædia Britannica*. 11th ed.

"Carlyle, Thomas," *Encyclopædia Britannica*. 11th ed.

*The Central Alps*. Ed. John Ball. The Alpine Guide, Part II. 1864. [Includes notes by Stephen.]

*The Dictionary of National Biography*. Vols. I–XXI, sole ed. 1885–1890. Vols. XXII–XXVI, ed. with Sidney Lee, 1890–1891. [Stephen also contributed hundreds of biographies.]

"The Eiger Joch," in *Peaks, Passes and Glaciers*. Second Series. Ed. E. S. Kennedy. 2 vols. 1862. II, 15–32. [*P.*]

"Evolution and Religious Conceptions," in *The Nineteenth Century: A Review of Progress*. New York, 1901. Pp. 370–383.

*A Guide to the Western Alps*. Ed. John Ball. The Alpine Guide, Part I. 1863. [Includes notes by Stephen.]

"James Dykes Campbell," a prefatory memoir to *Samuel Taylor Coleridge*. By James Dykes Campbell. 2nd ed. 1896. Pp. v–xxxviii.

"James Payn," biographical introduction to *The Backwater of Life or Essays of a Literary Veteran*. By James Payn. 1898. Pp. ix–xliv.

*Lectures and Essays*. By William Kingdon Clifford. Ed. with Frederick Pollock. 2 vols. 1879.

*Letters of John Richard Green*. Ed. Stephen. 1901.

"An Old Puzzle," in *Among My Books*. With a Preface by H. D. Traill. [1898]. Pp. 141–147. [Reprinted from *Literature*, II (1898), 286–287.]

"On Alpine Climbing," in *British Sports and Pastimes. 1868.* Ed. Anthony Trollope. 1868. Pp. 257–289. [Anon.]

"On Rowing," in *British Sports and Pastimes. 1868.* Ed. Anthony Trollope. 1868. Pp. 227–256. [Anon.]

"On the Choice of Representatives by Popular Constituencies," in *Essays on Reform.* 1867. Pp. 85–125.

"Perishable Books," in *Among my Books.* With a Preface by H. D. Traill. [1898.] Pp. 37–43, [Reprinted from *Literature,* I (1897), 176–178.]

"Preface," *A Marriage of Shadows.* By Margaret Veley. 1888. Pp. vii–xxiv.

"Prefatory Essay. The Growth of Toleration," *Encyclopædia Britannica.* 10th ed. XXVIII, vii-xix.

"Richardson's Novels. Introduction," *The Works of Samuel Richardson.* 12 vols. 1883. I, ix–lv.

"Thomas Carlyle," *The Warner Classics.* New York, 1897. IV, 33–62.

"The Uniformity of Nature," March 11, 1879. [Anon. Privately printed for the Metaphysical Society.]

*The Works of Henry Fielding, Esq.* Ed. Stephen. 10 vols. 1882. [Contains a biographical essay by Stephen, "Henry Fielding," I, iii–civ.]

"The Writings of W. M. Thackeray," *The Works of William Makepeace Thackeray.* 24 vols. 1879. XXIV, 315–378.


III. Contributions to Periodicals

*Alpine Journal**

"The Weisshorn," I (1863), 40–44.

"The Jungfrau-joch and the Viescher-joch," I (1863), 97–112. [*P.,* two articles.]

"The Best Form of Alpenstock for the High Alps," I (1864), 253–255.

"The Bietschhorn and Blümlis Alp," I (1864), 353–360. [*P.* (1936), Bietschhorn section only.]

"Ascent of the Rothhorn," II (1865), 67–79. [*P.*]

"Alpine Dangers," II (1866), 273–285. [*P.,* 1st ed. only. Retitled "The Dangers of Mountaineering."]

"The Eastern Carpathians," III (1867), 25–44. [*P.,* 1st ed. only.]

* Edited by Stephen, January 1868–May 1872.

"Ball's Alpine Guide," IV (1869), 282–288. [Anon. A review.]

"Recent Accidents in the Alps," IV (1869), 373–379.

"The Peaks of Primiero," IV (1870), 385–402. [P.]

"Alpine Notes," V (1871), 188–190. [Initialed.]

"Tyndall's Hours of Exercise in the Alps," V (1871), 285–288. [Anon. A review.]

"Round Mont Blanc," V (1872), 289–305.

"Mr. H. Dixon's Switzers," V (1872), 384–386. [Anon. A review.]

"The Mountain.—By Jules Michelet," V (1872), 386–388. [Anon. A review.]

"Mountaineering in the Sierra Nevada," V (1872), 389–396. [Anon. A review.]

"A New Pass in the Chain of Mont Blanc," VI (1874), 351–364. [P., retitled "The Col des Hirondelles." Not in 1st ed.]

"Alpine Dangers," VII (1875), 311–313, 404 [erroneously marked p. 304. Letters].

"The Effect of a Rarefied Atmosphere on Climbers," VIII (1877), 281–282. [A letter.]

"In Memoriam. Thomas Woodbine Hinchliff," XI (1882), 41–44.

"Alpine Accidents in 1887," XIII (1888), 467–469. [A letter.]

"In Memoriam. John Birkbeck," XV (1890), 277–281. [Initialed.]

"John Ormsby," XVIII (1896), 33–36.


*Cornhill Magazine**

"American Humour," XIII (1866), 28–43.

"Transylvania," XIV (1866), 567–585.

"The Regrets of a Mountaineer," XVI (1867), 539–555. [P.]

"Richardson's Novels," XVII (1868), 48–69. [H.]

"De Foe's Novels," XVII (1868), 293–316. [H.]

"Some Remarks on Travelling in America," XIX (1869), 321–339.

"A Cynic's Apology," XIX (1869), 574–582. ["A Cynic."]

"Idolatry," XIX (1869), 689–698. ["A Cynic."]

"Useless Knowledge," XX (1869), 41–51. ["A Cynic."]

"Vacations," XX (1869), 205–214. ["A Cynic."]

* Edited by Stephen, March 1871–December 1882.

"Arcadia," XX (1869), 588–597. ["A Cynic."]

"The Decay of Murder," XX (1869), 722–733. ["A Cynic."]

"National Antipathies," XXI (1870), 154–166. ["A Cynic."]

"Our Rulers—Public Opinion," XXI (1870), 288–298. ["A Cynic."]

"The Uses of Fools," XXI (1870), 465–476. ["A Cynic."]

"Social Slavery," XXI (1870), 566–577. ["A Cynic."]

"Oratory," XXII (1870), 87–97. ["A Cynic."]

"Literary Exhaustion," XXII (1870), 285–296. ["A Cynic."]

"Hours in a Library. No. I.—Sir Thomas Browne," XXIII (1871), 596–611. [*H.*]

"Hours in a Library. No. II.—Lord Chesterfield," XXIV (1871), 86–101.

"Hours in a Library. No. III.—Some Words About Sir Walter Scott," XXIV (1871), 278–293. [*H*].

"Hours in a Library. No. IV.—Thomas Fuller," XXV (1872), 28–44.

"Hours in a Library. No. V.—Horace Walpole," XXV (1872), 718–735. [*H.*]

"Hours in a Library. No. VI.—Nathaniel Hawthorne," XXVI (1872), 717–734. [*H.*]

"Thoughts of an Outsider: Public Schools," XXVII (1873), 281–292.

"The Late Lord Lytton as a Novelist," XXVII (1873), 345–354.

"Sunset on Mont Blanc," XXVIII (1873), 457–467. [*P.*, not in 1st ed.]

"Hours in a Library. No. VII.—Pope as a Moralist," XXVIII (1873), 583–604. [*H.*]

"Thoughts of an Outsider: the Public Schools Again," XXVIII (1873), 605–615.

"Housekeeping," XXIX (1874), 69–79.

"Hours in a Library. No. VIII.—Dr. Johnson's Writings," XXIX (1874), 280–297. [*H.*]

"A Bye-Day in the Alps," XXIX (1874), 675–685. [*P.*(1936).]

"Hours in a Library. No. IX.—Crabbe's Poetry," XXX (1874), 454–473. [*H.*]

"Mr. Lowell's Poems," XXXI (1875), 65–78. [Initialed "F.T."]

"Hours in a Library. No. X.—William Hazlitt," XXXI (1875), 467–488. [*H.*]

"Art and Morality," XXXII (1875), 91–101.

"Hours in a Library. No. XI.—Cowper and Rousseau," XXXII (1875), 439–457. [*H.*]

"The Youth of Swift," XXXIII (1876), 172–183. [Initialed "S."]

"Humour," XXXIII (1876), 318–326.

"Thoughts of an Outsider: the Ethics of Vivisection," XXXIII (1876), 468–478.

"Hours in a Library. No. XII.—Macaulay," XXXIII (1876), 563–581. [*H.*]

"Thoughts of an Outsider: International Prejudices," XXXIV (1876), 45–59.

"Hours in a Library. No. XIII.—Wordsworth's Ethics," XXXIV (1876), 206–226. [*H.*]

"Thoughts on Criticism, by a Critic," XXXIV (1876), 556–569.

"Heroes and Valets," XXXV (1877), 46–55.

"Hours in a Library. No. XIV.—Fielding's Novels," XXXV (1877), 154–171. [*H.*]

"The Alps in Winter," XXXV (1877), 352–362. [*P.*, not in 1st ed.]

"Hours in a Library. No. XV.—Charles Kingsley," XXXV (1877), 424–442. [*H.*]

"Genius and Vanity," XXXV (1877), 670–684.

"Hours in a Library. No. XVI.—Massinger," XXXVI (1877), 440–460. [*H.*]

"Hours in a Library. No. XVII.—Charlotte Brontë," XXXVI (1877), 723–739. [*H.*]

"War," XXXVII (1878), 478–489.

"Stray Thoughts on Scenery," XXXVIII (1878), 68–82.

"Hours in a Library. No. XVIII.—The First Edinburgh Reviewers," XXXVIII (1878), 218–234. [*H.*]

"Hours in a Library. No. XIX.—Landor's Imaginary Conversations," XXXVIII (1878), 667–686. [*H.*]

"Hours in a Library. No. XX.—Godwin and Shelley," XXXIX (1879), 281–302. [*H.*]

"Hours in a Library. No. XXI.—Gray and His School," XL (1879), 70–91. [*H.*]

"London Walks," XLI (1880), 222–238.

"Burton's 'Anatomy of Melancholy,' " XLI (1880), 475–490.

"Hours in a Library. No. XXII.—Sterne," XLII (1880), 86–106. [*H.*]

"Rambles Among Books. No. 1.—Country Books," XLII (1880), 662–679. [*H.*]

"The Moral Element in Literature," XLIII (1881), 34–50.

"George Eliot," XLIII (1881), 152–168. [*H.*]

"Thomas Carlyle," XLIII (1881), 349–358.

"Rambles Among Books. No. II.—Autobiography," XLIII (1881), 410–429. [*H.*]

"Authors for Hire," XLIII (1881), 684–702.

"Rambles Among Books. No. III.—The Essayists," XLIV (1881), 278–297.

"Hours in a Library. No. XXIII.—Carlyle's Ethics," XLIV (1881), 664–683. [*H.*]

"Senior Wranglers," XLV (1882), 225–234.

"Rambles Among Books. No. IV.—The State Trials," XLV (1882), 455–473. [*H.*]

"The Decay of Literature," XLVI (1882), 602–612.

"The Study of English Literature," LV (1887), 486–508. [Signed.]

"The Story of Scott's Ruin," LXXVI (1897), 448–465. [Signed. *S.*]

"James Payn," LXXVIII (1898), 590–594. [Signed.]

"In Memoriam. George Smith," LXXXIV (1901), 577–580. [Signed.]

## Fortnightly Review

"Balzac's Novels," XV (1871), 17–39. [*H.*]

"De Quincey," XV (1871), 310–329. [*H.*]

"Warburton," XVII (1872), 155–175. [*F.*]

"Are We Christians?" XIX (1873), 281–303. [*F.*]

"Taine's History of English Literature," XX (1873), 693–714.

"Mr. Maurice's Theology," XXI (1874), 595–617.

"Mr. Disraeli's Novels," XXII (1874), 430–450. [*H.*]

"William Law," XXIII (1875), 339–359. [*H.*, 1st ed. only.]

"Order and Progress," XXIII (1875), 820–834.

"The Value of Political Machinery," XXIV (1875), 836–852.

"An Agnostic's Apology," XXV (1876), 840–860. [*A.*]

"William Godwin," XXVI (1876), 444–461.

"The Scepticism of Believers," XXVIII (1877), 355–376. [*A.*]

"Dr. Newman's Theory of Belief," XXVIII (1877), 680–697, 792–810. [*A.*]

"Dreams and Realities," XXX (1878), 334–352. [*A.*]

"An Attempted Philosophy of History," XXXIII (1880), 672–695.

"Mr. Bradlaugh and His Opponents," XXXIV (1880), 176–187.

"Spinoza," XXXIV (1880), 752–772.

"Thomas Paine," LX (1893), 267–281.

"Pascal," LXVIII (1897), 1–18. [*S.*]


*Fraser's Magazine*

"University Organisation," LXXVII (1868), 135–153. [Signed "A Don."]

"The Comtist Utopia," LXXX (1869), 1–21.

"Mr. Lecky's *History of European Morals*," LXXX (1869), 273–284.

"The Baths of Santa Catarina," LXXX (1869), 635–648. [*P.*]

"Dr. Pusey and Dr. Temple," LXXX (1869), 722–737.

"The Broad Church," LXXXI (1870), 311–325. [Signed. *F.*]

"The Religious Difficulty," LXXXI (1870), 623–634. [Signed.]

"The Alps in the Last Century," LXXXII (1870), 167–180. [Signed. *P.*, retitled "The Old School."]

"Mr. Matthew Arnold and the Church of England," LXXXII (1870), 414–431. [Signed.]

"Athletic Sports and University Studies," LXXXII (1870), 691–704. [Signed.]

"Mr. Elwin's Edition of Pope," LXXXIII (1871), 284–301 [Initialed. *H.*, 1st. ed. only.]

"Mr. Voysey and Mr. Purchas," LXXXIII (1871), 457–468.

"The Future of University Reform," LXXXIV (1871), 269–281. [Signed.]

"Religion as a Fine Art," LXXXV (1872), 156–168. [Initialed. *F.*]

"Darwinism and Divinity," LXXXV (1872), 409–421. [Initialed. F.]

"Voltaire," LXXXV (1872), 678–691. [Initialed.]

"Social Macadamisation," LXXXVI (1872), 150–168. [Initialed.]

"A Bad Five Minutes in the Alps," LXXXVI (1872), 545–561. [F.]

"Shaftesbury's *Characteristics*," LXXXVII (1873), 76–93. [Signed. F.]

"The Fable of the Bees," LXXXVII (1873), 713–727. [Signed. F.]

"Jonathan Edwards," LXXXVIII (1873), 529–551. [Signed. *H.*]

"University Endowments," LXXXIX (1874), 323–335.

"Mr. Ruskin's Recent Writings," LXXXIX (1874), 688–701.

"Sidgwick's Methods of Ethics," XCI (1875), 306–325. [Signed.]

## Macmillan's Magazine

"An American Protectionist," VII (1862), 126–133.

"Ritualism," XVII (1868), 479–494.

"Mr. Whymper's 'Scrambles Amongst the Alps,'" XXIV (1871), 304–311.

"Henry Fawcett: In Memoriam," LI (1884), 130–133.

## Mind

[On the use of the word "speculatist"], III (1878), 294.

"Philosophic Doubt," V (1880), 157–181.

"On Some Kinds of Necessary Truth," XIV (1889), 50–65, 188–215.

"Henry Sidgwick," XXVI (1901), 1–17.

## National Review

"Biography," XXII (1893), 171–183.

"Matthew Arnold," XXII (1893), 458–477. [*S.*]

"Luxury," XXIII (1894), 29–48. [*SR.*]

"The Duties of Authors," XXIII (1894), 319–339. [*SR.*]

"A Substitute for the Alps," XXIII (1894), 460–467.

"The Choice of Books," XXV (1895), 165–182.

"Coleridge's Letters," XXV (1895), 318–327.

"The Evolution of Editors," XXVI (1896), 770–785. [S.]

"National Biography," XXVII (1896), 51–65. [S.]

"John Byrom," XXVII (1896), 208–221. [S.]

"Arthur Young," XXVII (1896), 489–504. [S.]

"Oliver Wendell Holmes," XXVII (1896), 626–641. [S.]

"Wordsworth's Youth," XXVIII (1897), 769–786. [S.]

"Gibbon's Autobiography," XXIX (1897), 51–67. [S.]

"Jowett's Life," XXIX (1897), 443–458. [S.]

"The Importation of German," XXIX (1897), 619–635. [S.]

"Johnsoniana," XXX (1897), 61–76. [S.]

"Life of Tennyson," XXX (1897), 371–390. [S.]

"The Browning Letters," XXXIII (1899), 401–415. [S.]

"Studies of a Biographer—Southey's Letters," XXXIII (1899), 740–757. [S.]

"The Cosmopolitan Spirit in Literature," XXXIV (1899), 378–391. [S.]

"John Donne," XXXIV (1899), 595–613. [S.]

"John Ruskin," XXXV (1900), 240–255. [S.]

"Lord Herbert of Cherbury," XXXV (1900), 661–673.

"Walter Bagehot," XXXV (1900), 936–950. [S.]

"James Anthony Froude," XXXVI (1901), 671–683. [S.]

"Emerson," XXXVI (1901), 882–898. [S.]

"Shakespeare as a Man," XXXVII (1901), 220–239. [S.]

"Anthony Trollope," XXXVIII (1901), 68–84. [S.]

"Did Shakespeare Write Bacon?" XXXVIII (1901), 402–406.

"Robert Louis Stevenson," XXXVIII (1902), 725–743. [S.]

"William Godwin's Novels," XXXVIII (1902), 908–923. [S.]

"James Spedding," XXXIX (1902), 241–257.

"Young's 'Night Thoughts,' " XXXIX (1902), 908–926.

"Browning's Casuistry," XL (1902), 534–552.

"Some Early Impressions," XLII (1903), 130–146, 208–224. [SEI.]

"Some Early Impressions—Journalism," XLII (1903), 420–436. [SEI.]

"Some Early Impressions—Editing," XLII (1903), 563–581. [*SEI.*]

## Nineteenth Century

"The Suppression of Poisonous Opinions," XIII (1883), 493–508, 653–666. [*A.*]

"Belief and Conduct," XXIV (1888), 372–389.

"Cardinal Newman's Scepticism," XXIX (1891), 179–201.

"Bishop Butler's Apologist," XXXIX (1896), 106–122.

"Thomas Henry Huxley," XLVIII (1900), 905–918. [*S.*]

"The Good Old Cause," LI (1902), 11–23.

"The Ascendancy of the Future," LI (1902), 795–810.

## Miscellaneous

"Up and Down Mount Blanc," *Chambers's Journal*, LVI (Christmas, 1866), 1–7, 30–32. [Fictional frame for a series of stories. Anon.]

"The Political Situation in England," *North American Review*, CVII (1868), 543–567.

"About Rowing," *St. Pauls*, I (1868), 319–333. [Anon. *B.*]

"Alpine Climbing," *St. Pauls*, I (1868), 470–485. [Anon. *B.*]

"The Religion of All Sensible Men," *North American Review*, CXXX (1880), 438–461. [*A.*]

"Chatham, Francis, and Junius," *English Historical Review*, III (1888), 233–249.

"Social Equality," *International Journal of Ethics*, I (1891), 261–288. [*SR.*]

"The Moral Sanction," *Agnostic Annual* (1893), pp. 3–10.

"Ethics and the Struggle for Existence," *Contemporary Review*, LXIV (1893), 162–170. [*SR.*]

"William Cobbett," *New Review*, IX (1893), 362–372, 482–493.

"Nansen," *International Journal of Ethics*, VIII (1897), 1–22.

"The Will to Believe," *Agnostic Annual* (1898), pp. 14–22.

"Right and Wrong in Politics," *Monthly Review*, II (Jan. 1901), 33–48.

"In Praise of Walking," *Monthly Review*, IV (Aug. 1901), 96–116. [*S.*]

"Romance and Science," *Pall Mall Magazine*, XXIV (1901), 105–113.

"New Lights on Milton," *Quarterly Review*, CXCIV (1901), 103–125. [Anon. *S.*]

"James Russell Lowell," *Quarterly Review*, CXCVI (1902), 61–81. [Anon.]